Guide to the
Battle of
Gettysburg

Edited by Jay Luvaas
and Harold W. Nelson

University Press of Kansas

The U.S. Army War College
Guides to Civil War Battles

© 1986 by the University Press of Kansas
All rights reserved

Published by the University Press of Kansas (Lawrence, Kansas 66049), which was organized by the Kansas Board of Regents and is operated and funded by Emporia State University, Fort Hays State University, Kansas State University, Pittsburg State University, the University of Kansas, and Wichita State University

Printed in the United States of America

10 9 8 7 6 5 4

The paper used in this publication meets the minimum requirements of the American National Standard for Permanence of Paper for Printed Library Materials Z39.48-1984.

PREFACE

Jay Luvaas has spent decades perfecting the methods embodied in this guidebook. I first joined him on a battlefield tour in 1971, when he was already a veteran of these intellectual campaigns. As a student of military history who had spent many years studying the subject in a traditional classroom, I was fascinated by Jay's ability to move a very disparate group to a carefully-chosen spot on the battlefield and bring the action at that point back to life by using the words of the participants. I have since watched him work the same magic on other battlefields with civilians, senior military leaders, and novice officers. Those who use this book will not be directly exposed to the decades of preparation, enthusiasm and sparkle that Jay brings to each of his battlefield excursions, but nothing else is missing.

Joining Jay on this splendid project is Colonel Harold Nelson. What Hal brings to this effort is a rare combination of training, education, and experience. He has been an Army officer for 25 years and expert on combined arms war. He has led American soldiers in the United States, Korea, Vietnam and Europe, recently commanded a field artillery battalion, and has been a joint staff officer at SHAPE. Moreover, he has been a serious student of the profession of arms for decades and holds a doctorate in Russian history from the University of Michigan. Most importantly, though, has been his superb contribution as a teacher in uniform – a soldier teaching soldiers – at West Point, the Command and General Staff College and the Army War College. Quite simply, he is the most gifted soldier-scholar I know.

Around the turn of the century, the U.S. Army took the lead for the federal government in preserving and marking Civil War battlefields, primarily so that those fields could be used as "outdoor classrooms" for the education of officers. When the U.S. Army War College was founded

iii

about the same time, its faculty and students assisted in the historical research and then benefited from the results by taking extensive staff rides over the old battlefields, discussing leadership, decision making, tactics and strategy. So too, the Staff College at Leavenworth. When the War College closed its doors during World War II, that practice ceased. When Jay Luvaas and Hal Nelson, who had taught history together at West Point, joined the War College faculty in 1982, they found an enthusiastic group of former colleagues at the U.S. Army Military History Institute eager to again take students to the Gettysburg battlefield using the old staff ride methods. Jay's approach is virtually identical to those methods, so they made rapid progress developing several staff rides, beginning with Gettysburg. Future volumes in this series will capture their insights into the other battlefields they frequent.

The U.S. Army War College's sponsorship of this project is a welcome symbol of the Army's renewed emphasis on battlefield staff rides. Senior leaders recognize that most warfighting skills do not change radically even though the outward features of war are transformed. Terrain may pose special challenges to today's fighter, but it is still important. When historical sources allow someone who fought the ground to speak to us of his battle on the spot where we stand, we all come much closer to understanding the essence of war. Soldiers and civilians who use this book can achieve that special insight.

Washington, D. C.
26 March 1986

William A. Stofft
Brig. Gen. U. S. A.
Chief of Military History

CONTENTS

MAPS

ACKNOWLEDGMENTS

This book would not have been published without the support of many people. Generals Lawrence, Healy, and Thompson, as successive Commandants of the U.S. Army War College, gave the sustained command emphasis on using old battlefields to reinforce modern lessons that established the need for this series of guides. Roy Strong and the U.S. Army War College Foundation facilitated commercial publication. John Votaw, Jim Bigelow, and Dennis McSweeney, as colleagues with a special interest in the Gettysburg Battlefield, helped us interpret major portions of the action. Mike Winey, and Randy Hackenburg of the U.S. Army Military History Institute gave expert assistance with photographs, and Cathy Georg Harrison of the National Park Service helped in many ways as the project matured. Paula Murphy's cheerful assistance was vital as we struggled with deadlines in the closing stages, and Mark Pfoutz stepped in to provide excellent maps. John Kallmann was much more than a publisher, providing creative wisdom, historical skill, and interpretive insight. Our wives were patient with a project that devoured countless weekends, and the members of The Regiment and the Army of the Cussewago added to both the enjoyment and the challenge of refighting an old battle. We thank all of them and the many others who have tramped the ground with us.

The Editors

Legend for Maps

☐	Confederate Lines
■	Union Lines
ılı ılı ılı	Artillery
⟵⟋	Attack and Retreat
▬	Woods
✕	Modern Roads

Scale is variable—See notations on maps

INTRODUCTION

This is not another *history* of the battle of Gettysburg. The task of the historian is to establish facts by extensive research and then, through explanation, interpretation, and appreciation, to shape the data and factors, forces and movements into a cohesive balance. What we have endeavored to do instead is to encourage the reader to function as his own historian by presenting first-hand accounts, nearly all of them written by officers who commanded units from the size of batteries and regiments to corps level and above, which convey the perceptions—or misperceptions—of the moment, the confusion of battle, and the problem of human behavior in combat.

These after-action reports place the reader at the side of the men who made decisions and fought over a particular piece of terrain without the homogenization that occurs almost inevitably as the historian processes his information and adds his own imaginative insights to recreate what probably happened. Many histories, especially of battles, tend to be anecdotal or impressionistic, weaving together a tapestry of first-hand narratives written over the span of half a century in such a way that the reader can almost smell the smoke and hear the trumpets blow. Others are inevitably distorted by what John Keegan has called "the rhetoric of battle history," which makes for stirring reading but in the process is apt to oversimplify or distort. Opposed to the romantic school is what the nineteenth-century theorist Jomini described as "purely military history . . . of a thankless and difficult kind" which, if it is to be useful to soldiers, requires details "as dry as they are remote." The tendency in this kind of didactic literature is to treat battles and campaigns "as if they were elaborate games of three-dimensional chess," or else to analyze a battle in such minute detail that it is possible for the reader to trace the position of all units at any given time.[1]

Nor is this a typical guide book, although it does endeavor to steer the reader around the battlefield. A guide book is factual and usually aimed at a broad audience. It must assume little knowledge on the part of the reader, it generally avoids controversial interpretation, and it seeks, by distilling events, to explain what happened at a given location. The battle that emerges from the guide book is usually a *sum* of all of the parts. In contrast, our assumption is that a battle is best understood by exploring in greater depth *some* of its intimate or vital parts.

This book owes its existence to the fact that the Army War College is located only 28 miles from Gettysburg. Since 1951, when the War College was moved to Carlisle Barracks, the annual Gettysburg tour has been a popular family outing. Every September a column of 15 or so school buses, loaded with an entire seminar, including spouses, teen-age children and enough provisions to last well into the following week, sets off for a day-long tour of the battlefield. The "guide" for each bus is usually one of the historians assigned to the War College, and this book originally was put together to equip the historian, who may in fact have been trained as a medievalist, with the information that he might need to interpret events at each designated stop. In some respects this volume represents an effort to achieve some degree of quality control in equipping our volunteer "guides" to interpret the battle. At some locations the guide will use the material given him to reconstruct what happened at a specific location; elsewhere he simply reads an after-action report or two, so that the audience, each responding to his own experiences, might recreate a commander's decision or some segment of the battle. The photocopied typescript was frequently borrowed throughout the year by students who wished to conduct their own tour of the battlefield, either to understand more of the battle or to share their experience with visiting friends and relatives. It was to meet this need that we first considered publishing our guidebook.

This effort also coincides with current attempts throughout the Army to revive the "Historical Staff Ride" that played a part in officer education before World War II and was traditionally the capstone of the academic year at the War College from 1909 until 1940. The Staff Ride operates at a somewhat higher level of analysis than a family tour and seeks to involve the participant in the battle in a variety of ways. It should demand somewhat greater preparation on the part of all participants as well as the leader. It seeks to enable the professional soldier to learn more about his trade through the study and analysis of an old battlefield in areas involving leadership, battle intelligence, the use of terrain, unit cohesion, tactics, the psychology of man in combat, or any other aspect of the military art that will always be applicable to some degree. As the guidance for the Army War College Staff Rides in the 1930's, the officers designated to present a given battle to the rest of the class worked with the following advice:

> Frequently, interest may be heightened by asking the listener what he would do if he were the commander in a situation that has been presented. It is not desirable to have the question considered by any of the listeners. Some will know the answer but all who do not will ask themselves the questions: "Now just what would I do."[2]

Officers conducting these Staff Rides in the old days obviously appreciated that history is often of greater value to the professional soldier in suggesting questions for him to ponder, drawing upon his own experience and insights, than in providing specific answers or formulas to be applied on some battlefield of the future.

Today officers who visit an old battlefield can still discover, as one student at the War College has written, that the experience refocusses attention "on the fundamentals of our profession—courage, fortitude, perseverance and selflessness." A few hours of quiet contemplation on a battlefield like Gettysburg can force a person to reflect on the meaning of some past event as a lesson worthy of consideration for future application. "There is something to be gained from walking those fields that will never be found on a computer terminal or Pentagon Briefing chart."[3]

Inevitably soldiers who have been in combat will be able to read their own experiences into the lesson. As a British General who commanded in the Falklands has observed from his recent visit to Chancellorsville,

> I found myself easily identifying with the men who fought there. Lee must have been terribly worried that Jackson's flank march would not succeed. . . . I bet he didn't show his concern but he must have been very tense inside. I could picture Jackson driving his men on through that hot, dusty wilderness, and his elation when his plan worked. I can fully understand his consuming impatience to get forward to conduct a personal reconnaissance—something every commander feels. It is so easy to visualize the chaos that ensued when Jackson was wounded, leaving no one to grip the situation and drive on to finish Hooker once and for all. I can even identify with Hooker alternatively taking council of his fears and deluding himself that his plan was working. . . . He was guilty of "making pictures". . . . The after-action reports by both sides reminded me that in the chaos of battle things may not be what they seem to be and that two people partici-

pating in the same incident may view it very differently. . . . Our visit reminded me . . . what an enormous amount Soldiers can learn from a study of old battlefields. The tactics in themselves are not so important, they may change. What is important is that battles are fought and commanded by men and they do not change. That Jackson went left flanking at Chancellorsville [or Longstreet went 'right flanking' at Gettysburg] is of academic interest. What is of greater interest is that good reconnaissance, the ability to think "on your feet" and adapt your plan as new information comes in . . . the ability to move fast and hit from an unexpected direction: to name but few of the lessons . . . are as relevant today, as they were in 1863. *All the manuals list the prerequisites for military success but only a study of how our predecessors applied, or failed to apply, the principles can breathe life into them.*[4]

Those who may assume that this volume will be of interest only to the military professional should be reassured that the methodology works equally well, if in somewhat different ways, for anyone who has ever visited a battlefield—or thinks that she might want to! Wives and families of War College students are no less interested than the soldier. The same is true of many foreign officers who know practically nothing about our Civil War. The authors share the friendship of a number of unusual men, representing all ages, many professions, and several sections of the country (indeed, several different countries) and the methodology works equally well with them all. It has been tested with cadets from West Point and various ROTC detachments as well as non-military students from liberal arts colleges. It works for alumni tours and Civil War Round Tables. On one occasion it even seemed to attract the interest of a busload of culturally deprived teenagers.

What these groups had in common is imagination, an ability to ask questions (of the material as well as the guide) and a little understanding of human nature at some level. (The teenager will identify with Joshua Chamberlain and the 20th Maine at Little Round Top fully as much as the new lieutenant or the former battalion commander, if in different ways.) This book does not deal with the operations leading to Gettysburg nor is it intended as a complete study of the battle. It says little about the vital subject of logistics, for example, and ignores, as do many of the histories, the cavalry battle between Gregg and Stuart on 3 July. Anyone wanting a full analysis of the battle should start with a book like Coddington's *The Gettysburg Campaign* and follow the sources that he cites.[5]

Historians use a wide variety of sources—diaries, letters, official reports, newspapers, memoirs, articles, and other histories—in recreating an historical event. In contrast we have depended almost exclusively on the Gettysburg volumes in the *War of the Rebellion: Official Records of the Union and Confederate Armies* recognizing that these are often flawed sources—poorly written in some cases, lacking perspective in others, frequently contradictory and occasionally even self-serving. These volumes do, however, contain detail not found elsewhere, they present the battle as it was remembered by the principal actors weeks or at most several months after the event, before other kinds of literature had crowded in to give a different shape to memory and perception, and they constitute the best kind of dialogue between participants and the modern soldier. Not everyone, however, has access to the *Official Records*, the time—or inclination—to read three bulky volumes on the Gettysburg campaign, or sufficient experience in tramping old battlefields to have worked out an appropriate methodology. This, in essence, is the rationale for publishing this volume.

This book can be read, as any history of the battle, during leisure hours at home. It can also serve as a reference source on a visit to the battlefield. To fight the battle as it is portrayed here could easily consume an entire day or longer; used selectively, however, it will illuminate any portion of the battlefield that the visitor has the time or inclination to visit. In either case, the instructions will take you from one stop to the next; there will be enough commentary on whatever you need to know to place the extracts from the *Official Records* in a meaningful context, and for that purpose a situation map is provided for each Stop. For a variety of reasons, not the least because the modern soldier must be familiar with a topographical map, these situation maps have troop positions imposed upon a modern topographical map, with features such as buildings, roads, and treelines drawn as they are known to have existed on the day of battle. An appendix provides sufficient information about weapons, formations and combined tactics to enable anyone who has no particular interest in the Civil War to comprehend and evaluate the tactical situations as they develop.

The reader should understand the importance of conducting his own tour in the order in which the battle was fought. This is essential, for it is the only way to get some sense of how the battle developed. Events on the second day can have little meaning without some knowledge of what had transpired the day before. To understand Longstreet's attack on the second day it is also necessary to follow him on his flank march, to understand in what way the concept that he and Lee seem to have had of Union positions the morning of 2 July was faulty, and to think about his relationship with Lee and their respective approaches to the situation. The soldier instinctively knows this; the civilian is probably more inclined to pass judgment and to become the partisan, which is part of the appeal to many who are attached to the Civil War but which has no place in this volume. Similarly, the decision to launch Pickett's charge can only be understood if one realizes what Lee had attempted on 2 July, while to interpret the movements and the fighting on July 1 and 2 as merely leading up to the climax of Pickett's charge is to distort the battle in its entirety. For all they knew, those who fell along McPherson's Ridge on 1 July believed that they had fought *the* battle at Gettysburg.

Finally, it is hoped that this book will serve two useful and distinct purposes. To some it will be an introduction to the battle of Gettysburg, while to others it may introduce a new and fascinating methodology. It is therefore at once a book for the beginner and a useful tool for the well-informed. It is also the first in a series of self guided tours which we hope will be of distinct help to the Army Staff Rides and of value to the long-time student of the Civil War.

Col. Harold W. Nelson
Dr. Jay Luvaas
Carlisle, Pennsylvania
24 February 1986

[1] Baron de Jomini, *Summary of the Art of War, or, a New Analytical Compend of the Principal Combinations of Strategy, of Grand Tactics and of Military Policy*, translated by Major O. F. Winship and Lieut. E. E. McLean (New York: G. P. Putnam and Co., 1854), p. 19; John Keegan, *The Face of Battle* (New York: The Viking Press, 1976), pp. 36 – 54; J. H. Plumb, "The Face of Battle," *The New York Times Book Review*. November 7, 1976, p. 2.

[2] Col. H. W. Huntley, Director, The Conduct of War Course. "Memorandum," The Army War College, May 5, 1937. U.S. Army Military History Institute, Carlisle Barracks, PA.

[3] Private information.

[4] Major General Sir Julian Thompson, "The Chancellorsville Battlefield: Personal Impressions." Copy in possession of the authors.

[5] Edwin B. Coddington, *The Gettysburg Campaign: A Study in Command* (New York: Charles Scribner's Sons, 1968).

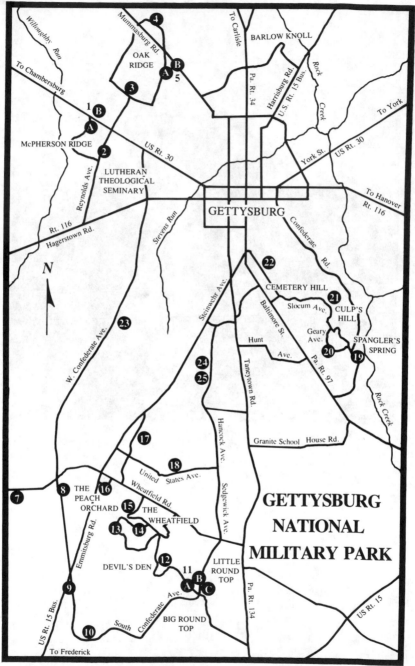

For Stop 6, see p. 5 5

THE FIRST DAY
WEDNESDAY 1 JULY 1863

Today, as in 1863, many roads lead to Gettysburg. No matter which one brings you there, you will begin this tour west of the town on McPherson Ridge, where the Battle of Gettysburg began. Stop 1 (refer to General Situation Map, opposite) is on this ridge where U.S. Highway 30, the old Chambersburg Road, approaches Gettysburg from the west. The National Park Service maintains a Guide/Information facility on the south side of the Highway in a small stone building. TURN SOUTH ON STONE AVENUE just east of this building. Drive south about 70 yards on Stone Avenue and TURN RIGHT into the small, rustic parking lot. You may want to use the facilities in the Park Service building before beginning the tour.

At the entrance to the parking lot, WALK ABOUT 50 YARDS SOUTH ON STONE AVENUE to the 150th Pennsylvania Monument. As you face east in the vicinity of this monument, looking over the snake rail fence, you see the McPherson barn to your left front. The ground slopes away from the barn toward the east for about a hundred yards and then rises gently to another ridge that is also a part of McPherson's Ridge. There are a few large trees in the declivity of the ridge almost directly east of you, marking the house site, and the church spire they frame is that of the chapel at the Lutheran Seminary. The cupola that was used as an observation post during the battle is nearby, but it is nearly obscured by vegetation in the summer. The ridge line identified by the spire is Seminary Ridge. You will also see the "National Tower" peeping over the trees a bit further south. That tower is on Cemetery Ridge, and it serves as a useful landmark from many points on the battlefield. Wherever you see that tower you will know the location of CEMETERY HILL, the key to the Union defensive position.

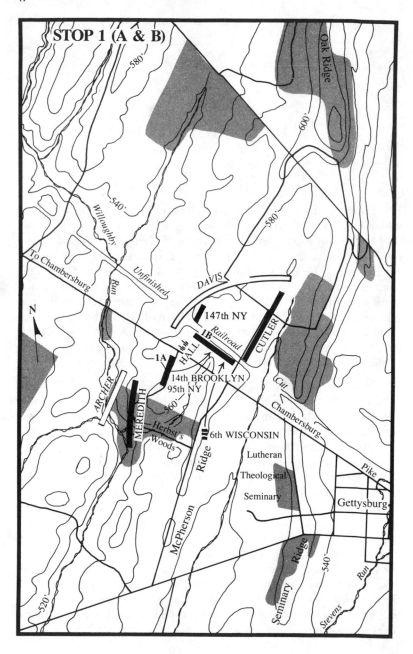

As you turn south, the woods directly in front of you are Herbst's Woods, continuing across Stone Avenue westward. As you look west, you see South Mountain on the skyline and a few houses and a rather large barn on the ridgeline. That is Herr Ridge, and Willoughby Run passes through the valley between Herr Ridge and McPherson's Ridge.

STOP 1, POSITION A

The first Union troops to occupy this position belonged to Brig. Gen. Jno. Buford's First Cavalry Division, which had entered Gettysburg the previous afternoon in time to drive out a Confederate infantry brigade which had been sent forward to "search the town for army supplies" and especially for shoes. The Confederates, commanded by *Brig. Gen. J.J. Pettigrew*, subsequently withdrew toward Cashtown, leaving pickets some 4 miles west of town. According to Buford,

> The night of the 30th was a busy night for the division. No reliable information of value could be obtained from the inhabitants, and but for the untiring exertions of many different scouting parties, information of the enemy's whereabouts and movements could not have been gained in time to prevent him from getting the town before our army could get up. By daylight on July 1, I had gained positive information of the enemy's position and movements, and my arrangements were made for entertaining him until General Reynolds [I Corps] could reach the scene. . . . Between 8 and 9 a.m., reports came in from the First Brigade (Colonel Gamble's) that the enemy was coming down from . . . Cashtown in force. Colonel Gamble made an admirable line of battle, and moved off proudly to meet him. [Buford's report is from *The War of the Rebellion: a compilation of the Union and Confederate Armies* (Washington 1880–1901) Series I, Volume XXVII, Part 1, pp. 926–27. Hereafter this source will be cited as *O.R.*, XXVII, Parts 1, 2, or 3 plus the page information.]

Report of Col. William Gamble, USA, commanding First Brigade, Buford's Division

> My brigade . . . about 1,600 strong . . . was placed in line of battle about 1 mile in front of the seminary . . . the Cashtown road being a little to the right of the center. . . . Three squadrons, part dismounted, were ordered to the front, and deployed as skirmishers

Chambersburg Turnpike (today's U.S. Route 30) looking west. Herr's Tavern is on the left in the distance. Willoughby Run is in the hollow. *Heth's* Confederate Division formed on the field at the left. c. 1890. Photo courtesy National Park Service (NPS).

to support the squadron on picket, now being driven back by the enemy's artillery and skirmishers. Our battery of six 3-inch rifled guns was placed in battery, one section [2 guns] on each side of the Cashtown road . . . and the other section on the right of the left regiment, to cover that flank. The enemy cautiously approached in column on the road, with three extended lines on each flank, . . . our skirmishers became engaged, and our artillery opened on the enemy's advancing column, doing good execution. The enemy moved forward; two batteries opened on us, and a sharp engagement of artillery took place. In a short time we were, by overpowering numbers, compelled to fall back about 200 yards to the next ridge and there make a stand. In the meantime our skirmishers, fighting under cover of trees and fences, were sharply engaged, did good execution, and retarded the progress of the enemy as much as could possibly be expected. . . . [O.R., XXVII, Part 1, p. 934.]

The Confederates, now moving upon Gettysburg in force, belonged to the Third Army Corps commanded by *Lieut. Gen. Ambrose P. Hill*, with *Maj. Gen. Henry Heth's* division in the lead. This division, accompanied by *Pegram's* battalion of artillery, had commenced its march at 5 a.m. and when it encountered Gamble's dismounted troopers some four hours later, *Heth* still did not know for certain what Union forces were in the vicinity of Gettysburg. He assumed that all that he had to deal with was Union cavalry, "most probably supported by a brigade or two of infantry."

Report of Maj. Gen. Henry Heth, CSA, commanding division, Hill's Corps

On reaching the summit of the second ridge of hills west of Gettysburg, it became evident that there were infantry, cavalry and artillery in and around the town. . . . My division, now within a mile of Gettysburg, was disposed as follows: *Archer's* brigade in line of battle on the right of the turnpike; *Davis'* brigade on the left of the same road, also in line of battle; *Pettigrew's* brigade and *Heth's* old brigade (*Colonel Brockenbrough* commanding) were held in reserve. *Archer* and *Davis* were now directed to advance, the object being to feel the enemy; to make a forced reconnaissance, and to determine in what force the enemy were . . . massing his forces on Gettysburg. Heavy columns of the enemy were soon encountered. *Davis*, on the left advanced, driving the enemy before him and capturing his batter-

The position of Meredith's Brigade 1 July 1863. Tree marks the spot of General Reynold's death. Photo c. 1865. Courtesy of the U.S. Army Military History Institute (USAMHI).

ies. . . . The brigade maintained its position until every field officer save two were shot down, and its ranks terribly thinned. . . .

On the right of the road, *Archer* encountered heavy masses in his front, and his gallant little brigade, after being almost surrounded by overwhelming forces in front and on both flanks, was forced back. . . . The enemy had now been felt, and found to be in heavy force . . . around Gettysburg. [*O.R.*, XXVII, Part 2, pp. 637–38.]

After checking the advance of the Confederates for several hours, Gamble's hard-pressed troopers were relieved by the timely arrival of two infantry brigades from Maj. Gen. John F. Reynolds' First Army Corps.

Brig. Gen. Lysander Cutler's brigade was the first to reach the scene. Reynolds himself detached two regiments—the 95th New York and the 14th Brooklyn [known also as the 84th New York Volunteers]—to deploy in the interval between Herbst's Woods, to your left, and Hall's 2d Maine Battery, which he already had ordered into position on the right of the Cashtown [Chambersburg] road. The remaining three regiments crossed the Cashtown road to meet the advance of *Davis'* Confederate brigade.

The second infantry unit to arrive was the famous 'Iron Brigade,' which the senior division commander in the corps, Maj. Gen. Abner Doubleday, had promptly sent into Herbst's Woods. This small piece of woods "possessed all the advantages of a redoubt, strengthening the center of our line, and enfilading the enemy's columns should they advance in the open spaces on either side." According to Doubleday:

> There was no time to be lost, as the enemy was already in the woods, and advancing at double-quick to seize this important central position and hold the ridge. The Iron Brigade, led by the Second Wisconsin in line, and followed by the other regiments, deployed *en échelon* without a moment's hesitation, charged with the utmost steadiness and fury, hurled the enemy back into . . . [Willoughby] run, captured, after a sharp and desperate conflict, nearly 1,000 prisoners . . . from *Archer's* brigade, and reformed their lines on the high ground beyond the ravine." [*O.R.*, XXVII, Part 1, 244–45.]

Report of Col. William W. Robinson, USA, commanding Seventh Wisconsin Infantry, Meredith's (Iron) Brigade

The brigade was immediately moved . . . to the point where the cavalry were engaged, where we formed . . . in position behind a grove of timber and slight elevation of land . . . [the cavalry] skirmishers dismounted and thrown forward of the ridge. Just at the time we came up, a brigade of the enemy's infantry was advancing upon the position. We were ordered to take position on the ridge in front of the cavalry as quickly as possible. I immediately formed companies, and threw the battalion forward into line in double-quick, and advanced to the top of the ridge. We had not halted to load, and no orders had been received to do so, for the reason, I suppose, that no one expected we were to be engaged so suddenly. I, however, gave the order to load during the movement, which was executed by the men while on the double-quick, so that no time was lost. . . .

Immediately in [front], and running parallel to and about 200 yards from my front, was a ravine, through which runs a small rivulet; from this ravine a heavy fire was opened. I was at first uncertain, in the dense smoke and from the near proximity of the fire, whether it was the enemy or the left wing of the Second Wisconsin.

At this moment Captain Wadsworth, of the division staff, rode up from the right. I asked could he tell what troops those were firing in the ravine. He pointed a little farther to the left up the ravine (where I saw the rebel battle-flag), and said it was the enemy, and that the general directed that we should drive them out. I moved the line forward to the crest of the ridge, delivered a volley, and gave the order to charge. The . . . Seventh Wisconsin, Nineteenth Indiana and Twenty-fourth Michigan rushed into the ravine with a yell. The enemy—what was left of them able to walk—threw down their arms, ducked through between our files, and passed to the rear. We moved up the opposite bank to the top of the hill, where I halted the line. . . . We had occupied our new position but a few minutes when Captain Richardson, of the brigade staff, brought an order to change front to the rear on the left battalion. While this evolution was being executed, General Meredith came up, and directed me to place my regiment in the grove on the right of the Second. I took the position indicated, my right resting on the open fields [the field immediately to your front as you stand at Stop 1, Position A, facing west], and threw out skirmishers to the front. In this position we lay some hours under a severe artillery fire. . . . I could see the movements of the enemy in our front. [*O.R.*, XXVII, Part 1, pp. 278–79.]

Report of Lieut. Col. S. G. Shepard, CSA, Seventh Tennessee Infantry, of operations of Archer's brigade

General Archer halted for a short time while a section of a battery opened fire. . . . He then deployed the brigade in line, and advanced directly upon the enemy through an open field. At the extreme side of the field there was a small creek [Willoughby Run] with a fence and undergrowth, which was some disadvantage to our line in crossing, but the brigade rushed across with a cheer, and met the enemy just beyond. We were not over 40 or 50 yards from the enemy's line when we opened fire. Our men fired with great coolness and deliberation, and with terrible effect, as I learned next day by visiting the ground.

We had encountered the enemy but a short time, when he made his appearance suddenly upon our right flank with a heavy force, and opened upon us a cross-fire. Our position was at once rendered untenable, and the right of our line was forced back. He made also a demonstration upon our left, and our lines commenced falling back, but owing to the obstructions in our rear (the creek, etc. . . .), some 75 of the brigade was unable to make their escape, General Archer among the rest. I saw General Archer a short time before he surrendered, and he appeared to be very much exhausted with fatigue. Being completely overpowered by numbers, and our support not being near enough to give us any assistance, we fell back across the field, and reformed just in rear of the brigade that had started in as our support. [*O.R.*, XXVII, Part 2, pp. 646–48.]

McPherson house and barn in 1880's. Today only the barn survives. (NPS)

Members of the Class of 1910, U.S. Army Military Academy, at the Reynolds statue. (USAMHI).

Now walk northward on STONE AVENUE, cross the Chambersburg pike (Route 30), and stand at POSITION B in the vicinity of the guns of Hall's Maine Battery and the equestrian statue of General Reynolds.

STOP 1, POSITION B

As the Iron Brigade fought for possession of Herbst's Woods, north of the Chambersburg road a desperate struggle was taking place between *Davis'* Confederate brigade and three regiments of Cutler's brigade. Because frontal assaults against artillery in position and properly supported by infantry on the flanks rarely if ever succeeded, *Davis'* brigade advancing from the west chose not to move directly up the hill against Hall's battery, but to endeavor instead to follow the low ground around to the north in an effort to outflank the position. If you stand behind one of Hall's 10 pounder Parrots and look to the west you can see this portion of the battle through the eyes of an artilleryman.

Report of Capt. James A. Hall, USA, Second Maine Battery, Wainright's Artillery Brigade, First Corps

We were in camp on the morning of July 1, at Marsh Creek, 4 miles from Gettysburg. At 9 a.m. marched, following the advance brigade [Cutler] of the First Division, First Army Corps, to the battle-field, about a half mile south and west of town, where we were ordered into position by General Reynolds on the right of the Cashtown road, some 400 yards beyond Seminary Hill. The enemy had previously opened a battery of six guns directly in our front at 1,300 yards distance, which they concentrated upon me as I went into position, but with little effect.

We opened upon this battery with shot and shell at 10.45 a.m., our first six shots causing the enemy to change the position of two of his guns and place them under cover behind a barn. In twenty-five minutes from the time we opened fire, a column of the enemy's infantry charged up a ravine on our right flank within 60 yards of my right piece, when they commenced shooting down my horses and wounding my men. I ordered the right and center sections to open upon this column with canister, and kept the left firing upon the enemy's artillery. This canister fire was very effective, and broke the charge of the enemy, when, just at this moment, to my surprise I saw my [infantry] support falling back without any order having been given me to retire. Feeling that if the position was too advanced for infantry it was equally so for artillery, I ordered the battery to retire by sections, although having no order to do so. The support falling back rapidly, the right section of the battery, which I ordered to take position some 75 yards to the rear, to cover the retiring of the other four pieces, was charged upon by the enemy's skirmishers and 4 of the horses from one of the guns shot. The men of the section dragged this gun off by hand.

As the last piece of the battery was coming away, all its horses were shot, and I was about to return for it myself when General Wadsworth [commanding First Division] gave me a peremptory order to lose no time, but get my battery in position near the town, on the heights [probably Cemetery Hill] to cover the retiring of the troops.

I sent a sergeant with 5 men after the piece, all of whom were wounded or taken prisoners. I had got near to the position I had been ordered to take, when I received another order from General Wadsworth to bring my guns immediately back . . . [along] the railroad grading leading out from town, which was swept at the time by two of the

The railroad cut, c. 1870. (NPS)

enemy's guns from the hills beyond, through the excavations at Seminary Hill. Having gotten onto this road, from its construction I could not turn from it on either side, and was obliged to advance 1,200 yards under this raking fire. . . .

Casualties first day, 18 men wounded and 4 taken prisoners; 28 horses killed and 6 wounded. . . . Fired during engagement, 635 rounds of ammunition. [*O.R.*, XXVII, Part 1, pp. 359–60.]

Some confusion exists as to events on this part of the field. Cutler reports that after sending the 14th Brooklyn and the 95th New York to support the left flank of Hall's battery he crossed the Cashtown road and deployed his three remaining regiments on the next ridge to your right, where the park road now crosses the railroad cut. Here he was struck on his right flank by "a vastly superior force of the enemy" — *Davis'* brigade.

To get a better view of this phase of the battle, you should now position yourself on the north side of the large equestrian statue of General Reynolds.

From this location you can discern the trace of the railroad cut about 100 yards to your front. About half a mile to your right front you will also notice a large monument silhouetted against the treeline on a ridge. This is the Peace Memorial, the ridge is Oak Ridge, and as you read about the events that swirled about your present position you should be aware that *Rodes'* Confederate division from *Ewell's* corps was slowly making its way through those woods a mile or two north of the Peace Memorial. They will not be a factor, however, in the fight about to take place for possession of this artillery position.

At the time of the battle the field on the other side of the railroad cut was in wheat. About 100 yards to the north and parallel to the railroad cut was a worm fence (probably about where you can see a part of a fence row), which intersected at right angles with a fence that ran along the crest from the Chambersburg road. Both this fence and the railroad cut are mentioned prominently in reports of the fighting in this sector.

Report of Brig. Gen. Lysander Cutler, U.S.A., commanding Second Brigade, Wadsworth's Division

The brigade . . . moved from camp early on the 1st instant (being the leading brigade of the corps) on toward Gettysburg. . . . When within about 2 miles of the town, I was ordered to move obliquely to the left across the fields to the ridge near the seminary, west of the town, where the enemy were already engaging our cavalry. I moved forward across the [unfinished] railroad with the Seventy-sixth New York Volunteers, One hundred and forty-seventh New York Volunteers, and the Fifty-sixth Pennsylvania Volunteers, immediately formed in line of battle, and found myself engaged with a vastly superior force of the enemy, advancing in two lines, at short range, in front and on my right flank. The Ninety-fifth New York Volunteers and the Fourteenth Brooklyn had been detached to the left, by order of General Reynolds, to support the Second Maine Battery and to hold the enemy in check until other troops could arrive.

The three regiments under my immediate command fought as only brave men can fight, and held their ground until ordered to fall back, by General Wadsworth, to the woods on the next ridge. The Fifty-sixth Pennsylvania and Seventy-sixth New York fell back. The One hundred and forty-seventh [New York] did not receive the order, in consequence of Lieutenant-Colonel Miller being wounded at the moment of receiving it. Major Harney held the regiment to its position until the enemy were in possession of the railroad cut on his left, when it was impossible for him to retire until relieved by a charge on the enemy from the left by the Sixth Wisconsin, Ninety-fifth New York, and Fourteenth Brooklyn, which resulted in capturing a large body of the enemy and enabling Major Harney to bring off the remainder of his regiment.

The loss of this gallant regiment was fearful . . . being 2 officers killed and 10 wounded, 42 men killed and 153 wounded—207 out of 380 men and officers within half an hour. The Seventy-sixth New York . . . went in with 348 men and 27 officers; their loss during the same time was 2 officers killed, 16 wounded, 27 men killed and 124 wounded within thirty minutes. The . . . Fifty-sixth Pennsylvania . . . went into action with 17 officers and 235 men, and lost 6 officers wounded, 1 mortally, and 8 men killed and 64 wounded at that point. [*O.R.*, XXVII, Part 1, p. 282.]

Cutler failed to mention—and perhaps he did not know—that the 147th New York did not fight alongside his other two regiments on the next ridge. As the following accounts prepared by survivors for the dedication of the regimental monument twenty-five years later, clearly demonstrate, the 147th New York fought on the same ridge where you now stand, roughly on line with Hall's battery and in a wheatfield on the far side of the railroad cut. Captain Hall himself verified the position years after the battle.

Captain James A. Hall to H. H. Lyman, July 19, 1888

I know there was a line of infantry on my immediate right. The first thing a battery commander would desire to know would be, how his flanks were protected; and of course I saw the infantry over there. As to their exact position, whether a prolongation of my line or a little retired, I cannot state definitely; but, certainly, not 300 yards in rear. General Reynolds, who put me in position, spoke to General Wadsworth at the moment, directing him to put a strong support on my right, which of itself would have caused me to keep an eye over there, and I there saw the line. . . . Let reason guide you. What was the infantry placed there for? To protect Hall's Battery. That infantry line was all there was to the right of said battery at that time, and was the extreme right of our line, with the enemy pressing the front and flank closely. Would any sane man, any corporal, have put the infantry support, in that critical period and situation, 300 yards in rear of the artillery it was to defend from a flank attack?

You know how difficult it is even the next day after a battle to tell just how things were [New York Monuments Commission for the Battlefields of Gettysburg and Chattanooga, *Final Report on the Battlefield of Gettysburg:*3 vols., Albany, 1900, III, 1006 – 7.]

A former captain in the 147th provided dramatic details of the kind not included in most after-action reports when the monument to the 147th New York Infantry regiment was dedicated in 1888. Because regulations stipulated that monuments must be situated on the brigade line unless the regiment had been officially detached, and because the brigade commander in this instance had erroneously included the 147th New York with his two remaining regiments on the next ridge to the rear (east), where REYNOLDS AVENUE today crosses the railroad cut, the part played by the 147th is often not noticed. In the dedication *Captain J. W. Pierce* reminded his old comrades of what had happened.

The distant reports of artillery tingled the ear as we marched up the Emmitsburg Pike. White circles of smoke rising in the air told of bomb bursts where the gallant cavalry boys were defending the line of Willoughby Run. . . . Orderlies with despatches dashed past us to the rear with the encouraging intelligence that "The rebs were thicker than blackberries beyond the hill." Pioneers were ordered to the front, fences were thrown down, and, as we passed into the fields near the Codori House, the fierce barking of Calef's Battery [Horse Artillery fighting alongside Gamble's dismounted cavalry] redoubled. With it came the order, "Forward, double-quick! Load at will!" Then was heard the wild rattle of jingling ramrods, as we moved towards the sound of the cannon. No straggling now; the old musket was clinched with firmer grasp. . . . We climbed the fence (at the crossing of the Fairfield Road) and passing to the south of the Seminary plunged headlong over the hill into the narrow valley between the Seminary and the McPherson House ridge. The air was full of flying fragments of shell from Confederate guns beyond Willoughby Run. The Fourteenth Brooklyn and Ninety-fifth New York were moved to the front of the McPherson House, from the rear of our column. Lieut. Col. Miller, not having any orders, halted . . . near the garden with a picket fence at the McPherson House, a few rods east of the stone basement barn on the south side of the pike and rode forward for orders. Hall's Battery . . . passed us in our rear, going to our right, across the Chambersburg Pike, and into position between the pike and railroad cut. Lieut. Col. Miller returned and ordered us by the flank to the right at a double-quick in rear of Hall's Battery, now in position on the third ridge. We crossed the railroad bed, and the moment the left of the regiment cleared it the order came, "By the left flank; guide centre!" We are now in the line of battle moving to the west. The Seventy-sixth New York and Fifty-sixth Pennsylvania, with the headquarters guard, had preceded us, moving along the rear of the second ridge, and were some distance to our right and rear, on the second ridge, and not on alignment with us.

While we were advancing in the wheatfield the battle opened on our right, and the bullets . . . were flying thick and fast as we marched rapidly towards our opponents. . . . We continued to advance in the nodding wheat of death until our left touched on the railroad cut, supporting Hall's Battery. "Lie down! fire through the wheat close to ground!" The battle was now on in all its fierceness. . . .

The firing of the enemy in my immediate front slackened, and the enemy retired towards the right. I moved my men forward a few yards further to the crest of the ridge . . . and discovered a line of Confederate skirmishers on our front, advancing . . . up a slope towards a rail fence [that ran north-south along the crest], firing as they advanced into Hall's Battery, while the battery was fighting for dear life. . . . I immediately ordered, "Left oblique, fire." The order was responded to by the two left companies. . . . Several rounds were fired into the skirmish lines . . . and I saw them return down the hill. . . . Hall's Battery had been fighting that skirmish line in a death grapple. "Artillery against skirmishers is like shooting mosquitoes with a rifle." . . . The moment the battery was relieved from the force of the attack it began to limber to the rear, and . . . disappeared in a cloud of dust on the Chambersburg Pike.

While this was taking place on the left, the battle reopened on the right with redoubled fury, and the cry came down the line, "They are flanking us on the right." The right companies, by Major Harney's orders, swung back on the south side of the rail fence [that ran parallel to, and about 100 yards north of the railroad cut]; the left front of the regiment was relieved of pressure from the enemy, who either laid concealed close under the ridge at the west end of the railroad cut, or had passed towards our fight. The fight was again fierce and hot. . . . Men fell all along the line.

I saw an officer ride down from Oak Hill in our rear, and wave his cap in retreat. To venture into this maelstrom between the railroad cut and that fence on the right was death. . . . Closer pressed the enemy. A regiment—the Fifty-fifth North Carolina—was pressing far to our right and rear, and came over to the south side of the rail fence. The colors drooped to the front. An officer in front of the centre corrected the alignment as if passing in review. It was the finest exhibition of discipline and drill I ever saw . . . on the battlefield. . . . Wadsworth seeing our peril ordered his adjutant general . . . to ride in and withdraw us. . . . He came through the leaden hail like a whirlwind across the old railroad cut and up the hill to Major Harney, who gave the command, "In retreat, march!". . . .

Finding the enemy so close upon us and the way open—the route we came in by—I followed several of my men into the railroad cut. A squad of Confederates were at the west end of the cut, behind some rails, and as we struck the bottom . . . they saluted us with all their guns. . . . I did not stay to dispute possession . . . and I climbed up the rocky face of the cut, on the south side, and made my way with many of our men across the meadow between the railroad cut and the Chambersburg Pike, crossed the pike . . . [and] joined . . . the regiment on the east slope of Seminary Ridge. . . . If we were ever "surrounded" we never knew it. If we were ever "rescued" by any troops . . . on that particular occasion, we were not aware of it. . . .

When Major Harney received the order to retire, we had occupied the ground nearly half an hour. The rear was open to Oak Hill [Seminary Ridge] and . . . the route over which we came from the Seminary was open and unobstructed. The ground that Hall's Battery occupied was unoccupied by the enemy. The only point where there was any opposition to our retreat was at the west end of that railroad cut. . . . The one hundred and forty-seventh . . . ran, pursued pell-mell by the enemy, most of the men crossing to the south side of the old railroad grading in the hollow between the second and third ridges, a very few only keeping on the north side of the grading and along in the railroad cutting through the second ridge, back towards Seminary Ridge. [*New York at Gettysburg*, III, pp. 990–94, 1004.]

Early in the action General Reynolds was killed in Herbst's Woods and Maj. Gen. Abner Doubleday, the senior division commander in I Corps, assumed command. Although he was hardly in a position to retrieve the situation caused by the retreat of Cutler's three regiments, he did organize an effective counter-attack against *Davis'* brigade. The 6th Wisconsin, of the Iron Brigade, had not participated in the attack against *Archer*; instead, along with the brigade guard of 2 officers and 100 men, this fine regiment had been held in reserve behind the Herbst Woods and was in the act of advancing to join the rest of the brigade when Doubleday sent it to the right, where Cutler's battle line was about to evaporate.

Report of Lieut. Col. Rufus R. Dawes, USA, Sixth Wisconsin
Infantry, Meredith's [Iron] Brigade, Wadsworth's Division

I marched by the right flank double-quick toward the point indicated. Before reaching a position where I could be of service, the enemy had succeeded in turning the flank, and, flushed with victory, was pressing rapidly in pursuit of our retreating line, threatening the rear of . . . Meredith's Iron Brigade, engaged in the woods on the left. I filed to the right and rear, to throw my line in front of the enemy, and moved by the left flank forward in line of battle upon his advancing line. My men kept up a steady double-quick, never faltering or breaking under the fire, which had become very galling. When my line had reached a fence on the Chambersburg turnpike, about 40 rods from the line of the enemy, I ordered a fire by file. This checked the advance of the rebels, who took refuge in a railroad cut . . . from which they opened a murderous fire upon us. I immediately ordered the men over the fence, with a view to charging the cut. The Ninety-fifth New York and Fourteenth Brooklyn [which had withdrawn from their original position between Hall's Battery and the woods] here joined on my left. . . .

The men of the whole line moved forward upon a double-quick, well closed, in face of a terribly destructive fire from the enemy. When our line reached the edge of the cut, the rebels began throwing down their arms in token of surrender. Adjt. Ed. P. Brooks, with promptness and foresight, moved a detachment of 20 men in position to enfilade the cut from the right, when the entire regiment in my front, after some murderous skirmishing by the most desperate, threw down their arms. . . .

The loss sustained by my command in this charge was not less than 160 men killed or wounded. [*O.R.*, XXVII, Part 1, pp. 275–76.]

Now you should return to your automobile and drive to STOP 2.

Turn RIGHT as you leave the parking lot, driving south on STONE AVENUE through Herbst's Woods. As you pass through the woods the road follows the battle line of the Iron Brigade and allows you a good view of the ravines and rough terrain before turning east, where the name of the road changes to MEREDITH AVENUE. As

View toward the location where Reynolds fell in Herbst Woods. Brady, July 1863. (NPS)

you leave the woods you will note the large field to the south (your right). Here Buford's cavalry reassembled to provide flank security before additional Union infantry lengthened the line of battle. The main axis of that line of battle is marked by the row of monuments that you see extending to your right as you approach the STOP sign.

Turn LEFT at the stop sign. Drive north on REYNOLDS AVENUE for about 100 yards to the parking extension near the north edge of Herbst's Woods, just short of the artillery position. Cross the road to a position near the snake rail fence. From here you should have a clear view of McPHERSON'S BARN, HERR RIDGE, THE REYNOLDS STATUE, the RAILROAD CUT, and the PEACE MEMORIAL. A few hundred feet behind you, near the east edge of the woods, is a monument marking the spot where Reynolds fell. It was also from this point that The Sixth Wisconsin moved forward in line of battle to the Chambersburg pike in his counterattack against *Davis'* brigade. In a paper written after the war, Colonel Dawes stated that he was not aware of the existence of the railroad cut until he had reached the Chambersburg pike; he had mistaken the maneuver of *Davis'* brigade for a retreat. [Col. Rufus Dawes, "With the Sixth Wisconsin at Gettysburg," reprinted in Ken Bandy, ed., *The Gettysburg Papers* (2 vols., Dayton, Ohio, 1978), I, pp. 218, 224.]

STOP 2.

After the repulse of *Archer* and the successful counterattack against *Davis'* brigade in the railroad cut, the Confederates fell back to Herr Ridge to reform. Meredith's Iron Brigade remained in the position it had staunchly defended in the morning, the men lying down much of the time to protect themselves from artillery fire from Confederate guns on Herr Ridge. Cutler's shattered regiments reformed in the woods near the Seminary and later moved back to reoccupy the original brigade line along this ridge (Reynolds Avenue) north of the highway. "Although reduced by a loss of half their numbers, the men bravely and cheerfully moved back to renew the fight." [*O.R.*, XXVII, Part 1, p. 282.]

Together with the 6th Wisconsin and Tidball's (Calef's) horse battery, which had been sent in to replace Hall's battery, Cutler's men held this ridge for about 45 minutes until Confederate artillery moving into position on Oak Ridge near the Peace Memorial caused the brigade once again to fall back to the woods on Seminary Ridge. When large bodies of *Rodes'* infantry could be seen forming at the edge of the woods behind the Confederate batteries, Cutler changed front to the right and assisted in the initial repulse of *Iverson's* brigade from *Rodes'* division early in the afternoon. The 6th Wisconsin and one of Cutler's regiments, the 14th Brooklyn, remained with Tidball's (Calef's) battery until enemy fire forced it to retire.

Meanwhile the remainder of the First Corps arrived. Doubleday, who had succeeded Reynolds in command of the corps when the latter was mortally wounded, placed Robinson's division in reserve on Seminary Ridge, with orders to throw up "some slight intrenchments" to serve as a fallback position. He directed Rowley to divide his division, sending Stone's brigade to plug the gap between the Iron Brigade and the position that Cutler had resumed north of the railroad cut along this ridge, and Biddle's brigade to strengthen the cavalry in the field south of Herbst's Woods (the line of monuments bordering Reynolds Avenue to the right of the last Stop sign.)

By this time the Confederates had massed for their second effort. *Heth's* whole division was thrown into line with three of his four brigades formed to the right of the Chambersburg road and supported by *Pender's* division deployed in similar fashion. This line was prolonged to the left by *Rodes'* division, which had reached Oak Ridge by early afternoon in time to join in the attack.

Stone's brigade, comprising three Pennsylvania regiments, bore the brunt of this attack.

Report of Col. Roy Stone, USA, commanding Second Brigade, Rowley's Division

I posted my brigade . . . between the two brigades of Wadsworth's division, upon the ridge in advance of Seminary Ridge, my right resting upon the Chambersburg or Cashtown road and left extending nearly to the wood occupied by General Meredith's [Iron] Brigade, with a strong force of skirmishers thrown well down the next slope, and the road held by a platoon of sharpshooters.

The skirmishers having to advance over an open field, without the slightest shelter, and under a hot fire from the enemy's skirmishers concealed behind a fence, did not stop to fire a shot, but, dashing forward at a full run, drove the rebel line from the fence, and held it throughout the day. As we came upon the field, the enemy opened fire upon us from two batteries on the opposite ridge, and continued it, with some intermissions, during the action. Our low ridge afforded slight shelter from this fire, but no better was attainable, and our first disposition was unchanged until between 12 and 1 o'clock, when a new battery upon a hill on the extreme right opened a most destructive enfilade of our line, and at the same time all the troops upon my right [Cutler] fell back nearly a half mile to the Seminary Ridge.

This made my position hazardous and difficult in the extreme, but rendered its maintenance all the more important. I threw one regiment (149th Pennsylvania) into the road, and disposed the others on the left of the stone building, to conceal them from the enfilading battery. My line thus formed a right angle facing north and west. Soon after, as the enemy's infantry was developed in heavy force upon the right, I sent another regiment (143rd Pennsylvania, Colonel Dana) to the right of the One hundred and forty-ninth. At about 1.30 p.m. the grand advance of the enemy's infantry began. From my position I was enabled to trace their formation for at least 2 miles. It appeared to be a nearly continuous line of deployed battalions, with other battalions in mass or reserve, their line being formed not parallel but obliquely to ours, their left first became engaged with the troops on the northern prolongation of Seminary Ridge. The battal-

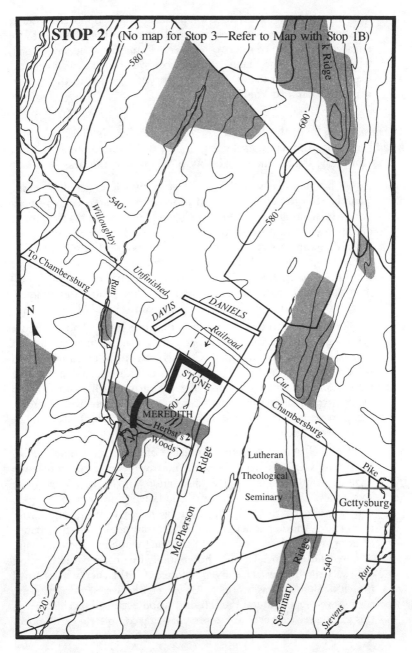

STOP 2 (No map for Stop 3—Refer to Map with Stop 1B)

ions engaged soon took a direction parallel to those opposed to them, thus causing a break in their line and exposing the flank of those engaged to the fire of my two regiments in the Chambersburg road. Though at the longest range of our pieces, we poured a most destructive fire upon their flanks, and, together with the fire in their front, scattered them over the fields.

Stone here refers to the attack of *Iverson's* brigade, *Rodes'* division, against the right flank of Baxter's brigade of Robinson's division, which had been sent from its original position near the Seminary to strengthen the right of the Union line. (See below, p. 37) Stone continues:

A heavy force was then formed in two lines parallel to the Chambersburg road, and pressed forward to the attack of my position. Anticipating this, I had sent Colonel Dwight (149th) forward to occupy a deep railroad cutting about 100 yards from the road, and when they came to a fence within pistol-shot of his line he gave them a staggering volley; reloading as they climbed the fence [the same fence that the 147th New York had contested earlier] and waiting till they came within 30 yards, gave them another volley, and charged, driving them back over the fence in utter confusion.

Returning to the cut, he found that the enemy had planted a battery which perfectly enfiladed and made it untenable, and he was obliged to fall back to the road. Colonel Dana [143rd] meanwhile had been engaged with the enemy directly in his front and preventing them from outflanking Colonel Dwight on the right, and Colonel Wister [150th] had been holding our original line, now the left front. Being wounded about this time and carried from the field, I cannot speak so definitely of the remainder of the action.

Colonel Wister assumed command of the brigade, and finding the enemy were advancing from the northwest, brought up his own regiment, and, making a new disposition, drove back that force. Again they advanced from the north, and, struggling over the railroad cut, came nearly to the road, but a vigorous bayonet charge drove them back. Another attack from the west was met by another change of front and repulsed. Colonel Wister being wounded, the command devolved on Colonel Dana, who continued to contest the position with varying fortunes until it was reported that the enemy had turned his left flank as well as his right. An officer who was sent to learn the truth of the report found the [Herbst] wood occupied by the enemy; this made a retreat necessary to prevent being completely surrounded, and the command fell back, making an occasional stand and fighting all the way to Seminary Ridge. There a firm stand was made and a battery brought off; thence the retreat was continued through the town, in which the troops suffered heavily from the fire of the enemy;, who already occupied the streets on both their flanks. . . .

No language can do justice to the conduct of my officers and men on the bloody "first day;" to the coolness with which they watched and awaited, under a fierce storm of shot and shell, the approach of the enemy's overwhelming masses; their ready obedience to orders, and the prompt and perfect execution, under fire, of all the tactics of the battle-field; to the fierceness of their repeated attacks, or to the desperate tenacity of their resistance.

They fought as if each man felt that upon his own arm hung the fate of the day and the nation. Nearly two-thirds of my command fell on the field. Every field officer save one was wounded and disabled. . . . To the courage and skill of regimental commanders is due in great measure the successful maintenance of the position. [O.R., XXVII, Part 1, pp. 329–31.]

Return to your car and read the following extract from Doubleday's *Report* in a position where you can view the Seminary and also the entire line along REYNOLDS AVENUE.

About 4 p.m. the enemy, having been strongly re-enforced, advanced in large numbers, everywhere deploying into double and triple lines, overlapping our left for a third of a mile, pressing heavily upon our right and overwhelming our center. It was evident *Lee's* whole army was approaching. Our tired troops had been fighting desperately, some of them for six hours. They were thoroughly exhausted, and . . . it became necessary to retreat. All my reserves had been thrown in, and the First Corps was now fighting in a single line. . . .

I now gave orders to fall back . . . [to] the intrenchments in front of the seminary. . . . From behind the feeble barricade of rails these brave men stemmed the fierce tide which pressed upon them incessantly, and held the rebel lines, which encircled them on three sides, at bay until the greater portion of the corps had retired. . . . The batteries [which] had all been brought back from their advanced positions and posted in Seminary Hill . . . greatly assisted the orderly retreat, retarding the enemy by their fire. . . .

The First Corps only consisted of about 8,200 men when it entered the battle. It was reduced at the close of the engagement to about 2,450. [*O.R.*, XXVII, Part 1, pp. 250–51.]

Despite these horrendous losses the regiments who fell back from the Herbst's Woods and the fields on either side maintained unit cohesion. On the left, Biddle's First Brigade "gradually fell back, firing," until it reached the cover of the rail breastworks thrown up in haste by Robinson's division, where it remained "fighting desperately and until time was afforded to most of our other troops, to the artillery, and to the ambulances to withdraw in an orderly manner." [*O.R.*, XXVII, Part 1, 313.] Outflanked on their left, the Iron Brigade was likewise forced to fall back. Told that they must hold the woods "to the last extremity," the hard-pressed men of the Iron Brigade did not move until ordered to retire to Seminary Ridge. The Second Wisconsion, although it had lost 233 of 302 engaged, made the movement "in good order, firing as we retired. About half the distance from where we commenced to retire to this new position, I faced the regiment to the front, and again moved to meet the advancing columns of the enemy, when I discovered the enemy closing in upon our left. I again faced the rear, and took up a position on the [Seminary] ridge." [*O.R.*, XXVII, Part 1, p. 274.] The Seventh Wisconsin likewise fell back deliberately "by the right of companies to the rear some 150 or 200 yards, halted, and wheeled into line again to support the other regiments in retiring. Then again retired about the same distance and again wheeled into line, and so on" to the foot of Seminary Ridge. [*O.R.*, XXVII, Part 1, p. 280.]

Report of Maj. Joseph A. Engelhard, CSA, Assistant Adjutant-General of operations of Pender's division, Hill's Corps

About 4 o'clock, *General Pender* ordered an advance . . . with instructions to pass *General Heth's* division, if found at a halt, and charge the enemy's position. . . . The division moved rapidly forward and passed the division . . . which seemed much exhausted and greatly reduced by several hours' hard and successful fighting. *General Lane*, on the extreme right, being annoyed by a heavy force of dismounted cavalry [Gamble] on his right flank, which kept up a severe enfilade fire, was so much delayed thereby that he was unable to attack the enemy in front. . . . *Colonel Perrin*, after passing *General Heth's* division, took advantage of a ravine to reform his line and moved rapidly forward, preserving an alignment with *General Scales*, on his left.

Upon ascending a hill in front, the brigade was met by a furious storm of musketry and shell from infantry posted behind temporary breastworks and artillery from batteries to the left of the road near Gettysburg. The brigade steadily advanced at a charge, reserving its fire, as ordered, easily dislodging the enemy from his several positions, and meeting with but little opposition, excepting from an enfilade fire from the artillery on the left, until it came within 200 yards of . . . the ridge upon which is situated the theological college.

The brigade, in crossing a line of fencing, received a most withering and destructive fire, but continued to charge without returning the fire of the enemy until reaching the edge of the grove which crowns the crest of the ridge. *Colonel Perrin*, here finding himself without support either on the right or left (*General Lane* having been delayed by the attack on his flank, and *General Scales'* brigade having halted to return the fire of the enemy after their brigade commander had been wounded), attacked the enemy determinedly in his immediate front with success, suffering greatly by an enfilade fire on both flanks, and then, dividing his command by ordering the two right regiments to change front to the right, and the two left regiments to change front to the left, he attacked the enemy posted on the right behind a stone wall and on the left behind a breastwork of rails in flank, easily routing them, driving them through the town to Cemetery Hill.

This movement caused the artillery on the left, which had continued to keep up a constant and destructive fire upon the advancing lines of the division, to limber up and move to the rear. Much of this artillery would have been captured, but the two left regiments met a second force of the enemy posted behind a stone fence to the left of the college, which was easily dislodged, but not in time to intercept the fleeing batteries. . . .

General Scales, on the left, with his left resting on the turnpike, after passing the troops of *General Heth*, advanced at a charge upon the flank of a brigade of the enemy   [*O R*, XXVII, Part 2, pp. 656–58.]

Report of Brig. Gen. A. M. Scales, CSA, commanding brigade, Pender's Division

We pressed on until coming up with the line in our front, which was at a halt and lying down. I received orders to halt, and wait for this line to advance. This they soon did, and pressed forward in quick time. That I might keep in supporting distance, I again ordered an advance, and, after marching one-fourth of a mile or more, again came upon the front line, halted and lying down. The officers on this part of the line informed me that they were without ammunition, and would not advance farther. I immediately ordered my brigade to advance. We passed over them, up the ascent, crossed the ridge, and commenced the descent just opposite the theological seminary. Here the brigade encountered a most terrific fire of grape and shell on our flank, and grape and musketry in our front. Every discharge made sad havoc in our line, but still we pressed on until we reached the bottom. . . . Our line had been broken up, and now only a squad here and there marked the place where regiments had rested.

Every field officer of the brigade had been disabled. [*O.R.*, XX-VII Part 2, pp. 669–70.]

RETURN TO YOUR CAR AND CONTINUE DRIVING NORTH TO STOP 3.

As you drive toward the STOP sign at the Chambersburg Pike, imagine what it must have been like for the men of the 6th Wisconsin, 160 of whom became casualties in the area between the highway and the railroad cut. Notice too how the artillery positions on OAK RIDGE, near the PEACE MEMORIAL, dominate this terrain, quickly causing Cutler's brigade to fall back for the second time to the protective woods on SEMINARY RIDGE.

Pause as you pass over the railroad tracks to appreciate the difficulty the cuts would pose for infantry. Colonel Dawes stated after the war that when his 6th Wisconsin marched across this railroad cut to join Cutler's brigade when it reoccupied this ridge, "at least one thousand muskets lay in the bottom of it." ["With the Sixth Wisconsin at Gettysburg," Ken Bandy, ed., *The Gettysburg Papers*, 2 vols., Dayton, Morningside Bookshop, 1978; vol. I, p. 375.]

Continue driving north until you come to the "T" intersection. Drive directly across the "T" intersection and turn left into the small turnout on the north side of BUFORD AVENUE. Park there. You need not dismount while reading the narrative for this stop.

STOP 3

From here you can see why *Davis'* Confederate brigade kept edging toward the north when making its initial attack in the morning. Not wanting to attack Hall's Maine Battery head-on, the Brigade edged toward its left where it would be sheltered somewhat by the high ground to your left-front. The terrain inevitably would have drawn the attacking Confederates toward the car rather than assaulting the 147th New York directly from the Willoughby Run valley. By moving in this direction before launching their attacks, the Confederates could strike Cutler's two remaining regiments at an oblique angle and get into the rear of the 147th New York. The "high hill" mentioned in his report is the hill to your left front. It is not high and from here it does not look much like a hill, but if you look to your left as you turn to the right about 100 yards ahead, and picture the 147th New York posted behind a fence, it might look more like a hill.

Report of Brig. Gen. Joseph R. Davis, CSA, *commanding brigade and Heth's Division*

About 10.30 o'clock a line of battle was formed—with the Forty-second Mississippi . . . on the right; Fifty-fifth North Carolina . . . on the left, and Second Mississippi . . . in the center—skirmishers thrown forward, and the brigade moved forward to the attack . . . driving in the enemy's skirmishers, and came within range of his line of battle, which was drawn up on a high hill in a field a short distance in front of a railroad cut. The engagement soon became very warm After a short contest the order was given to charge, and promptly obeyed. The enemy made a stubborn resistance, and stood until our men were within a few yards, and then gave way, and fled in much confusion, but rallied near the railroad where he again made a stand, and, after desperate fighting, with heavy loss on both sides, he fled in great disorder toward the town, leaving us in possession of his com manding position and batteries.

After a short interval, he again returned in greater numbers, and the fight was renewed, and, being opposed by greatly superior numbers, our men gave way under the first shock of his attack, many officers and men having been killed or wounded, and all much exhausted by the excessive heat; but the line was promptly formed, and carried to its former position, and, while there engaged, a heavy force was observed moving rapidly toward our right [probably the 14th Brooklyn and the 95th New York], and soon after opened a heavy fire on our right flank and rear.

In this critical condition, I gave the order to retire, which was done in good order, leaving some officers and men in the railroad cut, who were captured, although every effort was made to withdraw all the commands. This was about 1 p.m. About 3 p.m. a division of *Lieutenant-General Ewell's* corps came up on our left, moving in line perpendicular to ours, and the brigade was again moved forward, and, after considerable fighting, reached the suburbs of the town, into which the enemy had been driven. The men, being much exhausted by the heat and severity of the engagement, were here rested, and about sunset were ordered to bivouac about 1 mile to the rear.

In this day's engagement the losses in men and officers were very heavy; of 9 field officers present, but 2 escaped unhurt . . . A large number of the company officers were killed or wounded. [*O.R.*, XXVII, Part 2, pp. 649–50.]

Now you can proceed on **BUFORD AVENUE** toward STOP 4. Just before **BUFORD AVENUE** turns right, heading toward OAK RIDGE, take a quick look to your left at the "high hill in a field a short distance in front of a railroad cut," where the 147th was posted. Only from this angle is it perceived as a "hill", but to make the main assault from here would have been a costly business.

Follow **BUFORD AVENUE** north, cross the **MUMMASBURG ROAD**, and proceed to the parking lot in front of the **PEACE MEMORIAL**. Park your car there and walk up the hill to the pair of 10-pounder Parrots positioned east of the Memorial.

As you face south from this position you can easily identify McPHERSON'S BARN, HERBST WOODS, HERR RIDGE, and the NATIONAL TOWER on Cemetery Ridge. Whatever its esthetic shortcomings, the National Tower serves throughout the tour as a useful point of reference, indicating the location of the key terrain in the Union line.

View west from the seminary cupola, c. 1870. (NPS)

In the foreground you will see a small house located on the north side of the Mummasburg Road. Across the road from that house, and beyond the field, you will see a line of monuments ending in a woods. That point of the woods marks the objective of *Rodes'* attack.

STOP 4

Ewell's Corps, which had reached Carlisle, Pennsylvania, on 27 June, approached Gettysburg from the *north*. In response to orders, on 30 June *Ewell's* Corps began its march to rejoin the main body of the Army of Northern Virginia in the vicinity of Cashtown. The first to reach the scene was Rodes' division, which that morning had left Heidlersburg for Biglerville (then known as Middletown), where he turned his column south to join *Hill's* Corps, then reported to be moving on Gettysburg.

The view that he describes is now before you.

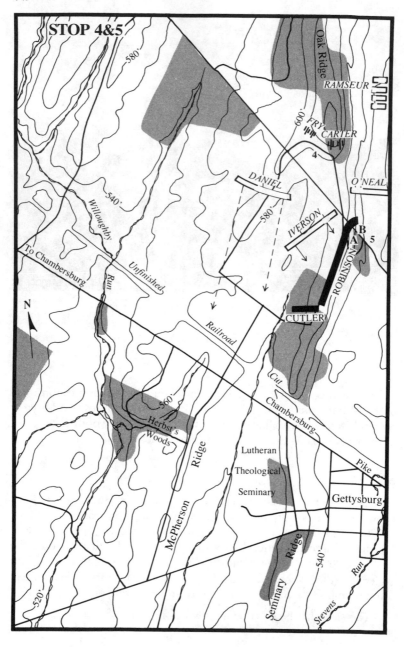

Report of Maj. Gen. R. E. Rodes, CSA, commanding division, Ewell's Corps

When within 4 miles of the town, to my surprise, the presence of the enemy there in force was announced by the sound of a sharp cannonade, and instant preparations for battle were made.

On arriving on the field, I found that by keeping along the wooded [Oak] ridge . . . I could strike the force of the enemy with which *General Hill's* troops were engaged upon the flank, and that, besides moving under cover, whenever we struck the enemy we could engage him with the advantage in ground.

The division was, therefore, moved along the summit of the ridge, with only one brigade deployed at first, and finally, as the enemy's cavalry had discovered us and the ground was of such character as to admit of cover for a large opposing force, with three brigades deployed; *Doles* on the left, . . . *O'Neal* . . . in the center, and *Iverson* on the right, the artillery and the other two brigades moved up closely to the line of battle. The division had to move nearly a mile before coming in view of the enemy's forces, excepting a few mounted men, and finally arrived at a . . . prominent hill on the ridge whence the whole of that portion of the force opposing *General Hill's* troops could be seen. To get at these troops properly, which were still over half a mile from us, it was necessary to move the whole of my command by the right flank, and to change direction to the right.

While this was being done, *Carter's* [artillery] battalion was ordered forward, and soon opened fire upon the enemy, who at this moment, as far as I could see, had no troops facing me at all. He had apparently been surprised; only a desultory fire of artillery was going on . . . but before my dispositions were made, the enemy began to show large bodies of men in front of the town, most of which [Robinson's division] were directed upon the position which I held, and almost at the same time a portion of the force opposed to *General Hill* [Cutler's brigade] changed position so as to occupy the woods on the summit of the same ridge I occupied. . . . Either these last troops, or others which had hitherto been unobserved behind the same body of woods, soon made their appearance directly opposite my center.

Being thus threatened from two directions, I determined to attack with my center and right, holding at bay still another force [two divisions of Howard's Eleventh Corps] then emerging from the town (apparently with the intention of turning my left) with *Doles'* brigade,

. . . trusting to this gallant brigade thus holding them until *General Early's* division arrived, which I knew would be soon, and which would strike this portion of the enemy's force on the flank before it could overpower *Doles.*

At this moment *Doles'* brigade occupied the open plain between the Middletown road [present route #34] and the foot of . . . [Oak] ridge. . . . The Alabama brigade [*O'Neal*], with a wide interval between it and *Doles'*, extended from this plain up the slope of the ridge; *Daniel's* brigade supported *Iverson's*, and extended some distance to the right of it; *Ramseur* was in reserve. All the troops were in the woods excepting *Doles'* and a portion of . . . *O'Neal's* brigades, but all were subjected to some loss or annoyance from the enemy artillery. . . .

Finding that the enemy was rash enough to come out from the woods to attack me, I determined to meet him when he got to the foot of the hill I occupied, and, as he did so, I caused *Iverson's* brigade to advance, and at the same moment gave in person to *O'Neal* the order to attack, indicating to him precisely the point to which he was to direct the left of the four regiments then under his orders. . . . *Daniel* was at the same moment instructed to advance to support *Iverson*, if necessary; if not, to attack on his right as soon as possible.

Carter's whole battalion was by this time engaged hotly—a portion from the right, the remainder from the left of the hill—and was subjected to a heavy artillery fire in return. *Iverson's* brigade attacked handsomely, but suffered very heavily from the enemy's musketry from behind a stone wall along the crest of the ridge. The Alabama brigade went into action in some confusion, and with only three of its regiments . . . the Fifth having been retained by my order, and . . . the Third having been permitted by *Colonel O'Neal* to move with *Daniel's* brigade. The three . . . regiments moved with alacrity (but not in accordance with my orders as to direction). . . . It was soon apparent that we were making no impression upon the enemy, and hence I ordered forward the Fifth Alabama to their support; but, to my surprise . . . I found that *Colonel O'Neal*, instead of personally superintending the movements of his brigade, had chosen to remain with his reserve regiment. The result was that the whole brigade . . . was repulsed quickly, and with loss . . .

Iverson's left being thus exposed, heavy loss was inflicted upon his brigade. His men fought and died like heroes. His dead lay in a distinctly marked line of battle. His left was overpowered, and many of his men, being surrounded, were captured.

General Daniel's gallant brigade, by a slight change in the direction of *Iverson's* attack, had been left too far to his right to assist him directly, and had already become engaged . . . [with] the enemy, strongly posted in a railroad cut. [*O.R., XXVII*, Part 2, pp. 552–54.]

Report of Brig. Gen. Alfred Iverson, CSA, commanding brigade, Rodes' Division

Learning that the Alabama brigade, on my left, was moving, I advanced at once, and soon came in contact with the enemy, strongly posted in woods and behind a concealed stone wall. My brigade advanced to within 100 yards, and a most desperate fight took place. I observed a gap on my left, but presumed that it would soon be filled by the advancing Alabama brigade . . . *Brigadier-General Daniel* came up to my position, and I asked him for immediate support, as I was attacking a strong position. He promised to send me a large regiment. . . . At the same time, I pointed out to *General Daniel* a large force of the enemy who were about to outflank my right, and asked him to take care of them. He moved past my position, and engaged the enemy [Stone's brigade] some distance to my right, but the regiment he had promised me . . . did not report to me at all. . . . I then found that this regiment had formed on the right of the Third Alabama, which was on my right, and could not be used in time to save my brigade, for *Colonel O'Neal's* brigade had in the meantime advanced on my left, and been almost instantaneously driven back, upon which the enemy, being relieved from pressure, charged in overwhelming force . . . and captured nearly all that were left unhurt in three regiments of my brigade.

When I saw white handkerchiefs raised, and my line of battle still lying down in position, I characterized the surrender as disgraceful; but when I found afterward that 500 of my men were left lying dead and wounded on a line as straight as a dress parade, I exonerated, with one or two disgraceful individual exceptions, the survivors, and claim for the brigade that they nobly fought and died without a man running to the rear. . . .

I endeavored, during the confusion among the enemy incident to the charge and capture of my men, to make a charge with my remaining regiment and the Third Alabama, but in the noise and excitement I presume my voice could not be heard. The fighting here ceased on my part. . . . [*O.R.*, XXVII, Part 2, pp. 579–80.]

RETURN TO YOUR CAR FOR THE SHORT DRIVE TO STOP 5. Before departing, however, please notice the top of an Observation Tower protruding above the trees on the distant ridge to the south.

This was the point where *General Robert E. Lee,* who had not yet reached the battlefield, would plan to move two divisions of *Lieut. Gen. James Longstreet's* First Army Corps with the hope of rolling up the Union left flank on the second day of the battle. *Longstreet* was ordered to move his corps under the cover provided by **HERR RIDGE**, in plain view slightly to your right.

Leave the parking lot moving in an easterly direction, and follow the road as it bends south toward the **MUMMASBURG ROAD** (STOP sign). Cross the Mummasburg Road, drive about 100 yards to the **OAK RIDGE OBSERVATION TOWER**, and park in the parking lot beyond the tower.

STOP 5, POSITION A

From the south end of the parking lot walk down the road that follows the stone wall to the SOUTHWEST. Proceed about 100 yards to the vicinity of the 83rd New York Infantry Monument. From this position you have a clear view of the Union defensive position as *Iverson* attacked from the direction of the Peace Memorial.

Report of Brig. Gen. John C. Robinson, USA, commanding Second Division, First Corps

On the morning of . . . the 1st, the division marched from Emmitsburg, bringing up the rear of the column, and . . . was placed . . . in reserve near the seminary. Almost immediately after taking this position I received notice that the enemy was advancing a heavy column of infantry on the right of our line of battle, when I sent the Second Brigade, under Brigadier-General Baxter, to meet it. Orders being received at this time to hold the Seminary, the First Brigade under Brigadier General Paul, was set at work to intrench the ridge on which it was situated. I then rode to the right of the line, to superintend the operations there.

On my arrival, I found my Second Brigade so placed as to cover our right flank, but with too great an interval between it and the line of the First Division. I at once directed General Baxter to change front forward on his left battalion, and to close this interval, toward which the enemy was making his way. By the time this change was effected, the whole front of the brigade became hotly engaged, but succeeded in repulsing the attack. The enemy, however, soon after brought up fresh forces in increased masses, when, finding the position so seriously threatened, I . . . brought up the First Brigade, and placed part of it in the position first occupied by Baxter's brigade, and the remaining battalions as a support to his second position. The enemy now made repeated attacks on the division, in all of which he was handsomely repulsed, with the loss of three flags and about 1,000 prisoners. . . .

The division held this position on the right—receiving and repelling the fierce attacks of a greatly superior force, not only in front, but on the flank, and, when the enemy's ranks were broken, charging upon him and capturing his colors and men—from about noon until nearly 5 p.m., when I received orders to withdraw. These orders not being received until all other troops (except Stewart's battery) had commenced moving to the rear, the division held its ground until outflanked right and left, and retired fighting.

From the nature of the enemy's attacks, frequent changes were rendered necessary, and they were made promptly under a galling fire. No soldiers ever fought better. . . .

This division went into battle with less than 2,500 officers and men, and sustained a loss of 1,667, of which 124 were commissioned officers. [*O.R.*, XXVII, Part 1, pp. 289–91.]

STOP 5, POSITION B

Walk back to the parking lot. Position yourself near the stone wall on the east side of the lot. From here you can easily spot the NATIONAL TOWER on Cemetery Ridge. To the left of the tower, roughly on a line with the large black-roofed building in the valley, you should be able to detect the top of a small steel observation tower on CULP's HILL. Shifting much further to the left and on the same general line as a transmission tower on the skyline, you should be able to discern BARLOW'S KNOLL with its clump of trees and line of monuments in the plain about ¾ of a mile to the east.

Report of Maj. Gen. Oliver O. Howard, USA, commanding Eleventh Army Corps

At 3.30 a.m. July 1, orders were received . . . to move the Eleventh Corps to within supporting distance of the First Corps, which was to move to Gettysburg. I immediately sent an aide-de-camp to General Reynolds [commanding the Left Wing] to receive his orders.

At 8 a.m. orders were received from him directing the corps to march to Gettysburg. The column was at once set in motion. . . . On approaching the town, heavy artillery firing was heard. . . .

On hearing of the death of General Reynolds, I assumed command of the left wing, instructing General Schurz to take command of the Eleventh Corps. After an examination of the general features of the country, I came to the conclusion that the only tenable position for my limited force was . . . Cemetery Ridge . . . [which] commanded every eminence within easy range. The slopes toward the west and south were gradual, and could be completely swept by artillery. To the north, the ridge was broken by a ravine running transversely. . . .

Learning from General Doubleday . . . that his right was hard pressed, and receiving continued assurance that his left was safe and pushing the enemy back, I ordered the First and Third Divisions of the Eleventh Corps to seize and hold a prominent height on the right of the Cashtown road and on the prolongation of Seminary Ridge. . . .

About 12.30 [p.m.] General Buford sent me word that the enemy was massing between the York and Harrisburg roads, to the north of Gettysburg, some 3 or 4 miles from the town. . . . Prisoners . . . taken by the First Corps . . . reported that we were engaging *Hill's* corps, or a portion of it, and that an aide of *General Longstreet* had arrived, stating that he would be up with one division in a short time. About this time the head of column of the Eleventh Corps . . . passed through the town. . . .

The news of *Ewell's* advance from the direction of York was confirmed by reports from General Schurz, General Buford, and . . . my aide-de-camp, who had been sent in that direction to reconnoiter. I therefore ordered General Schurz to halt his command, to prevent his right flank being turned, but to push forward a thick line of skirmishers, to seize the point first indicated [Oak Ridge] as a relief and support to the First Corps. . . .

About . . . 2.45 p.m. the enemy showed himself in force in front of the Eleventh Corps. His batteries could be distinctly seen on a prominent slope between the Mummasburg and the Harrisburg roads. From this point he opened fire upon the Eleventh Corps, and also more or less enfilading Robinson's division, of the First Corps. . . .

At 3.20 the enemy renewed his attack upon the First Corps. . . . Earnest requests were made upon me for re-enforcements, and General Schurz, who was engaged with a force of the enemy much larger than his own, asked for a brigade to be placed *en échelon* on his right. I had then only two small brigades in reserve, and had already located three regiments from these in the edge of the town . . . and I felt sure that I must hold the point where I was [Cemetery Hill] as an ultimate resort. [*O.R.*, XXVII, Part 1, pp. 701–704.]

Report of Maj. Gen. Carl Schurz, USA, commanding Third Division and Eleventh Corps

. . . Signs were apparent of an advance of the enemy upon my line, especially the right. . . . Feeling much anxiety about my right, which was liable to be turned if any of the enemy's forces were advancing by the Heidlersburg road, I dispatched one of my aides . . . with the request to have one brigade of the Second Division placed upon the north side of the town, near the railroad depot, as an *échelon* to the First Division. My intention was to have that brigade in readiness to charge upon any force the enemy might move around my right.

After having taken the necessary observations on my extreme left, I returned to the Mummasburg road, where I discovered that General Barlow had moved forward his whole line, thus losing on his left the connection with the Third Division; moreover, the Second Brigade, of the First Division, had been taken out of its position *en échelon* behind the right of the First Brigade. I immediately gave orders to re-establish the connection by advancing the right wing of the Third Division. . . .

Suddenly the enemy opened upon the First Division from two batteries placed near the Harrisburg road, completely enfilading General Barlow's line. . . . Soon afterward . . . the enemy appeared in our front with heavy masses of infantry, his line extending far beyond our right. It was now clear that the two small divisions under my command, numbering hardly over 6,000 effective men when going into battle, had a whole corps of the rebel army to contend against.

A movement to the rear became at once necessary, but before any orders to that effect could be transmitted, my whole line was engaged, and the Second Brigade, First Division, whose flank had been most exposed . . . fell back in considerable disorder. . . . The Third Division had meanwhile to sustain a furious attack. According to orders, it fell back toward the town in good order. . . . Being flanked right and left, the situation of that division was most trying. The retreat through the town, protected by part of our artillery was effected as well as could be expected under such circumstances, the streets being filled with vehicles of every description and overrun with men of the First Corps. A considerable number of men, who became entangled in cross streets and alleys, were taken prisoners. . . .

It was after 5 o'clock when the Eleventh Corps occupied the position on Cemetery Hill. . . . [O.R., XXVII, Part 1, pp. 728–30.]

The retreat of the Eleventh Corps through Gettysburg forced the withdrawal of what was left of the First Corps still on Seminary Ridge, thus for all practical purposes ending the fighting on July 1. From STOP 5 the standard tour moves on to the second day of the battle.

If you have time to spare and a special interest in the action around BARLOW'S KNOLL, you may wish to invest an extra 20–30 minutes for this two-mile automobile excursion. Those who prefer to proceed directly to STOP 6 should remain here and turn to p. 59, where the tour resumes.

EXCURSION

Leave the Parking lot at the southeast corner. The road doubles back as it goes down the hill, and you will approach the Mummasburg road from the south near some railroad tracks. TURN RIGHT ON THE MUMMASBURG ROAD. Proceed for about 0.3 mile, TURN LEFT and stop briefly at the first turnout (45TH NEW YORK INFANTRY). From this spot you can look back to the McLEAN house and barn on your left rear which mark the general area of the attack earlier in the afternoon of O'Neal's Alabama brigade. The blue building on your right marks the vicinity of Doles' position before he joined in the final attack against the Eleventh Corps.

Report of Lieutenant Colonel Adolphus Dobke, USA, Forty-fifth New York Infantry, First Brigade, Third Division, Eleventh Corps

At about 1:30 p.m. a long line of the enemy [O'Neal's Brigade] moved on the extreme right of the First Corps, passing the left of the Forty-fifth, and offering the flank to the Forty-fifth. . . . The left wing of our regiment at once gave fire at very short distance (50 or 100 yards) with such terrible effect that, in result with the combination of the fire from the extreme right of the First Corps, the whole of the enemy's line halted, gradually disappeared on the same spot where they stood, and the remainder, finding they could not retrace their steps, surrendered, partly to the First Corps and a great number to the Forty-fifth Regiment, which prisoners were at once sent to the rear. . . . In the most raging fire and the most horrible scenes . . . not a single man flinched, but all were cheering, and fulfilled their duties nobly.

So we remained under fire until about 4 p.m., when the First Corps, on our left gave way, and exposed our left flank, and at the same time heavy columns were moving on us in front and in the right, when the . . . Regiment was ordered to retreat. . . . Only one-third of the equipped men of the Forty-fifth . . . assembled at the cemetery behind the stone fence, and two-thirds of the regiment were lost. [*O.R.*, XXVII, Part 1, pp. 734–35.]

Continue on HOWARD AVENUE, cross the CARLISLE ROAD (STOP sign) and drive the remaining 0.3 mile to BARLOW'S KNOLL. Stop at the turnout on the knoll.

Report of Maj. Gen. Jubal A. Early, CSA, commanding division, Ewell's Corps

On arriving in sight of [Gettysburg] . . . on the direct road from Heidlersburg, I discovered that *General Rodes'* division was engaged with the enemy to the right of me . . . occupying a position in front of Gettysburg. . . . I immediately ordered my troops to the front, and formed my line across the Heidlersburg road, with *Gordon's* brigade on the right, *Hoke's* brigade (under *Avery*) on the left, *Hays'* brigade in the center, and *Smith's* brigade in the rear of *Hoke's*. *Jones'* battalion of artillery was posted in a field on the left of the Heidlersburg road . . . so as to fire on the enemy's flank, and, as soon as these dispositions could be made, a fire was opened upon the enemy's infantry and artillery by my artillery with considerable effect.

Gordon's brigade was then ordered forward to the support of *Doles'* brigade, which was on *Rodes'* left, and was being pressed by a considerable force . . . which had advanced . . . to a wooded hill [Barlow's Knoll] on the west side of Rock Creek . . . and as soon as *Gordon* was fairly engaged with this force, *Hays'* and *Hoke's* brigades were ordered forward in line, and the artillery, supported by *Smith's* brigade, was ordered to follow. [*O.R.*, XXVII, Part 2, p. 468.]

Report of Brig. Gen. J. B. Gordon, CSA, commanding brigade, Early's Division

About 3 p.m. I was ordered to move my brigade forward to the support of *Major-General Rodes'* left. The men were much fatigued from long marches, and I therefore caused them to move forward slowly until within about 300 yards of the enemy's line, when the advance was as rapid as the nature of the ground and a proper regard for the preservation of my line would permit. The enemy had succeeded in gaining a position upon the left flank of *Doles'* brigade, and in causing these troops to retreat. This movement . . . would necessarily have exposed his right flank, but for the precaution he had taken to cover it by another line. It was upon this line, drawn up in a strong position on the crest of a hill, a portion of which was woodland, that my brigade charged. Moving forward under heavy fire over rail and plank fences, and crossing a creek whose banks were so abrupt as to prevent a passage excepting at certain points, this brigade rushed upon the enemy with a resolution and spirit . . . rarely excelled. The enemy made a most obstinate resistance until the colors on portions of the two lines were separated by a space of less than 50 paces, when his line was broken and driven back, leaving the flank which this line had protected exposed to the fire from my brigade. An effort was here made by the enemy to change his front and check our advance, but the effort failed, and this line, too, was driven back in the greatest confusion, and with immense loss in killed, wounded, and prisoners. Among the latter was a division commander (General Barlow) who was severely wounded. I was here ordered . . . to halt.

I had no means of ascertaining the number of the enemy's wounded by the fire of this brigade, but if there were in the usual proportion to his killed, nearly 300 of whom were buried on the ground where my brigade fought, his loss in killed and wounded must have exceeded the number of men I carried into action. Neither was it possible for me to take any account of the prisoners sent to the rear, but the division inspector credits this brigade with about 1,800. I carried into action about 1,200 men. . . . [*O.R.*, Part 2, XXVII, pp. 492–93.]

Report of Maj. Gen. Early, (continued)

Gordon advanced . . . over the hill . . . and across the fields toward the town, until he came to a low ridge, behind which the enemy had another line of battle, extending beyond his left. I directed him to halt here, and then ordered *Hays* and *Avery*, who had been halted on the east side of Rock Creek . . . to advance toward the town, on *Gordon's* left, which they did in fine style, encountering and driving back into the town in great confusion the second line of the enemy.

A nineteenth century view of East Cemetery Hill. (USAMHI)

. . . A very large number of prisoners were captured in the town . . . their number being so great as really to embarrass us. . . .

While these operations were going on with my division, I saw, farther to the right, the enemy's force on that part of the line falling back and moving in comparatively good order on the right of the town toward the range of hills in the rear. . . . As soon as my brigades had entered the town, I rode into that place myself, and, after ascertaining the condition of things, I rode to find *General Ewell* and *General Rodes,* or *General Hill,* for the purpose of urging an immediate advance upon the enemy before he should recover from his evident dismay, in order to get possession of the hills to which he had fallen back with the remnant of his forces. . . . Shortly after meeting with *General Ewell* I communicated my views to him, and was informed that *Johnson's* division was coming up, and it was determined with this division to get possession of a wooded hill [Culp's Hill] to the left of Cemetery Hill, which it commanded, but this division arrived at a late hour and its movement having been delayed by the report of the advance [of the enemy] on the York road, no effort to get possession of the wooded hill on the left of the town was made that night. [*O.R.,* XXVII, Part 2, 469–70.]

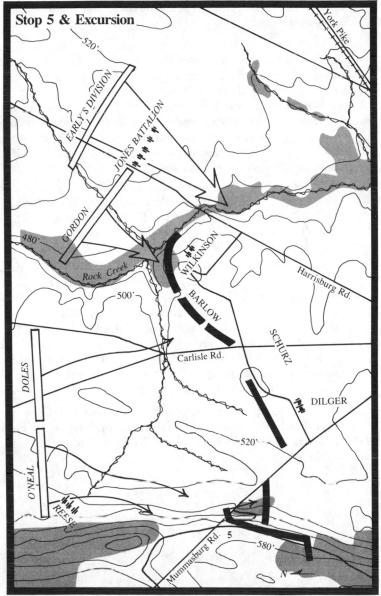

Stop 5 & Excursion

1" = 1500'

*Report of Lieut. Gen. Richard S. Ewell, CSA, commanding
Second Army Corps*

My loss on this day was less than 2,900 killed, wounded, and missing. The enemy had fallen back to a commanding position known as Cemetery Hill . . . and quickly showed a formidable front there. On entering the town, I received a message from the commanding general to attack this hill, if I could do so to advantage. I could not bring artillery to bear on it, and all the troops with me were jaded by twelve hours' marching and fighting, and I was notified that *General Johnson's* division (the only one of my corps that had not been engaged) was close to the town.

Cemetery Hill was not assailable from the town, and I determined, with *Johnson's* division, to take possession of a wooded hill to my left . . . commanding Cemetery Hill. Before *Johnson* got up, the enemy was reported moving to outflank our extreme left, and I could see what seemed to be his skirmishers in that direction.

Before this report could be investigated by *Lieut. T. T. Turner,* aide-de-camp of my staff, and *Lieut. Robert D. Early,* sent for that purpose, and *Johnson* placed in position, the night was far advanced. . . . On my return to my headquarters, after 12 o'clock at night, I sent orders to *Johnson* . . . to take possession of this hill [Culp's hill]. . . . *General Johnson* stated in reply . . . that . . . he had sent a reconnoitering party to the hill [which] on nearing the summit, was met by a superior force of the enemy. . . . Day was now breaking, and it was too late. . . . [*O.R.*, XXVII, Part 2, pp. 445–46.]

Now turn around and retrace your route to OAK RIDGE to pick up the tour directions carrying you on to the second day of the battle. Park in the area beside the Observation Tower and turn the page to continue the tour.

THE SECOND DAY
THURSDAY 2 JULY 1863

The first day of battle at Gettysburg is what soldiers today call an 'encounter engagement:' it was not fought according to any preconceived plan, units came piecemeal to the field, almost nothing was known of the terrain or enemy troop dispositions, and command and control problems, particularly on the side of the Confederates, prevented any unity of action until late in the day.

Lee had arrived during *Rodes'* attack the previous day. Although he still did not intend to bring on a general engagement, the arrival of *Early's* division presented an opportunity for a tactical victory that he could not resist. By the time the Confederates had swept the Eleventh Corps from the fields north of Gettysburg and forced the First Corps back from Seminary Ridge through the town, *Lee* had determined to renew the conflict the following day. He gave discretionary orders to *Ewell* to "push those people" off Cemetery Hill that evening "if practicable," while to *Lieutenant General Peter Longstreet*, the veteran commander of the First Army Corps, he revealed his intention to attack the Union left flank the next day. For reason already explained in his after-action report, *Ewell* decided not to assault Cemetery Hill, and by the time he could get a reconnoitering party to Culp's Hill, superior Union forces occupied that position as well. "Day was now breaking, and it was too late."

Historians have argued for years whether or not an attack against Cemetery Hill on the night of July 1 would have succeeded. For the purposes of this tour, however, we are concerned not whether *Ewell's* decision was the correct one, but, accepting the fact of the decision, to understand *Lee's* remaining options as he saw them. His central thoughts are explained in the detailed report of the Pennsylvania campaign that he completed six months after the battle.

Report of General R. E. Lee, CSA, commanding the
Army of Northern Virginia

The enemy gave way on all sides, and was driven through Gettysburg with great loss. . . . More than 5,000 prisoners, exclusive of a large number of wounded, three pieces of artillery, and several colors were captured. Our own loss was heavy. . . . The enemy retired to a range of hills south of Gettysburg, where he displayed a strong force of infantry and artillery.

It was ascertained from the prisoners that we had been engaged with two corps . . . and that the remainder of that army, under General Meade, was approaching Gettysburg. Without information as to its proximity, the strong position which the enemy had assumed could not be attacked without danger of exposing the four divisions present, already weakened and exhausted by a long and bloody struggle, to overwhelming numbers of fresh troops. *General Ewell* was, therefore, instructed to carry the [Cemetery] hill . . . if he found it practicable, but to avoid a general engagement until the arrival of the other divisions of the army. . . . He decided to await *Johnson's* division . . . which had marched from Carlisle by the road west of the mountains to guard the trains of his corps, and consequently did not reach Gettysburg until a late hour.

In the meantime the enemy occupied the point which *General Ewell* designed to seize [Culp's Hill], but in what force could not be ascertained owing to the darkness. An intercepted dispatch showed that another corps had halted that afternoon 4 miles from Gettysburg. Under these circumstances, it was decided not to attack until the arrival of *Longstreet*, two of whose divisions [those of *Hood* and *McLaws*] encamped about 4 miles in the rear during the night. . . .

It had not been intended to deliver a general battle so far from our base unless attacked, but coming unexpectedly upon the whole Federal Army, to withdraw through the mountains with our extensive trains would have been difficult and dangerous. At the same time we were unable to await an attack, as the country was unfavorable for collecting supplies in the presence of the enemy, who would restrain our foraging parties by holding the mountain passes with local and other troops. A battle had, therefore, become in a measure unavoidable, and the success already gained gave hope of a favorable issue.

The enemy occupied a strong position, with his right upon two commanding elevants adjacent to each other [Culps Hill and Cemetery Hill]. . . . His line extended thence upon the high ground *along the Emmitsburg road*, with a steep ridge in rear, which was also occupied. This ridge was difficult of ascent, particularly the two hills above mentioned as forming its northern extremity, and a third at the other end [Little Round Top], on which the enemy's left rested. Numerous stone and rail fences along the slope served to afford protection to his troops and impede our advance. In his front, the ground was undulating and generally open for about three-quarters of a mile. . . .

It was determined to make the principal attack upon the enemy's left, and endeavor to gain a position from which it was thought that our artillery could be brought to bear with effect. *Longstreet* was directed to place the divisions of *McLaws* and *Hood* on the right of *Hill*, partially enveloping the enemy's left, which he was to drive in.

General Hill was ordered to threaten the enemy's center, to prevent re-enforcements being drawn to either wing, and to co-operate with his right division in *Longstreet's* attack.

General Ewell was instructed to make a simultaneous demonstration upon the enemy's right [at Culp's Hill], to be converted into a real attack should opportunity offer. [*O.R.*, XXVII, Part 2, pp. 317–19.]

Report of Lieutenant General James Longstreet, CSA, commanding First Army Corps

The command reached Chambersburg . . . on the 27th, and a halt of two days was made for rest. On the night of the 28th, one of my scouts came in with information that the enemy had passed the Potomac, and was probably in pursuit of us. The scout was sent to general headquarters, with the suggestion that our army concentrate east of the mountains, and bear down to meet the enemy.

I received orders . . . to move part of my command, and to encamp it at Greenwood. The command, excepting *Pickett's* division, which was left to guard our rear at Chambersburg, moved on the morning of the 30th, and the two divisions and battalions of Reserve Artillery got into camp at Greenwood about 2 o'clock in the afternoon. . . .

On the next day, the troops set out for Gettysburg, excepting *Pickett's* division, not yet relieved from duty at Chambersburg, and *Law's* brigade, left by *Hood* on picket at New Guilford. Our march was greatly delayed . . . by *Johnson's* division, of the Second Corps, which came into the road from Shippensburg, and the long wagon trains that followed him. *McLaws* division, however, reached Marsh Creek, 4 miles from Gettysburg, a little after dark, and *Hood's* division got within nearly the same distance of the town about 12 o'clock at night. *Law's* brigade was ordered forward to its division during the day, and joined about noon on the 2d. Previous to his joining, I received instructions from the commanding general to move, with the portion of my command that was up, around to gain the Emmitsburg road, on the enemy's left. The enemy, having been driven back . . . the day previous, had taken a strong position extending from the hill at the cemetery along the Emmitsburg road. [*O.R.*, XXVII, Part 2, p. 358.]

Neither *Hood* nor *McLaws*, *Longstreet's* two division commanders on the controversial 'flank march', submitted after-action reports of Gettysburg. *Hood* wrote briefly about it in his book *Advance and Retreat*, and in 1879, *McLaws* explained before the Georgia Historical Society what had happened from his point of view. His account is essential for understanding both the march itself and the frame of mind of the principals involved. Although many authorities place the meeting between *Lee* and *Longstreet* on Seminary Ridge, there is strong internal evidence in this and the following accounts that points to *Herr Ridge*, slightly more than a mile to the west, as the site where the events described by *McLaws* took place. *Lee* was too good a commander to have caused the tired troops of *Hood* and *McLaws* to have marched nearly to Seminary Ridge only to have them return to a position west of Herr Ridge before commencing the flank march: this would have involved an extra two miles and would have brought the troops forward over the dismal battleground of 1 July, where *Heth's* battered division was endeavoring to reform, something no experienced general would do unless it were necessary. And if the Confederate column was nearly as far forward as Seminary Ridge, why would *Lee's* engineer have led them behind Herr Ridge when they easily could have avoided detection simply by following the low ground near Willoughby Run, which they ultimately did. Moreover, as the italicised passages in the following accounts reveal, there are other reasons why the conversation could not have occurred in the vicinity of *Lee's* headquarters just north of the Chambersburg pike, as many have assumed. *McLaws* recalls:

On the 30th June my command was put in march towards Gettysburg, and camped, I think, at or near Greencastle. . . . Before moving on the first, I received orders to follow in rear of *Johnson's* division of *Ewell's* corps, which had been detached from the corps to conduct *Ewell's* trains west of the mountains, while the rest of the corps came by the shortest route to *General Lee's* headquarters.

Accordingly I had my division ranged alongside of the road to Gettysburg by eight o'clock on the 1st of July . . . and had not been long in place before *Johnson's* division appeared. After it had passed I went to *Major Fairfax*, of *General Longstreet's* staff, and asked if I should follow the troops or wait until *Ewell's* train had passed. *Fairfax* rode to *General Longstreet* to find out, and shortly returned with directions to wait until the train had passed. As the train appeared to be a very long one I had its rate of travel timed as it passed over a known distance, and computed its length to be over fourteen miles.

At any rate it was not until after four o'clock that it had passed, and I then took up the line of march to the front. About five o'clock . . . we heard distinctly the sound of cannon, and . . . the men quickened their pace to the music of the guns. The march was continued, and about ten P.M. I met *General Longstreet* in the road and he . . . directed me to go into camp at the water course [Marsh Creek], then some miles distant, which I reached a little after twelve at night, and camped or rather rested. Some time after my arrival I received orders from *General Longstreet* to continue the march at four A.M., but the order was afterwards countermanded, with directions not to leave until sunrise.

The march was continued at a very early hour, and my command reached the hill overlooking Gettysburg early in the morning. Just after I arrived *General Lee* sent for me — *as the head of my column was halted within a hundred yards of where he was* — and I went at once and reported. *General Lee* was sitting on a fallen tree with a map beside him. After the usual salutation, *General Lee* remarked: "General, I wish you to place your division across this road," pointing on the map to about the place I afterwards went to [near the Peach Orchard], *and directing my attention to about the place across the country from where we were, the position being a commanding one;* "and I wish you to get there if possible without being seen by the enemy." The place he pointed out was about the one I afterwards went to, and the line he marked out on the map for me to occupy was one perpendicular to the Emmittsburg road. . . . "Can you get there? . . . Can you do it?"

I replied that I knew of nothing to prevent me, but would take a party of skirmishers and go in advance and reconnoitre. He said "*Major Johnston*, of my staff, has been ordered to reconnoitre the ground, and I expect he is about ready." I then remarked, "I will go with him."

Just then *General Longstreet*, who, when I came up, was walking back and forth some little distance from General Lee, and hearing my . . . request to reconnoitre, spoke quickly and said: "No, sir, I do not wish you to leave your division," and then, pointing to the map, said: "I wish your division placed so," running his finger in a direction perpendicular to that pointed out by *General Lee. General Lee* replied: "No, General, I wish it placed . . . just the opposite." I then reiterated my request to go with *Major Johnston*, but *General Longstreet* again forbade it. *General Lee* said nothing more, and I left them, and, joining my command, put it under cover under a line of woods a short distance off. *General Longstreet* appeared as if he was irritated and annoyed, but the cause I did not ask.

When I rejoined my command I sent my engineer officer . . . to go and join *Major Johnston*, and gave him instructions what to observe particularly, as he was an officer in whom I had confidence, but was ordered back. I then reconnoitred myself for my own information, and was soon convinced that *by crossing the ridge where I then was*, my command could reach the point indicated by *General Lee*, in a half hour, without being seen. I then went back to the head of my column and sat on my horse and saw in the distance the enemy coming, hour after hour, onto the battlefield.

[Major General Lafayette McLaws, "Gettysburg," *Southern Historical Society Papers*, vol. VII (1879), pp. 67–69.]

Drive out of the parking lot along the stone wall past position 5A. Follow that road into the grove and turn right at the first intersection to return to Reynolds Avenue. Turn left on Reynolds, cross the railroad tracks to US Highway 30. Turn right on Highway 30; drive 0.8 mile to the brick building on your left known now—and at the time of the battle—as HERR's TAVERN. Just beyond the tavern turn left onto HERR RIDGE ROAD and drive 0.7 mile to the STOP sign. It was probably in this general area where *Lee* and *McLaws* discussed the

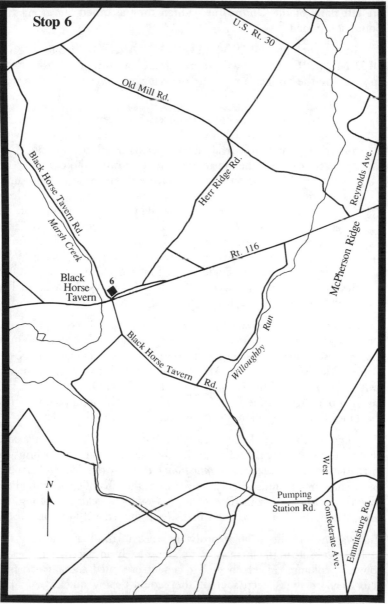

Stop 6

Black Horse Tavern

6

$1'' = 3000'$

N

coming march designed to bring two of *Longstreet's* divisions beyond the left flank of the Union line, which they assumed lay along the Emmitsburg road.

Turn right onto OLD MILL ROAD. After about 0.8 mile on OLD MILL ROAD you will approach a small bridge. Pause at the approach to the bridge to read the overview of *Longstreet's* orders and his subsequent narrative.

> *[General Lee's]* . . . engineer officers had been along the line far enough to find a road by which the troops could move and be concealed from the Federal signal stations [on Little Round Top.] About 11 o'clock on the morning of the 2d he ordered the march, and put it under the conduct of his engineer officers, so as to be assured that the troops would move by the best route and encounter the least delay in reaching the position designated by him for the attack on the Federal left, at the same time concealing the movements then under orders from view of the Federals. *McLaws'* division was in advance, with *Hood* following. [Lt. Gen. James Longstreet, "Lee's Right Wing at Gettysburg," Robert Underwood Johnson and Clarence Clough Buel, eds., *Battles and Leaders of the Civil War* (4 vols., New York: The Century Company, 1887), III, 340.

Evidently *Lee* and *Longstreet* already had a faulty concept of the Union position, which was still back along Cemetery Ridge at the time that *Lee* issued his orders: not until several hours later did Maj. Gen. Daniel Sickles order his Third Army Corps forward to occupy the higher ground in the area of the Devil's Den and the Peach Orchard, and it was nearly 4 p.m. by the time Brig. Gen. Andrew E. Humphrey's division of the Third Corps moved into position along the Emmitsburg Road.

Major General E. M. Law, commanding the last brigade in *Hood's* division to reach Herr Ridge, mentions that he "found the other brigades of *Hood's* division *resting about a mile from the town*, on the Chambersburg road. These troops undoubtedly moved from the Chambersburg road on your right, marching from right to left across these fields and along the open, flat ground bordering the small stream immediately to your front.

The wagons and the artillery probably stuck to the roads, leaving the more direct route to the infantry, which most likely advanced in a series of company columns, in which each regiment presented about 15–20 files across and 20 ranks deep so that they could deploy quickly into the standard two-rank fighting line.

McLaw's division, which had occupied Herr Ridge, used a different route. *Brig. Gen. J. B. Kershaw*, who commanded the lead brigade in the division on that occasion, wrote that earlier in the morning his troops moved southward behind the crest of Herr Ridge where the brigade "was halted at the end of the lane leading to Black Horse Tavern, situated some five hundred yards to our right." His brigade and at least one other, commanded by *Brig. Gen. P. J. Semmes*, followed *Kershaw's* brigade down the lane to the road that we shall follow to Black Horse Tavern.

Now cross the bridge and drive on for another 0.5 mile to the STOP sign.

Anderson's division of *Hill's* Corps, which had not been involved in the fighting on the first day, bivouacked the night of July 1st on the high ground to the right of the STOP sign. Not until this division moved forward early on the 2nd to extend the Confederate line southward along Seminary Ridge was *McLaws* division of *Longstreet's* corps able to advance from its bivouac along Marsh Creek to Herr ridge, where it remained until *Longstreet's* march began shortly after noon. *McLaws* recalled that his division was put in motion about 1 p.m.

At the STOP sign ("T" intersection), turn left. Drive 0.3 mile and turn left again, just short of the bridge, onto BLACK HORSE TAV-ERN ROAD. The creek on your right is Marsh Creek, where many of *Longstreet's* troops had encamped on the night of July 1st. Most of the buildings that you will pass on the road to BLACK HORSE TAVERN were here at the time of the battle.

As you top the rise beyond the Independent Brethren Church, 0.2 mile down the road, you can see HERR RIDGE to your left front. At some point within the next half mile you should be able to discern three large silos clustered on a farm on the far side of HERR RIDGE. These will serve as a useful landmark, for they stand at about the place where *McLaws'* lead brigade, commanded by *Brigadier General Joseph B. Kershaw*, rested until receiving the order "to move under cover of the hills toward the right, with a view to flanking the enemy in that direction, if cover could be found to conceal the movement. [*O.,R.*, XXVII, Part 2, p. 366.]

After 0.8 mile on the BLACK HORSE TAVERN ROAD you cross another small bridge. This is over the same small run you paused at while reading the operational concept for July 2nd, and here *Hood's* divisions, marching across the fields, joined this road.

Black Horse Tavern from Marsh Creek Bridge on Fairfield Road, c. 1890. (NPS)

At 1.8 miles on **BLACK HORSE TAVERN ROAD** you come to the tavern, the private residence on your left when you reach the **STOP** sign at the **FAIRFIELD** or Hagerstown road. Stop about 10 yards short of the **STOP** sign, pulling well to the side of the road. From this position you can look across the **FAIRFIELD** road to your left front toward a large rounded hill—the spot from which *Longstreet* and *McLaws* made their visual reconnaissance.

STOP 6

McLaws' division, or at least the brigades of *Kershaw* and *Semmes*, had left Herr Ridge by marching down an old lane that entered the BLACK HORSE TAVERN ROAD near the stone house about 500 yards to your rear. *McLaws*, who was riding with *Major Johnston* of *Lee's* staff "some distance ahead" of *Kershaw's* lead brigade, resumes the narrative.

Suddenly, as we rose a hill on the road we were taking, the [Little] Round Top was plainly visible, with the flags of the signal men in rapid motion. I sent back and halted my division and rode with *Major Johnston* rapidly around the neighborhood to see if there was any road by which we could go into position without being seen. Not finding any I joined my command and met *General Longstreet* there, who asked, "What is the matter?" I replied, "Ride with me and I will show you that we can't go on this route, according to instructions, without being seen by the enemy." We rode to the top of the hill and he at once said, "Why this won't do. Is there no way to avoid it?" I then told him of my reconnoissance in the morning, and he said: "How can we get there?" I said: "Only by going back—by counter-marching." He said: "Then all right," and the movement commenced. But as *General Hood*, in his eagerness for the fray (and he bears the character of always being so), had pressed on his division behind mine so that it lapped considerably, creating confusion in the counter-march, *General Longstreet* rode to me and said: "General, there is so much confusion, owing to *Hood's* division being mixed up with yours, suppose you let him countermarch first and lead in the attack." I replied: "General, as I started in the lead, let me continue so;" and he replied, "Then go on," and rode off. [McLaws, "Gettysburg," *S.H.S.P.*, VII, 69.]

Kershaw, who had halted his column at the FAIRFIELD ROAD while *Longstreet* and *McLaws* reconnoitered the route, then counter-marched up the lane "beyond the point at which we had before halted," crossed the ridge by a country road to a tributary of Willoughby Run, and then marched southward in columns of companies along Willoughby Run, hidden the entire way from the Union signal station on LITTLE ROUND TOP by the trees that lined SEMINARY RIDGE.

McLaws may have been in error in attributing the overlapping of his column by *Hood's* division to his aggressive temperament: his line of march down the small stream to Marsh Run and then along the Black Horse

Tavern road would inevitably have created a choke point where the lane taken by *Kershaw* and *Semmes* joins this road.

The decision to countermarch the divisions of *McLaws* and *Hood* remains controversial. At best it delayed *Longstreet's* attack by precious hours. Nor does it seem to have been necessary, as a postwar letter from *General E. P. Alexander*, who then commanded *Longstreet's* reserve artillery, reveals.

> About 8 or 9 A.M. we reached the vicinity of the field, and the guns were halted in a wood, and I reported in person to *Generals Lee* and *Longstreet*, who were together on a hill in rear of our lines. I was told that we were to attack the enemy's left flank, and was directed to take command of my own battalion . . . (and) *Henry's* battalion [36 guns] . . . and to reconnoitre the ground and co-operate with the infantry in the attack. I was especially cautioned in moving up the guns to avoid exposing them to the view of the signal station of the enemy's on Round Top mountain. I do not remember seeing or hearing anything at this time of *Longstreet's* infantry, nor did I get the impression that *General Lee* thought there was any unnecessary delay going on. I had just arrived, and knew nothing of the situation, and my instructions were to reconnoitre the flank to be attacked, and choose my own positions and means of reaching them. This duty occupied me . . . one or two hours, when I rode back and in person conducted my own battalion to the school-house on Willoughby run. At one point the direct road leading to this place came in sight of the enemy's signal station, but I turned out of the road [to the right] before reaching the exposed part, and passing through some meadows a few hundred yards, regaining the road without coming in sight. I then went about hunting up the other battalions which were attached to the infantry. . . . While thus engaged I came upon the head of an infantry column . . . standing halted in the road where it was in sight of Round Top. . . . For some reason, which I cannot now recall, they would not turn back and follow the tracks of my guns, and I remember a long and tiresome waiting . . . My general recollection is that nearly three hours were lost in that delay and countermarch. . . . ["Letter from General E. P. Alexander . . .", *S.H.S.P.*, IV, pp. 101–102].

Obviously *Hood's* division could not follow *Alexander's* artillery after *McLaws* had commenced his countermarch. Nor did any of the Confederates seem aware that earlier in the morning Humphrey's division from the Union Third Army Corps had approached Black Horse Tavern from your right, along the Fairfield road. Already the Confederates appeared to "occupy that road in strong force," and Humphreys, afraid to bring on an engagement here while the rest of the Union army was three miles away, retraced his steps and joined the Third Corps on Cemetery Ridge.

We will not follow *Longstreet's* divisions as they countermarched north behind Herr Ridge to the area beyond the three silos, nearly to the point at which you headed west on OLD MILL ROAD. Instead we will save time by crossing Herr ridge here to rejoin the approach march in the next valley.

Turn left onto **FAIRFIELD ROAD** and immediately turn right on **BLACK HORSE TAVERN ROAD**. As this road proceeds up the western slope of **HERR RIDGE**, do not follow *Alexander's* guns but instead bear left at the fork to stay on the main road. When you crest **HERR RIDGE**, you will see **BIG ROUND TOP** against the skyline directly to your front. (Little Round Top no longer is visible from this location, presumably because the trees on **SEMINARY RIDGE** are somewhat taller now than at the time of the battle.)

Continue on this road through the first intersection. Shortly you will see the valley of **WILLOUGHBY RUN** ahead of you. As you cross the bridge you rejoin *Longstreet's* approach march along the open and level ground to your left. Follow the Run for about 0.5 mile until you come to a STOP sign on **MILLERSTOWN ROAD** (also called **PUMPING STATION ROAD**.) Here *Longstreet's* column turned left and marched toward **SEMINARY RIDGE**. You should do likewise: proceed 0.1 mile on **MILLERSTOWN ROAD** and then stop at the turn out on the right side of the road. The large gray metal tower to your front is on Confederate Avenue and was erected by the US Army when it developed the park near the turn of the century so that soldiers could study the field. The farm to your right front is the Eisenhower Farm, which can be visited only by Park Service bus. Tickets are available at the Gettysburg National Military Park Visitor Center.

STOP 7

McLaws' Division was marching along this road toward Seminary Ridge when the following incident occurred. *McLaws* recalls:

After very considerable difficulty [recalled *McLaws*], owing to the rough character of the country in places and the fences and ditches we had to cross, the countermarch was effected, and my troops were moving easily forward along a road with fences on the side not giving room enough for a company front, making it necessary to break files to the rear, when *General Longstreet* rode up to me, and said: "How are you going in?" and I replied, "That will be determined when I can see what is in my front." He said: "There is nothing in your front; you will be entirely on the flank of the enemy." I replied, "Then I will continue my march in columns of companies, and after arriving on the flank as far as is necessary will face to the left and march on the enemy." He replied, "That suits me," and rode away.

My head of column soon reached the edge of the woods, and the enemy [in the Peach Orchard] at once opened on it with numerous artillery, and one rapid glance showed them to be in force much greater than I had, and extending considerably beyond my right. My command, therefore, instead of marching on as directed, by head of column, deployed at once. *Kershaw*, a very cool, judicious and gallant gentleman, immediately turned the head of his column and marched by flank to right, and put his men under cover of a stone wall. *Barksdale*, the fiery, impetuous Mississippian, following, came into line on the left of *Kershaw*, his men sheltered by trees and part of a stone wall and under a gentle declivity. . . . I hurried back to quicken the march of those in rear, and sent orders for my artillery to move to my right and open fire, so as to draw the fire of the opposite artillery from my infantry. . . . I had in my division about six thousand, aggregate. . . . Well, six thousand men standing in line would occupy over a mile, and in marching in the manner and over the roads we came they would extend a mile and a half. So . . . to form line of battle by directing troops across the country broken by fences and ditches requires considerable time, and it was difficult . . . to get the artillery in position.

While this was going on I rode forward, and getting off my horse, went to some trees in advance and took a good look at the situation, and the view presented astonished me, as the enemy was massed in my front, and extended to my right and left as far as I could see.

The firing on my command showed to Hood in my rear that the enemy was in force in my front and right, and the head of his column was turned by *General Longstreet's* order to go on my right, and as his troops appeared, the enemy opened on them, developing a long line to his right even, and way up to the top of Round Top. Thus was presented a state of affairs which was certainly not contemplated when the original plan or order of battle was given, and certainly was not known to *General Longstreet* a half hour previous. [McLaws, "Gettysburg," *S.H.S.P.*, VII, pp. 69–70.]

Continue in the same direction on the **MILLERSTOWN ROAD** for 0.5 mile to **WEST CONFEDERATE AVENUE**. Turn right on **WEST CONFEDERATE AVENUE** and drive 0.1 mile to the parking lot beside the tower. Park there and dismount: you can either ascend the tower or cross the stone wall on the east side of the parking lot near the 20-pound Parrot guns and use one of the numerous unimproved paths through the woods to gain a vista toward the east. As you leave the woodline, you will see the **PEACH ORCHARD**, the **EMMITSBURG ROAD**, and the **ROUND TOPS** arrayed in front of you.

STOP 8

Report of Brigadier General J. B. Kershaw, CSA, commanding brigade, McLaw's Division

Arriving . . . on the road leading across the Emmitsburg road by the peach orchard, then in possession of the enemy, the lieutenant-general commanding directed me to advance my brigade and attack the enemy at that point, turn his flank, and extend along the cross-road, with my left resting toward the Emmitsburg road. . . . About 3 p.m. the head of my column came into the open field in front of a stone wall, and in view of the enemy. I immediately filed to the right along and in front of the wall, and formed line of battle under cover of my skirmishers, then engaged with those of the enemy, these extending along the Emmitsburg road.

In the meantime, examining the position of the enemy, I found him to be in superior force in the orchard, supported by artillery, with a main line of battle intrenched in the rear and extending to and upon the rocky mountain [Little Round Top] to his left far beyond the point at which his flank had supposed to rest. To carry out my instructions, would have been, if successful in driving him from the orchard, to present my own right and rear to a large portion of his line of battle. I therefore communicated the position of things to the major-general commanding, and placed my line in position under cover of the stone wall. Along this wall the division was then formed, *Semmes* in reserve to me and *Barksdale* on my left, supported by *Wofford*, in reserve. Artillery was also placed along the wall to my right, and *Colonel De Saussure's* Fifteenth South Carolina Regiment was thrown beyond it to protect it. *Hood's* division was then moving in our rear toward our right, to gain the enemy's left flank, and I was directed to commence the attack so soon as *General Hood* became engaged, swinging around toward the peach orchard, and at the same time establishing connection with Hood, on my right, and co-operating with him. It was understood he was to sweep down the enemy's line in a direction perpendicular to our then line of battle. I was told that *Barksdale* would move with me and conform to my movement.

These directions I received in various messages from the lieutenant-general and the major-general commanding, and in part by personal communication with them. In my center front was a stone house [the ROSE HOUSE] and to the left of it a stone barn, both about 500 yards from our line, and on a line with the crest of the orchard hill. Along the front of the orchard, and on the face looking toward the stone house, the enemy's infantry was posted. Two batteries of artillery were in position, the one in rear of the orchard, near the crest of the hill, and the other some 200 yards farther back, in the direction of the rocky mountain. Behind the stone house, on the left, was a morass; on the right a stone wall running parallel with our line of battle. Beyond the morass some 200 yards was a stony hill, covered with heavy timber and thick undergrowth, extending some distance toward the enemy's main line, and inclining to our left, and in rear of the orchard and the batteries described. Beyond the stone wall, and in line with the stony hill, was a heavy forest, extending far to our right. From the morass a small stream ran through this wood along the base of the mountain toward the right. Between the stony hill and this forest was an interval of about 100 yards, which was only sparsely

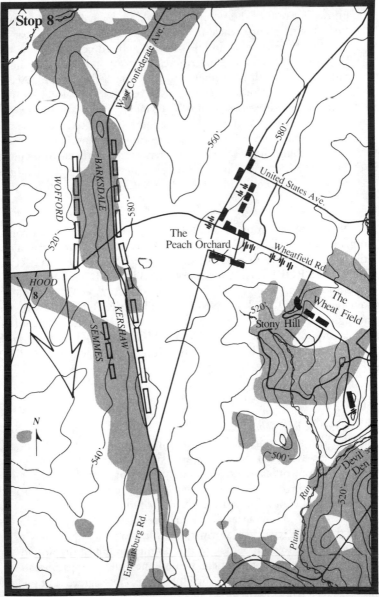

covered with scrubby undergrowth, through which a small road ran in the direction of the mountain. Looking down this road from the stone house, a large wheat-field was seen. In rear of the wheat-field . . . was the enemy's main line of battle, posted behind a stone wall. Under my instructions, I determined to move upon the stony hill, so as to strike it with my center, and thus attack the orchard. Accordingly, about 4 o'clock, when I received orders to advance, I moved at once in this direction, gradually changing front to the left. The numerous fences in the way, the stone building and barn, and the morass, and a raking fire of grape and canister [from Union batteries posted behind the peach orchard], rendered it difficult to retain the line in good order; but notwithstanding these obstacles, I brought my center to the point intended. [*O.R.*, XXVII, Part 2, pp. 367–68.]

Now return to your automobile and leave the parking lot continuing south on **WEST CONFEDERATE AVENUE**. After driving 0.6 mile you will come to a **STOP** sign at the **EMMITSBURG ROAD (BUSINESS ROUTE 15)**. Cross the **EMMITSBURG ROAD** and continue another 0.4 mile on **CONFEDERATE AVENUE** (its name has now become **SOUTH CONFEDERATE AVENUE**. You will pass through a grove with a picnic area on the right. Just beyond the woods on the right is the **ALABAMA MONUMENT**. Pull off to the side there. Looking back to your left rear you will see **LITTLE ROUND TOP**.

STOP 9

Major General John B. Hood was severely wounded in the arm soon after his division launched its attack and only two of his four brigade commanders wrote after-action reports of the battle, so it is difficult to determine from official accounts exactly what happened above the regimental level. *Brigadier General E. M. Law*, who commanded the brigade on the right of *Hood's* line and who succeeded to command of the division after *Hood* was hit by an artillery shell, recalled twenty years after the battle that upon receiving information from scouts and prisoners to the effect that there were no Union troops on the summit of Big Round Top, he had urged a flank movement behind the Round Tops instead of a frontal attack against the left of the Union line. *Hood* agreed "but said that his orders were positive to attack in front, as soon as the left of the corps should get in position." *Law* protested the order and *Hood* forwarded the

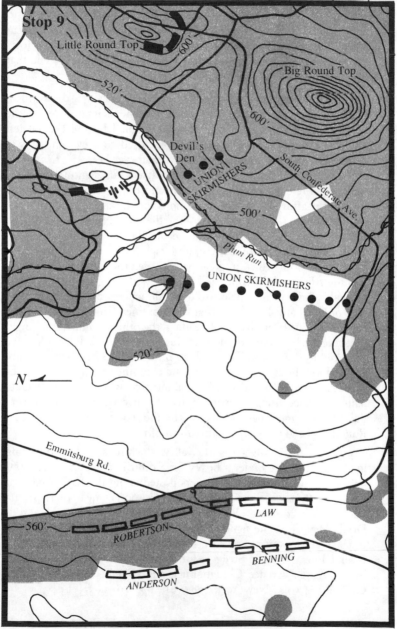

Stop 9

Little Round Top

600'

Big Round Top

520'

600'

Devil's
Den

UNION
SKIRMISHERS

South Confederate Ave.

500'

Phau Run

UNION SKIRMISHERS

520'

Emmitsburg Rd.

LAW

560'

ROBERTSON

BENNING

ANDERSON

1" = 1000'

protest to *Longstreet* with his own endorsement, but to no avail. Within minutes a staff officer from *Longstreet* arrived with the positive order to "begin the attack at once." *Hood* turned to *Law* and said simply: "You hear the order?" "Just here," *Law* concluded, "the battle of Gettysburg was lost." *Law* must have been in the immediate vicinity to describe the scene that you now see to your left.

The Confederate line of battle occupied a ridge, partly wooded, with a valley intervening between it and the heights held by the Federal troops in front. The position occupied by the Federal left wing in front of us was now fully disclosed to view, and it was certainly one of the most formidable it had ever been the fortune of any troops to confront. Round Top rose like a huge sentinel guarding the Federal left flank, while the spurs and ridges trending off to the north of it afforded unrivaled positions for the use of artillery. The puffs of smoke rising at intervals along the line of hills, as the Federal batteries fired upon such portions of our line as became exposed to view, clearly showed that these advantages had not been neglected. The thick woods which in great part covered the sides of Round Top and the adjacent hills concealed from view the rugged nature of the ground, which increased fourfold the difficulties of the attack. . . . Our order of attack . . . was that the movement should begin on the right, my brigade on that flank leading, the other commands taking it up successively toward the left. It was near 5 o'clock P.M. when we advanced to the attack. The artillery on both sides had been warmly engaged for about fifteen minutes, and continued to fire heavily until we became engaged with the Federal infantry, when the Confederate batteries ceased firing to avoid injury to our own troops, who were then, for the most part, concealed by the woods about the base of Round Top and the spurs to the north of it. . . .

Advancing rapidly across the valley which separated the opposing lines, – all the time under a heavy fire from the batteries, – our front line struck the enemy's skirmishers posted along the farther edge of the valley. Brushing these quickly away, we soon came upon their first line of battle, running along the lower slopes of the hills known as Devil's Den. . . . The fighting soon became close and severe. . . . In order to secure my right flank, I extended it well up on the side of Round Top. . . . ["The Struggle for Round Top," Robert Underwood Johnson and Clarence Clough Buel, eds., *Battles and Leaders of the Civil War* (4 vols., New York, 1884), III, pp. 320–21, 323–24.]

Proceed on South Confederate Avenue nearly 0.4 mile. The road bends to the east and descends into a valley as you pass the right flank of the Confederate line. As you approach the 0.4 mark you will see a turnout on the left side of the road with a field beyond a fringe of trees. Stop here where you can get a good view of the field and the SLYDER farm some 400 yards to your left.

STOP 10

You are now in about the middle of *Law's* line as his brigade sweeps ahead through the woods to the right and across the fields on your left. The 4th Alabama, which was assigned to the left of the brigade line, advanced "at the double-quick across a plowed field for half a mile, the enemy's batteries playing upon us with great effect until we arrived at a stone fence [at the western end of the field to your left rear] beyond which the enemy's first line of infantry was posted, which position we soon succeeded in carrying with the bayonet. Then, having reached the foot of the mountain, the command halted a few minutes to reform the line." (*O.R.*, XXVII, Part 2, p. 391.) The 15th Alabama occupied the center of the brigade when the line of battle was formed, but during the advance *Law* ordered the two regiments on the right to move by the left flank across the rear in an effort to plug the widening gap between his own brigade and that of *Robertson*, which was attacking farther on the left. This threw the 15th Alabama on the extreme right of *Law's* line, where it encountered Union sharpshooters posted behind a stone fence.

Report of Col. William C. Oates, CSA, Fifteenth Alabama Infantry, Law's brigade, Hood's corps

After crossing the fence, I received an order from *Brigadier-General Law* to left-wheel my regiment and move in the direction of the heights on my left, which order I failed to obey, for the reason that when I received it I was rapidly advancing up the mountain [Big Round Top], and in my front I discovered a heavy force of the enemy. Besides this, there was great difficulty in accomplishing the maneuver at that moment, as the regiment on my left . . . was crowding me on the left, and running into my regiment, which had already created considerable confusion. In the event that I had obeyed the order, I should have come in contact with the regiment on my left, and also have exposed my right flank to an enfilading fire from the enemy. I therefore continued to press forward, my right passing over the top of the mountain, on the right of the line [*O.R.*, XXVII, Part 2, p. 393.]

Had you been at this location "about 4.30" on the afternoon of July 2nd, you could have seen the lines of *Law's* regiments sweeping forward across the fields on your left. Keep in mind that these troops had marched "without interruption 24 miles to reach the battle-field, and advanced at the double-quick step fully a mile to engage the enemy" over "a very rough and rugged road—the worst cliffs of rocks there could have been traveled over." [*O.R.*, XXVII, Part 2, pp. 394, 395.] As *Law's* brigade edged to the right to cover Big Round Top, *Law* was forced to shift two regiments to the left of his line to plug the gap between his brigade and that of *Robertson*. Inadvertently these regiments passed behind the two right regiments of *Robertson's* brigade, with the result that they participated in the fight for the Devils Den while the 4th and 5th Texas infantry of *Robertson's* brigade found themselves joining in the attack over the fields to your left.

The 5th Texas, which occupied the right of *Robertson's* brigade and thus was the regiment of direction, "moved forward in good order."

Report of Lieut. Col. K. Bryan, CSA, Fifth Texas Infantry, Robertson's Brigade, Hood's Division

The enemy had a line of sharpshooters at the foot of the first height, behind a stone fence, about three-fourths of a mile from our starting point, which distance was passed over by our line at a double-quick and run. At our approach, the enemy retired to the top of the first height [the wooded heights to your left front], protected by a ledge of rocks. A short halt was made at the stone fence, to enable those who had fallen behind to regain their places. When the command "Forward" again fell from the lips of our gallant colonel, every man leaped the fence, and advanced rapidly up the hillside. The enemy again fled at our approach, sheltering himself behind his fortified position on the top of the second height [Little Round Top], about 200 yards distance from the first. [*O.R.*, XXVII, Part 2, p. 412.]

This is also the area of a controversial cavalry charge late in the afternoon of July 3rd. Brig. Gen. J. Kilpatrick, commanding the Third Cavalry Division, ordered two brigades to attack the rear of the Confederate lines from the wooded heights behind you. Merritt's brigade drove the enemy some distance along the Emmitsburg road, while Brig. Gen. E. J.

Farnsworth was ordered to charge through the woods and across the fields of Slyder's farm. The 1st West Virginia cavalry charged against the 1st Texas infantry guarding the Confederate right flank some 300–400 yards behind you over ground "very adverse in every particular," penetrated some distance behind the Confederate lines, and were ultimately surrounded and forced to cut their way back to the Union lines. "Any one not cognizant of the *minutiae* of this charge upon infantry, under cover of heavy timber and stone fences, will fail to form a just conception of its magnitude." [*O.R.*, XXVII, Part 1, p. 1019] Another column, from the 1st Vermont, galloped with drawn sabers and in columns of fours through the Confederate skirmish line, across the fields and over the fences until it reached a lane running by the Slyder house. Turning to the right, the column moved up the lane into the woods on your left front, where it met the fire of an Alabama regiment that had been pulled out of the main Confederate lines a few hundred yards ahead of you. Jumping over the stone wall bordering the lane, this column reformed beneath the crest of the hill.

Meanwhile a second column from the 1st Vermont, led by Farnsworth himself, skirted the woods behind you and swept in a great circle to the right, crossing the field from left to right just a short distance to your left. It then made a great sweep to the left, over the high ground and around to the vicinity of the Devil's Den, where it encountered severe enemy fire. A portion of the regiment completed the circle to re-enter the Union lines a short distance to the west of where they had started; Farnsworth with a few others galloped back to the high ground on your left front. Here they joined the other column in attacking two Alabama regiments drawn out of the line. Farnsworth himself was killed. He lost about 65 out of 350 men who made the charge, and his troopers brought in about 100 prisoners. Farnsworth's charge had no effect upon the battle.

Proceed 1.0 mile on SOUTH CONFEDERATE AVENUE. About midway between the turnout on your left and the parking lot at the top of the grade, you may see the rock wall that comes diagonally into the road on your right. This is the line constructed by *Hood's* men after their repulse at Little Round Top. One hundred yards to your left it also marks the position where skirmishers from the Union brigade on Little Round Top first encountered Law's brigade.

Continue on the road that winds through the woods around BIG ROUND TOP until you come to the DO NOT ENTER signs. Here the road becomes one way coming down off LITTLE ROUND TOP. Turn left at the intersection and drive about 100 yards to park in the turnout on either side of the road. Dismount and walk downhill to the point where a large boulder is worked into the rail fence on your right. Neither the road nor the fences were here at the time of the assault against LITTLE ROUND TOP. (If you prefer, you can also reach the summit of Little Round Top by *walking* back along the road you have just driven and turning left at the intersection. Turn left again when you reach the parking areas along the side of the road. Stand in front of the tall stone tower while reading the next selections from the *Official Records*.

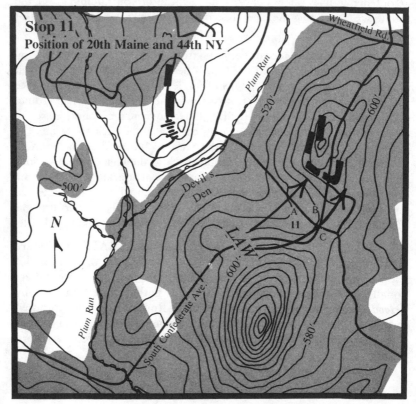

Stop 11
Position of 20th Maine and 44th NY

1" = 1000'

STOP 11, POSITION A

Hood's regiments emerged from the woods to find Col. Strong Vincent's brigade strongly posted on the hill in front, with "the right . . . thrown forward to the front of the ledge of rocks" about 50 yards from where you are standing. [*O.R.*, XXVII, Part 1, p. 617.]

Report of Maj. John P. Bane, CSA, Fourth Texas Infantry, Robertson's Brigade

Many of the officers and men had been killed and wounded up to this time. Finding it impossible to carry the heights by assault with my thinned ranks, I ordered my command to fall back in the skirt of timber, the position then occupied being enfiladed by the batteries on the left and exposed to heavy fire of musketry in my immediate front. Being joined by the Fifth Texas on my right, I again attempted to drive the enemy from the heights by assaults, but with like results. Again, being re-enforced by the Forty-eighth Alabama . . . and the Forty-fourth . . . we again charged their works, but were repulsed, and then, under the order of *General Law,* I ordered my command to fall back under cover of the timber, on a slight elevation within short range of the enemy. [*O.R.*, XXVII, Part 2, p. 411.]

Report of Lieut. Col. K. Bryan, CSA, Fifth Texas Infantry (continued)

From this position we failed to drive them. . . . owing to the rocky nature of the ground over which we had to pass, the huge rocks forming defiles through which not more than 3 or 4 men could pass abreast, thus breaking up our alignment and rendering its reformation impossible. Notwithstanding the difficulties to overcome, the men pressed on to the pass of the precipitous stronghold, forming and securing the enemy's second position, many of our officers and men falling in passing the open space between the heights. Here we halted, there being small clusters of rocks far below the elevated position of the enemy, which gave us partial protection. From this position we were enabled to deliver our fire for the first time with accuracy.

Both the colonel and Lieut. Col. having been wounded at this point, the command of the Fifth Texas devolved upon *Maj. J. C. Rogers,* who continues the report.

The order to fall back came from some unknown source, and, finding that the regiments on our right and left had retired, it became necessary to follow. I therefore gave the order for the regiment to about-face and retire to the rear, which they did in good order until they reached the position mentioned in *Colonel Bryan's* report as the second position of the enemy, and here were halted and reformed, in connection with the other regiments. From the exhausted condition of the men, it was deemed necessary to remain here for a few moments.

The regiments were again ordered forward, which they did in the most gallant manner, and regained their first position, which they held as long as it was tenable; and a farther advance being impracticable, owing to the nature of the ground . . . they again retired to an open space about 50 yards in rear, when here it was discovered for the first time that nearly two-thirds of our officers and men had been killed and wounded.

Only a few moments were here consumed to allow the men to recover their breath, when, in obedience to orders, I again moved the regiment forward to attack the enemy in their impregnable position. The coolness and determination of the men and officers were equal to the occasion. They advanced boldly over the ground strewn with the bodies of their dead and dying comrades to the base of what they knew to be an impregnable fortification. We held this position until it was discovered that we had no supports either on the right or left, and were about to be flanked, and therefore were again compelled to retire, which the regiment did in good order to the point mentioned in *Colonel Bryan's* report . . . which place we were ordered to hold at all hazards, which we did. Just before day on the morning of the 3rd, orders reached me that breastworks must be thrown up, and the position held. The order was obeyed [*O.R.*, XXVII, Part 2, pp. 412–13.]

Now you should move up to the small plateau under the large pine tree directly above this position. You can either climb the fence here or walk down to the hiker's passage and follow the hiking trail back up the hill. You are now on the contour line held by Vincent's brigade. Note the improvised breastworks of rocks thrown up just before the Confederate attack and probably strengthened at subsequent intervals in the fight.

Breastworks on the south side of Little Round Top, 6 July 1863. Photo courtesy Library of Congress (LC).

STOP 11, POSITION B

The monument higher on the hill behind you commemorates the actions of the 16th Michigan, which originally occupied the extreme left of Vincent's brigade line. After deploying two companies as skirmishers the 16th "was ordered at double-quick; to the right of the brigade"—probably at this spot, since the rest of the brigade occupied this contour line and to occupy a position farther up the slope of the hill would have permitted attacking Confederates to take advantage of the dead ground that you have just walked over. This position also more nearly corresponds to the distances and descriptions contained in the following extracts. The 44th New York Infantry on the left also threw out a company as skirmishers. "When they had advanced about 200 yards, they met the enemy advancing in three lines of battle."

Report of Lieut. Col. Freeman Conner, USA, Forty-fourth New York Infantry, Vincent's Brigade, First Division, Fifth Army Corps

Orders were immediately given by Capt. L. S. Larrabee, commanding the company, to fall back upon the battalion. . . . The enemy continued to advance until the first line came within about 40 yards of our line. Upon their first appearance we opened a heavy fire upon them, which was continued until they were compelled to retreat. After they had disappeared in our immediate front, we turned our fire upon those who had advanced in the hollow to our right, and continued it until we were out of ammunition . . .

After we had been engaged about one hour, Colonel Vincent, commanding brigade, was wounded. [*O.R.*, XXVII, Part 1, p. 630.]

Report of Col. James C. Rice, USA, Forty-fourth New York Volunteers, commanding Brigade, First Division, Fifth Army Corps

The brigade, under the command of the late Colonel Vincent, was detached from the division and ordered into position at about 4 p.m. . . . on the extreme left of our line of battle. The Twentieth Maine occupied the extreme left of the brigade line, the Sixteenth Michigan the extreme right . . . while the Eighty-third Pennsylvania and Forty-fourth New York occupied the center. The muskets taken into action by the brigade numbered about 1,000.

The ground occupied by the brigade in line of battle was nearly that of a quarter circle, composed mostly of high rocks and cliffs on the center, and becoming more wooded and less rugged as you approached the left. The right was thrown forward to the front of the ledge of rocks, and was much more exposed than other parts of the line. A comparatively smooth ravine extended along the entire front, perhaps 50 yards from our line, while on the left and beyond a high and jagged mountain rises, called Round Top. . . .

The brigade had scarcely formed line of battle and pushed forward its skirmishers when a division [actually a brigade] of the enemy's forces . . . made a desperate attack along the entire line. . . . He approached in three columns, with no skirmishers in advance. The object of the enemy was evident. If he could gain the vantage ground occupied by this brigade, the left flank of our line must give way, opening to him a vast field for successful operations in the rear of our entire army.

Stone breastworks near summit of Little Round Top, Brady c. 15 July 1863 (LC)

To effect this object the enemy made every effort. Massing . . . his force, he tried for an hour in vain to break the lines of the Forty-fourth New York and Eighty-third Pennsylvania, charging again and again within a few yards of these unflinching troops. At every charge he was repulsed with terrible slaughter. Despairing of success at this point, he made a desperate attack upon the extreme right of the brigade, forcing back a part of the Sixteenth Michigan. The regiment was broken, and, through some misunderstanding of orders . . . it was thrown into confusion, but being immediately supported by the One hundred and fortieth New York Volunteer, the line became again firm and unbroken. . . .

The enemy again attacked the center with great vigor, and the extreme left with desperation. [*O.R.*, XXVII, Part 1, p. 617.]

Breastworks on extreme Union left on Little Round Top. (USAMHI)

As the fighting rages along the left of the brigade line, you should follow the unimproved path directly up the slope of Little Round Top. You will note several small stone breastworks and a significant stone "redoubt" thrown up by Union troops, possibly reinforcements sent after the fight for Little Round Top was over. Stop when you get to the crest of the hill, in the vicinity of the 12th and 44th New York Monument.

The troops who held this portion of the line belonged to Weed's brigade, 2nd Division, Fifth Army Corps, which had been led to the crest of Little Round Top by Maj. Gen. G. K. Warren, chief engineer of the Army of the Potomac. The leading regiment, the 140th New York, had arrived just in time to charge down the hill to save the right flank of the 16th Michigan, an action that cost the life of Col. O'Rorke. Hazlett's battery followed this regiment and went into battery on the summit. The remaining regiments of the brigade, which had been sent into a narrow valley some distance to the front in support of a battery that had been

View from Little Round Top looking west, Brady c. 15 July 1863 (USAMHI)

commandeered by the Third Corps, returned at the double quick to the crest of Little Round Top to secure and hold the position. "As soon as the regiments had their positions, men from each regiment were advanced down the slope to the front, in among the rocks, and . . . actively engaged the enemy during the rest of that day. At night this ridge, naturally strong, was strengthened by building a stone wall about half way down the slope, wherever the rocks offered no protection to the men. [*O.R.*, XXVII, Part 1, p. 652.]

Now move north along the crest of Little Round Top to the vicinity of the battery of 10-pound Parrot guns. Here you get a fine panoramic view of the battlefield.

At your extreme right, north along CEMETERY RIDGE, you can view CEMETERY HILL and appreciate the extent to which it dominated the Union line. Little Round Top is somewhat higher in elevation, but no more than one battery can be employed here. As a matter of fact, during *Pickett's* charge on July 3rd, Hazlett's battery at this location "could only

Summit of Little Round Top looking toward Big Round Top (USAMHI).

use . . . two pieces, as the others could not be run far enough to point them to the right" as the Confederates approached the center of the Union lines. Even so, these two guns did frightful damage. The commander of a Virginia regiment mentioned that the battery "posted on the mountain, about one mile to our right . . . enfiladed nearly our entire line with fearful effect, sometimes as many as 10 being killed and wounded by the bursting of a single shell." [*O.R.*, XXVII, Part 2, p. 386; Benjamin F. Rittenhouse, "The Battle of Gettysburg as seen from Little Round Top," Ken Bandy, ed., *The Gettysburg Papers*, 2 vols., Morningside Press, Dayton, Ohio, II, p. 526.]

West of CEMETERY HILL you can easily discern the fields crossed by ten Confederate brigades during *Pickett's* charge. The object point – and the point of furthest advance – was that conspicious clump of trees that you can see on the Union line.

Little Round Top from Wheatfield Road, Brady 1863 (USAMHI)

Looking around to the west, you should be able to see the three silos that marked the location of *Kershaw's* brigade on Herr ridge. This will give some idea of the distance covered by *Longstreet's* two divisions before they were in position to launch their attack.

The woods directly in front conceal the WHEATFIELD, although you can see a park road running into it from WHEATFIELD ROAD, which is the historic road that connected Cemetery and Seminary Ridges. Beyond the woods, where you can see traffic moving along the Emmitsburg Pike, stands the PEACH ORCHARD.

Devil's Den is that conspicuous pile of boulders at your left front. Had you been standing in your present location anytime during July 3rd, you would have been exposed to the deadly fire of sharpshooters concealed in and about the rocks of Devil's Den. On the evening of July 2nd, you could have seen Confederate battle lines along the park avenue running from Devil's Den to Wheatfield Road, in the valley below.

Various views from the summit of Little Round Top: *Top page opposite:* Wheatfield and Peach Orchard, 1885 (USAMHI).
Bottom page opposite: Along the Union line to Cemetery Hill, 1885 (USAMHI)
Above: View toward north and Cemetery Hill, Brady 1863 (LC).

Now move a few yards off the crest of Little Round Top toward the east, onto the Park Service road, and walk south on that road until you see the sign for the 20th Maine Monument, on your left. Follow the asphalt path to the left that leads to that monument. Stop about 10 yards short of the monument.

STOP 11, POSITION C

You are now on the line of the 20th Maine, one of four regiments in Vincent's brigade, Fifth Corps, that had been rushed to help stem the Confederate advance into the Wheatfield and had been diverted to Little Round Top at the last minute to hold the Union left flank against *Long-street's* assault. In fighting off repeated assaults by two regiments in *Law's* Alabama brigade, Colonel Joshua Chamberlain and his 20th Maine fought one of the greatest small-unit actions of the war. The new US Army's Leadership Manual, FM22-100, devotes the first 12 pages to this part of the battle as a case study of leadership and unit cohesion in battle. The rock wall to your right, on the forward slope of the hill, was the battle line of the 20th Maine. The wall on the higher ground to your left was erected by another brigade that moved into the area during the night.

Report of Col. Joshua L. Chamberlain, USA, Commanding Twentieth Maine Infantry, Vincent's Brigade, First Division, Fifth Army Corps

After an hour or two of sleep by the roadside just before day-break, we reached the heights southeasterly of Gettysburg about 7 a.m., July 2. Massed at first with the rest of the division . . . we were moved several times farther toward the left. . . , expecting every moment to be put into action and held strictly in line of battle. . . .

Somewhere near 4 p.m. a sharp cannonade, at some distance to our left and front, was the signal for a sudden and rapid movement of our whole division in the direction of this firing, which grew warmer as we approached. Passing an open field in the hollow ground in which some of our batteries were going into position, our brigade reached the skirt of a piece of woods, in the farther edge of which there was a heavy musketry fire, and when about to go forward into line we received . . . orders to move to the left at the double-quick, when we took a farm road crossing Plum Run in order to gain a rugged mountain spur called Granite Spur, or Little Round Top.

The enemy's artillery got range of our column as we were climbing the spur, and the crashing of the shells among the rocks and the tree tops made us move lively along the crest. . . . Passing to the southern slope of Little Round Top, Colonel Vincent indicated to me the ground my regiment was to occupy, informing me that this was the extreme left of our general line, and that a desperate attack was expected in order to turn that position, concluding by telling me I was to "hold that ground at all hazards." That was the last word I heard from him.

In order to commence by making my right firm, I formed my regiment on the right into line, giving such direction to the line as should best secure the advantage of the rough, rocky, and stragglingly wooded ground.

The line faced generally toward a more conspicuous eminence southwest of ours, which is known as Sugar Loaf, or Round Top. Between this and my position intervened a smooth and thinly wooded hollow. My line formed, I immediately detached Company B, Captain Morrill commanding, to extend from my left flank across this hollow as a line of skirmishers, with directions to act as occasion might dictate, to prevent a surprise on my exposed flank and rear.

The artillery fire on our position had meanwhile been constant and heavy, but my formation was scarcely complete when the artillery was replaced by a vigorous infantry assault upon the center of our brigade to my right, but it very soon involved the right of my regiment and gradually extended along my entire front. The action was quite sharp and at close quarters.

In the midst of this, an officer from my center informed me that some important movement of the enemy was going on in his front, beyond that of the line with which we were engaged. Mounting a large rock, I was able to see a considerable body of the enemy moving by the flank in rear of their line engaged, and passing from the direction of the foot of Great Round Top through the valley toward the front of my left. The close engagement not allowing any change of front, I immediately stretched my regiment to the left, by taking intervals by the left flank, and at the same time "refusing" my left wing, so that it was nearly at right angles with my right, thus occupying about twice the extent of our ordinary front, some of the companies being brought into single rank when the nature of the ground gave sufficient strength or shelter. My officers and men understood my wishes so well that this movement was executed under fire, the right wing keeping up fire, without giving the enemy any occasion to seize or even to suspect their advantage. But we were not a moment too soon; the enemy's flanking column having gained their desired direction, burst upon my left, where they evidently had expected an unguarded flank, with great demonstration.

We opened a brisk fire at close range, which was so sudden and effective that they soon fell back among the rocks and low trees in the valley, only to burst forth again with a shout, and rapidly advanced, firing as they came. They pushed up to within a dozen yards of us before the terrible effectiveness of our fire compelled them to break and take shelter.

They renewed the assault on our whole front, and for an hour the fighting was severe. Squads of the enemy broke through our line in several places, and the fight was literally hand to hand. The edge of the fight rolled backward and forward like a wave. The dead and wounded were now in our front and then in our rear. Forced from our position, we desperately recovered it, and pushed the enemy down to the foot of the slope. The intervals of the struggle were seized to remove the wounded (and those of the enemy also), to gather ammunition from the cartridge boxes of disabled friend or foe on the field, and even to secure better muskets than the Enfields, which we found did not stand service well. Rude shelters were thrown up of the loose rocks that covered the ground.

Captain Woodward, commanding the Eighty-third Pennsylvania Volunteers, on my right, gallantly maintaining his fight, judiciously and with hearty co-operation made his movements conform to my necessities, so that my right was at no time exposed to a flank attack.

The enemy seemed to have gathered all their energies for their final assault. We had gotten our thin line into as good a shape as possible, when a strong force emerged from the scrub wood in the valley [to the left], as well as I could judge, in two lines in *échelon* by the right, and, opening a heavy fire, the first line came on us as is they meant to sweep everything before them. We opened on them as well as we could with our scanty ammunition snatched from the field.

It did not seem possible to withstand another shock like this now coming on. Our loss had been severe. One-half of my left wing had fallen, and a third of my regiment lay just behind us, dead or badly wounded. At this moment my anxiety was increased by a great roar of musketry in my rear, on the farther or northerly slope of Little

Round Top, apparently on the flank of the regular brigade [Weed], which was in support of Hazlett's battery on the crest behind us. The bullets from this attack struck into my left rear, and I feared that the enemy might have nearly surrounded the Little Round Top, and only a desperate chance was left for us. My ammunition was soon exhausted. My men were firing their last shot and getting ready to "club" their muskets.

It was imperative to strike before we were struck by this overwhelming force in a hand-to-hand fight, which we could not probably have withstood or survived. At that crisis, I ordered the bayonet. The word was enough. It ran like fire along the line, from man to man, and rose into a shout, with which they sprang forward upon the enemy, now not 30 yards away. The effect was surprising; many of the enemy's first line threw down their arms and surrendered. An officer fired his pistol at my head with one hand, while he handed me his sword with the other. Holding fast by our right, and swinging forward our left, we made an extended "right wheel," before which the enemy's second line broke and fell back, fighting from tree to tree, many being captured, until we had swept the valley and cleared the front of nearly our entire brigade.

Meantime Captain Morrill with his skirmishers (sent out from my left flank), with some dozen or fifteen of the U.S. Sharpshooters who had put themselves under his direction, fell upon the enemy as they were breaking, and by his demonstrations, as well as his well-directed fire, added much to the effect of the charge.

Having thus cleared the valley, and driven the enemy up the western slope of the Great Round Top, not wishing to press so far out as to hazard the ground I was to hold by leaving it exposed to a sudden rush of the enemy, I succeeded (although with some effort to stop my men, who declared they were "on the road to Richmond") in getting the regiment into good order and resuming our original position.

Four hundred prisoners, including two field and several line officers, were sent to the rear. These were mainly from the Fifteenth and Forty-seventh Alabama Regiments, with some of the Fourth and Fifth Texas. One hundred and fifty of the enemy were found killed and wounded. . . . We went into the fight with 386, all told—358 guns. Every pioneer and musician who could carry a musket went into the ranks. Even the sick and foot-sore, who could not keep up in the march, came up as soon as they could find their regiments, and took

Devil's Den Boulders at gorge area (NPS).

their places in line of battle. . . . Some prisoners I had under guard, under sentence of court-martial, I was obliged to put into the fight, and they bore their part well, for which I shall recommend a commutation of their sentence.

The loss, so far as I can ascertain it, is 136–30 of whom were killed, and among the wounded are many mortally. [*O.R.*, XXVII, Part 1, pp. 622–26.]

Later that evening the remnants of the 20th Maine, about 200 men and entirely out of ammunition, pressed up Big Round Top "in a very extended order" to seize and fortify the crest. In the darkness they captured 25 additional prisoners, including a staff officer who had commanded *Law's* brigade. The following noon the regiment was withdrawn and sent as a reserve to the center of the Union line, where *Pickett's* charge was about to occur. They returned to this area the day after the battle to bury the dead and look after the wounded, "marking each grave by a head-board made of ammunition boxes, with each dead soldier's name cut upon it."

Near the monument there is a path leading down the hill to a small parking area. Walk down the path, turn right on the road and walk back to your automobile.

Drive down toward DEVIL'S DEN, turning left at the "T" intersection. You can either park in the area near the comfort station, which will be on your left, and walk up the asphalt path to the site of the 4th New York Battery atop Devil's Den, or you can follow the road to the top of the ridge and stop near the 10 Pounder Parrott guns. If there is adequate space to park, walk to the top of the rocks on your right where you can get a good view.

Devil's Den, Posed Soldier on Rocks, c. 1865 (NPS).

STOP 12

You are now on the left flank of the Union line when *Longstreet* launched his attack. Meade had originally intended to occupy the line on Cemetery Ridge, extending the Third Corps on his left to Little Round Top, but Maj. Gen. Daniel E. Sickles, commanding the Third Corps, decided early in the afternoon to move his corps some 500 yards forward to occupy higher ground along the Emmitsburg road near the Peach Orchard. Birney's division held the sector stretching from Devil's Den to the Peach Orchard, with Brig. Gen. J. H. Hobart Ward's brigade deployed along this ridge. Smith's battery of rifled guns was posted on the left of Ward's line, where it could command the gorge at the base of Big Round Top. The Second U.S. Sharpshooters formed a skirmish line half a mile in advance.

*Report of Brig. Gen. J. H. Hobart Ward, USA, commanding
Second Brigade, First Division, Third Army Corps*

They had scarcely obtained the position designated before the skirmishers of the enemy issued from a wood [along Seminary Ridge] in front, followed by heavy lines of infantry. Captain Smith's battery of rifled guns, posted on the eminence on my left, opened on the advancing enemy . . . the enemy replying from a battery near the Emmitsburg road. The supports of the first two lines were now coming up in column *en masse*, while we had but a single line of battle to receive the shock. Our skirmishers were now forced to draw back. My line awaited the clash. To the regiments on the right, who were sheltered in a wood, I gave directions not to fire until they could plainly see the enemy; to those who were on my left, not to fire at a longer distance than 200 yards.

The enemy had now approached, . . yelling and shouting. My command did not fire a shot until the enemy came within the distance prescribed, when the whole command fired a volley. This checked the enemy's advance suddenly, which gave our men an opportunity to reload, when another volley was fired into them. The enemy now exhibited much disorder, and, taking advantage of this circumstance, I advanced my right and center with a view of obtaining a position behind a stone wall, about 160 yards in advance, and which the enemy was endeavoring to reach. While advancing, the rear columns of the enemy pressed forward to the support of the advance, who rallied and again advanced. This time our single line was forced back a short distance by the heavy columns of the enemy. In this manner for the space of one and a half hours did we advance and retire, both parties endeavoring to gain possession of the stone wall. . . . The enemy now concentrated his force on our extreme left, with the intention to turn our left flank through a gorge between my left and Sugar Loaf hill [Big Round Top.] The Fortieth New York was dispatched to cover the gorge which they did most effectually. Our men, now much exhausted and nearly destitute of ammunition, were relieved by a portion of the Second and Fifth Corps, when we retired and bivouacked for the night. . . . The number of effective men in the brigade when they engaged the enemy was not 1,500, while the loss is nearly 800. Out of 14 field officers, we lost 8.[*O.R.*, XXVII, Part 1, pp. 493–94.]

Outing on rocks of Devil's Den. Man in the foreground wears the ribbon of a guide, 1910. Photo from publisher's archive.

Today's view toward Devil's Den from Little Round Top. Harold W. Nelson photo (HWN)

Report of Captain James E. Smith, USA, Fourth New York Battery

In compliance with instructions . . . I placed two sections [4 guns] of my battery on a hill (near the Devil's Cave) on the left of General Birney's line, leaving one section, together with caissons and horses, 150 yards in the rear. The Fourth Maine Regiment was detailed as support, forming line in rear under cover of a hill. On my left, extending half way to the Emmitsburg road, was a thick wood, in which I requested Lieutenant Leigh, aide-de-camp to General Ward, to place supports. He informed me that a brigade had already been placed there, but this must have been a mistake.

About 2.30 the enemy opened fire on my right and front from several guns. . . . I was ordered . . . to return their fire. . . . Twenty minutes later I discovered the enemy was endeavoring to get a section of light 12-pounder guns in position on my left and front, in order to enfilade this part of our line, but I succeeded in driving them off before they had an opportunity to open fire. Soon after, a battery of six light 12-pounders marched from the woods near the Emmitsburg road, and went in battery in the field in front, about 1,400 yards distant. A spirited duel immediately began . . . lasting nearly twenty minutes, when *Anderson's* brigade, of *Hood's* division . . . charged upon us. The rebel battery then left the field, and I directed my fire upon the infantry.

At this time I requested the officer in command of the Fourth Maine Regiment to place his regiment in the woods on my left . . . but my request was not complied with. I used case shot upon the advancing column until it entered the woods, when I fired shell until they emerged from the woods on my left flank, in line of battle 300 yards distant; then I used canister with little effect, owing to numerous large rocks, which afforded excellent protection to their sharpshooters. I saw it would be impossible for me to hold my position without assistance, and therefore called upon my supports, who gallantly advanced up the hill and engaged the enemy. Fighting became so close that I ordered my men to cease firing, as many of the Fourth Maine had already advanced in front of the guns. I then went to the rear and opened that section of guns, firing obliquely through the gully, doing good execution.

At this time the Sixth New Jersey Volunteers . . . and Fortieth New York . . . came to our support. These regiments marched down the gully, fighting like tigers, exposed to a terrific fire of musketry, and, when within 100 yards of the rebel line, the Fourth Maine, which still held the hill, were forced to retreat. Very soon afterward the Fortieth New York and Sixth New Jersey Regiments were compelled to follow. . . .

When I left three guns on the hill (one having been sent to the rear disabled), I was under the impression we would be able to hold that position, but, if forced to retreat, I expected my supports would save the guns, which, however, they failed to do. . . . I feared if I removed them the infantry might mistake the movement for a retreat. In my opinion, had supports been placed in the woods, as I wished, the hill could not have been taken. [*O.R.*, XXVII, Part 1, pp. 588–89.]

The force attacking Ward's brigade comprised three regiments from *Law's* brigade, two from *Robertson's*, *Bennings* brigade, and a portion of *G. T. Anderson's* brigade. *Law's* men fought mostly in the "gorge" separating Little Round Top and the Devil's Den. The 44th Alabama emerged from the woods into the gorge to receive "a deadly volley at short range, which in a few seconds killed or disabled one-fourth their number."

Report of Col. William F. Perry, CSA, Forty-fourth Alabama Infantry, Law's Brigade, Hood's Division

When at a short distance from the stone fence near the base of the mountain, *General Law* informed me that he expected my regiment to take a battery which had been playing on our line from the moment the advance began. This battery was situated, not on the mountain itself, but on a rugged cliff which formed the abrupt termination of a ridge that proceeded from the mountain, and ran in a direction somewhat parallel with it, leaving a valley destitute of trees and filled with immense bowlders. . . . This valley, not more than 300 paces in breadth, and the cliff on which their artillery was stationed, were occupied by two regiments of the enemy's infantry.

The direction of the regiment after crossing the stone fence was such that a march to the front would have carried it to the right of the enemy's position. It was, therefore, wheeled to the left, so as to confront that position, its left opposite the battery, and its right extending toward the base of the mountain. This movement was executed under fire, and within 200 yards of the enemy. The forward movement was immediately ordered, and was responded to with an alacrity and courage seldom, if ever, excelled on the battle-field. As the men emerged from the forest into the valley . . . they received a deadly volley at short range, which in a few seconds killed or disabled one-fourth their number. Halting without an order from me, and availing themselves of the shelter which the rocks afforded, they returned the fire. Such was their extreme exhaustion—having marched without interruption 24 miles to reach the battle-field, and advanced at a double quick step fully a mile to engage the enemy—that I hesitated for an instant to order them immediately forward. Perceiving very soon, however, that the enemy were giving way, I rushed forward, shouting to them to advance. It was with the greatest difficulty that I could make myself heard or understood above the din of battle. The order was, however, extended along the line, and was promptly obeyed, The men sprang forward over the rocks, swept the position, and took possession of the heights, capturing 40 or 50 prisoners around the battery and among the cliffs.

Meanwhile the enemy had put a battery in position on a terrace of the mountain to our right [Little Round Top], which opened upon us an enfilading fire of grape and spherical case shot. A sharp fire of small-arms was also opened from the same direction [probably from the 44th New York]. This was not destructive, however, owing to the protection afforded by the rocks. Soon the enemy appeared moving down upon our front in heavy force. At this critical moment, *General Benning's* brigade of Georgians advanced gallantly into action. His extreme right, lapping upon my left, swarmed over the cliffs and mingled with my men. It was now past 5 p.m. The conflict continued to rage with great fury until dark. Again and again the enemy in great force attempted to dislodge us from the position and retake the battery, in each case with signal failure and heavy loss. [*O.R.*, XXVII, Part 2, p. 394.]

Report of Brig. Gen. J. B. Robertson, CSA, commanding brigade, Hood's Division

The division arrived on the ground . . . but a few minutes before we were ordered to advance. I therefore got but a glance at the field on which we were to operate before we entered upon it. I was ordered to keep my right well closed on *Brigadier-General Law's* left, and to let my left rest on the Emmitsburg pike. I had advanced but a short distance when I discovered that my brigade would not fill the space between *General Law's* left and the pike . . . and that I must leave the pike, or disconnect myself from *General Law*. Understanding . . . that the attack . . . was to be general, and that the force of *General McLaws* was to advance simultaneously with us on my immediate left, and seeing at once that a mountain held by the enemy in heavy force with artillery to the right of *General Law's* center was the key to the enemy's left, I abandoned the pike and closed on *General Law's* left. This caused some separation of my regiments, which was remedied as promptly as the numerous stone and rail fences that intersected the field through which we were advancing would allow.

Today's view of the stone wall west of Devil's Den as seen by Confederate attackers (HWN).

As we advanced through this field for half a mile we were exposed to a heavy and destructive fire of canister, grape and shell . . . and from the enemy's sharpshooters from behind the numerous rocks, fences, and houses in the field.

As we approached the base of the mountain, *General Law* moved to the right, and I was moving obliquely to the right to close on him when my whole line encountered the fire of the enemy's main line, posted behind rocks and a stone fence. The Fourth and Fifth Texas . . . while returning the fire and driving the enemy before them, continued to close on *General Law*, to their right. At the same time the First Texas and Third Arkansas . . . were hotly engaged with a greatly superior force. '. . . while at the same time a heavy force appeared and opened fire on *Colonel Manning's* left [3rd Arkansas]. . . . On discovering this heavy force on my left flank, and seeing that no attack was being made by any of our forces on my left, I at once sent a courier to *Major General Hood*, stating that I was hard pressed on my left; that *General McLaws'* forces were not engaging the enemy to my left (which enabled him to move fresh troops from that part of his line down on me), and that I must have reinforcements.

Lieutenant-Colonel Work, with the First Texas Regiment, having pressed forward to the crest of the hill and driven the enemy from his battery, I ordered him to the left, to the relief and support of *Colonel Manning*   With this assistance, *Colonel Manning* drove the enemy back, and entered the woods after him, when the enemy reoccupied the hill and his batteries in *Colonel Work's* front, from which *Colonel Work* again drove him.

For an hour and upward, these two regiments maintained one of the hottest contests, against five or six times their number, that I have witnessed. The moving of *Colonel Work* to the left, to relieve *Colonel Manning* while the Fourth and Fifth Texas were closing to the right on *General Law's* brigade, separated these two regiments from the others. . . . After finding that I could not move the First and Third to the right to join them, I sent to recall them . . . but my messenger found two of *General Law's* regiments on the left of my two . . . and did not find these regiments at all. . . . I sent a request to *General Law* to look to them. . . . My courier, sent to *General Hood*, returned, and reported him wounded and carried from the field. I sent a messenger to *Lieutenant-General Longstreet* for re-enforcements, and at the same time to *Generals Anderson* and *Benning*, urging them to hurry up to my support. They came up, joined us, and fought gallantly, but as fast as we could break on line of the enemy, another fresh one would present itself, the enemy re-enforcing his lines in our front from his reserves at the base of the mountain . . . and from his lines to our left. Having no attack from us in his front, he threw his forces from there on us. . . .

When night closed the conflict, late in the evening, I was struck above the knee, which deprived me of the use of my leg, and prevented me from getting about the field. I retired some 200 yards to the rear, leaving the immediate command with *Lieutenant-Colonel Work* . . . under whose supervision our wounded were brought out and guns secured, and our dead on that part of the field were buried the next day. About 2 o'clock that night, the First Texas and Third Arkansas were moved by the right to the position occupied by the Fourth and Fifth . . . where the brigade remained during the . . . 3rd, keeping up a continuous skirmishing with the enemy's sharpshooter. [*O.R.*, XXVII, Part 2, pp. 404–5.]

Report of Brig. Gen. Henry L. Benning, CSA, commanding brigade, Hood's Division

In order to get to the place they assigned me, in the Rear of *General Law*, it was necessary to move the brigade 500 or 600 farther to the right. Having done this, I advanced in line of battle. A wood intervened between us and the enemy, which, though it did not prevent their shells from reaching us and producing some casualties, yet completely hid them from our view. On emerging from the woods, their position became visible. Before us, at the distance of 600 or 800 yards, was an oblong mountain peak, or spur [Devil's Den], presenting to us a steep face, much roughened by rocks. To the right, 400 or 500 yards from the peak, was the main mountain itself [Little Round Top], with a side that looked almost perpendicular. Its summit overlooked the peak just sufficiently to command it well. On the summit of the peak were three pieces of artillery, and a little in advance of them, on a sort of uneven, irregular shelf, were three others. To the right and left of the battery, as well as immediately in its rear, were lines of infantry. This formed the enemy's first line of battle.

On the top of the mountain itself, and a little to the right of the peak, were five other guns. These commanded our approaches to the peak for nearly the whole way. To the right and left of these guns extended the enemy's second line of infantry. Where that line crossed the gorge running between the peak and the mountain, a point 500 or 600 yards in the rear of the peak, were two other guns. This we ascertained when the right of the brigade reached the gorge, by the terrible fire from them which swept down the gorge.

Thus, what we had to encounter were thirteen guns, and two, if not more, lines of infantry posted on mountain heights. The intervening spur over which we had to march to reach the first line was nearly all open. Our own first line became visible advancing about 400 yards in our front. The part of it in our front I took to be *Law's* brigade, and so I followed it. In truth, it was *Robertson's*, *Law's* being farther to the right. This I did not discover until late in the fight, a wood on the right concealing from me most of *Law's* brigade. My line continued to follow the first line, halting once or twice to preserve its interval. At length I saw that the first line would not be able alone to carry the peak, so I advanced without halting again.

When my line reached the foot of the peak, I found there a part of the First Texas, struggling to make the ascent . . . The part of the First Texas . . . falling in with my brigade, the whole line commenced ascending the rugged . . . steep [incline] and, on the right, crossing the gorge. The ground was difficult — rocks in many places presenting, by their precipitous sides, insurmountable obstacles, while the fire of the enemy was very heavy and very deadly. The progress was, therefore, not very rapid, but it was regular and uninterrupted. After awhile the enemy were driven from their three front guns. The advance continued, and at length they were driven completely from the peak, but they carried with them the three rear guns on its summit, its sudden descent on the other side favoring the operation, so that we captured only the three front guns. These were 10-pounder Parrots. A number of prisoners also were taken — More, I suppose than 100.

The peak being thus taken and the enemy's first line driven behind his second, I made my dispositions to hold the ground gained, which . . . appeared a difficult task. The shells of the enemy from the adjacent mountain were incessantly bursting along the summit of the peak, and every head that showed itself was the target for a Minié ball. Several attempts by flank movements were made to dislodge us, but by the gallantry of the regiments on the right and left they all failed. . . .

Our loss was heavy, not less than 400 in killed, wounded and missing. Of this number, an unusually large proportion were killed and badly wounded. . . . At the close of the day the fighting ceased, and I employed the night in arranging my line, establishing pickets, and removing the wounded. The last was a work of great labor, as, owing to some fault or mistake in the surgeon having charge of the brigade ambulances, but two of them made their appearance, so that the labor to the litter bearers became very heavy [O.R., XXVII, Part 2, pp. 414–16.]

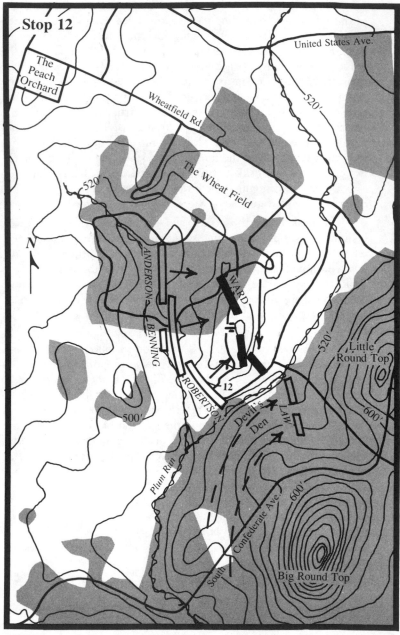

Stop 12

The Peach Orchard

United States Ave.

Wheatfield Rd.

520'

The Wheat Field

520'

N

ANDERSON

BENNING

WARD

520'

Little Round Top

ROBERTSON

12

Devil's Den

LAW

600'

500'

Plum Run

South Confederate Ave.

600'

Big Round Top

1" = 1000'

Return to your automobile and proceed about 0.4 mile. When you reach the first intersection, take a sharp left onto CROSS AVENUE. After following this twisting road through the woods back toward the Confederate lines for about 0.7 mile, you will come to a left turnout at the marker indicating the point where *Kershaw's* brigade crossed to engage Union troops in the vicinity of the WHEATFIELD. The line of monuments that you pass on the crest to the right indicates the advanced position of Brooke's Brigade, Caldwell's division, from the Second Corps, which at a somewhat later stage will drive Confederates out of the WHEATFIELD, a hundred or so yards to your right, to the shelter of a stone wall in the field on your left.

STOP 13

Dismount at the marker and walk to the rail fence. From this position you can look north past the ROSE HOUSE toward the PEACH ORCHARD, to the salient of Sickles' advanced line. You can also look northwest toward the tower on Confederate Avenue where you first encountered *Kershaw's* brigade in the process of deploying for his attack. And a few hundred feet to the west you will see a line of scattered tall trees; this marks the stone wall where elements of the brigades of *Semmes* and *Kershaw* reformed after having been driven from the WHEATFIELD. The stony hill that figures prominently in *Kershaw's* report is a short distance beyond the morass, on your right front. *Kershaw* provides the details of his attack.

Under my instructions I determined to move upon the stony hill, so as to strike it with my center, and thus attack the orchard on its left rear. About 4 o'clock I received the order to move, at a signal from *Cabell's* artillery. They were to fire for some minutes, then pause, and then fire three guns in rapid succession. At this I was to move without further orders. I communicated these instructions to the commanders of each of the regiments . . . directing them to convey them to the company officers. They were told, at the signal, to order the men to leap the wall [by the observation tower] without further orders, and to align the troops in front of it. Accordingly, at the signal, the men leaped over the wall and were promptly aligned; the word was given, and the brigade moved off . . . with great steadiness and precision, followed by Semmes with equal promptness. *General Longstreet* accompanied me in his advance on foot, as far as the Emmitsburg road.

All the field and staff officers were dismounted on account of the many obstacles in the way. When we were about the Emmitsburg road, I heard *Barksdale's* drums beat the assembly, and knew *then* that I should have no immediate support on my left, about to be squarely presented to the heavy force of infantry and artillery at and in rear of the Peach Orchard.

The 2d and 8th South Carolina regiments and *James's* (Third) battalion constituted the left wing of the brigade, and were then moving majestically across the fields to the left of the lane leading to Rose's, with the steadiness of troops on parade. They were ordered to change direction to the left, and attack the batteries in rear of the Peach Orchard, and accordingly moved rapidly on that point. In order to aid this attack, the direction of the 3rd and 7th regiments was changed to the left, so as to occupy the stony hill and wood.

After passing the buildings at Rose's, the charge of the left wing was no longer visible from my position; but the movement was reported to have been magnificently conducted until the [Union] cannoneers had left their guns and the caissions were moving off, when the order was given to "move *by the right flank*", by some unauthorized person, and was immediately obeyed by the men. The Federals returned to their guns and opened on these doomed regiments a raking fire of grape and canister, at short distance, which proved most disastrous, and for a time destroyed their usefulness. Hundreds of the bravest and best men of Carolina fell, victims of this fatal blunder.

While this tragedy was being enacted, the 3d and 7th regiments were conducted rapidly to the stony hill. In consequence of the obstructions in the way, the 7th Regiment had lapped the 3rd a few paces, and when they reached the cover of the stony hill I halted the line at the edge of the wood for a moment, and ordered the 7th to move by the right flank to uncover the 3d Regiment, which was promptly done. It was, no doubt, this movement, observed by someone from the left, that led to the terrible mistake which cost so dearly. [J. B. Kershaw, "Kershaw's Brigade at Gettysburg," *Battles and Leaders*. III, pp. 334–36.]

Dead Confederate soldier near Rose Farm. (USAMHI)

You will resume *Kershaw's* account of the fight for the Stony Hill when you reach the scene, where the details of his tactical maneuvers will become more intelligible. Bear in mind that when he was forced out of that key position his right wing fell back to the stone wall in the field and to the buildings at Rose's.

Now return to your automobile and continue driving in the same direction. As you cross the bridge over the "morass," look up to your left for a good view of the STONY HILL that features in Confederate accounts. It does not seem like much of a hill, but place a staunch Union brigade on its crest and it would probably look more formidable. After you emerge into the lower edge of the Wheatfield, stop just before the road curves away from the woodline toward the center of the field. The monument on your right depicting a soldier crouching behind a stone wall is the 17th Maine monument. The actual stone wall that sheltered this regiment is clearly visible at the edge of the treeline.

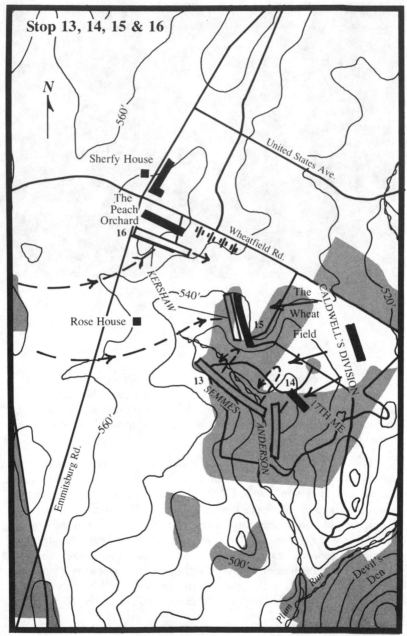

Stop 13, 14, 15 & 16

1" = 1000'

STOP 14

Major General David B. Birney, commanding the First Division of Sickles' Third Army Corps, had originally placed Ward's brigade on the ridge just north of Devil's Den and Graham's brigade in the Peach Orchard: Col. Regis de Trobriand's Third Brigade occupied the Stony Hill that you observed on your left just as your car was emerging from the woods. Because the obvious points of attack were on the left flank, resting on the Devil's Den, and the salient at the Peach Orchard, de Trobriand's brigade was "in column by regiments, ready to support either of the other two brigades according to circumstances." As soon as the Union artillery opened fire, de Trobriand sent one regiment to the Peach Orchard to support Graham's brigade, and when Ward's brigade was attacked near the Devil's Den he sent another—the 17th Maine—to cross the Wheatfield to occupy this stone wall and "fill a gap open there." Soon afterwards he was ordered to send still another regiment to support Ward's brigade by holding the gorge east of Devil's Den, leaving but two regiments to hold the vital terrain at the Stony Hill. [*O.R.*, XXVII, Part 1, p. 520.]

Report of Lieut. Col. Charles B. Merrill, USA, 17th Maine Infantry, de Tobriand's Brigade, First Division, Third Army Corps

About 4 p.m., the brigade of General Ward having become actively engaged with the enemy on our left, I was ordered by Colonel de Trobriand to march my regiment to connect with and support the line of General Ward. . . . The regiment at once moved [from the woods to the left of Winslow's battery on the high ground in the Wheatfield] by the left flank, and, crossing an interval between the two brigades, our line was formed behind a stone wall, which afforded a strong position. We opened fire upon the enemy, then within 100 yards of us. The contest became very severe, the enemy at times being driven back by our line, and then by superior numbers compelling us in turn to give way. The ground was hotly contested, but we held our position till, finding the right of my regiment outflanked and exposed to a murderous fire from the enemy's reinforcements, I was obliged to form a new line, changing the right wing of the regiment into position at a right angle with the left. This movement was executed in good order, under a heavy fire from the advancing foe. In this position we continued the fight, checking the enemy till, receiving orders to retire, we fell back across a wheat field in our rear to the edge of the woods.

At this point, Major General Birney rode upon the field and directed our line to advance. With cheers for our gallant commander, the regiment moved quickly forward, and pouring into the enemy volley upon volley, their advance was checked. The contest was now of a most deadly character, almost hand to hand, and our loss was very severe. [18 killed, 112 wounded 2 missing] In the color guard of 10, but 3 escaped uninjured.

Our ammunition being exhausted and fresh troops [from the Second Corps] having arrived to take our places, we were ordered to withdraw from the field, which we did in good order. A new line was then formed but a short distance to the rear, where we bivouacked for the night. [*O.R.*, XXVII, Part 1, p. 522.]

The guns that you see on the higher ground 200 yards to the northeast were light 12 pounders belonging to Winslow's battery. According to the commander of the Artillery Brigade, Third Army Corps, "from the position of the battery and of the infantry supporting, it was deemed best for a time to fire solid shot into the woods over our troops, who were fighting in front under protection of a stone wall. This fire was very effective (as such use of solid shot always is when troops are engaged in woods, the moral effect being at least equal to the physical), and was continued till our troops in front fell back of his battery, when Captain Winslow used case shot, 1 and 1½ second fuse, ending with canister. . . . The position of Captain Winslow's battery did not seem to be very good, owing to the nearness of the woods on all sides. . . ." [*O.R.*, XXVII, Part 1, p. 583.]

Report of Capt. George B. Winslow, USA, Battery D, First New York Light Artillery

The position assigned my battery was near the left of the line, in a small wheat-field. . . . A battery of the enemy posted nearly in my front opened between 3 and 4 p.m. upon our lines. I could only see the smoke of their guns as it rose above the tree tops, but, by command of General Hunt, fired a few rounds of solid shot in that direction, probably with no effect, as it was evidently beyond the range of my guns. Soon after, the two lines of infantry became hotly engaged, but I was unable from my obscure position to observe the movements of the troops, and was compelled to estimate distances and regulate my fire by the reports of our own and the enemy's musketry.

By direction of Major-General Birney, I opened with solid shot, giving but sufficient elevation to clear our own troops in front, and firing in the direction of the heaviest musketry, lessening the range as our troops fell back and the enemy advanced. Our line of skirmishers fell back on their supports at the edge of the woods, little, if any more than 400 yards from the front of my guns. This line was a weak one and soon fell back, but by using shell and case shot at about one degree elevation, and from 1 to 1½ second fuse, I kept the enemy from advancing from the cover of the woods. Having been just directed by General Birney, through an aide, to closely watch the movements and look for a route upon which I might withdraw in case it became necessary, I rode through the woods on my left, perhaps 200 yards in width, and found our line there formed perpendicular to my own, instead of parallel, as I had supposed, facing from me and closely pressed by the enemy. This line soon fell back irregularly, but slowly, passing in front of and masking my guns. A portion of Smith's battery, on my left, also withdrew by my rear.

The enemy's advance being within 25 yards of my left, and covered by woods and rocks, I ordered my left section limbered, with a view of moving it a short distance to the left and rear. Before this was accomplished, the enemy had advanced under cover of the woods upon my right, and was cutting down my men and horses. Having no supports in rear, and being exposed to a heavy fire of musketry in front and upon both flanks, I deemed it necessary to withdraw in order to save my guns, which was done by piece in succession from the left, continuing to fire until the right and last piece was limbered. . . . Meeting Major-General Sickles and Captain Randolph immediately after leaving the field, I was ordered by them to move my battery to the rear, and refit as far as possible. [*O.R.*, XXVII, Part 1, p. 587.]

The Confederates who disputed possession of the stone wall belonged to Brigadier *General George T. Anderson's* brigade of *Hood's* division. Originally deployed on the left of *Hood's* division, in support of *Robertson's* Texas brigade, *Anderson's* Georgians moved forward to the front line soon after *Robertson* became engaged in the fighting around Devil's Den. "A vigorous charge was [then] made, which dislodged the enemy from a stone fence running diagonally with the line of battle."

Report of Col. W. W. White, CSA, commanding Anderson's brigade, Hood's Division

The supports not coming up in time, and the enemy coming up on our left flank, General *[George T.] Anderson* changed the front of the left wing of the Ninth Georgia Regiment, which occupied the extreme left of the brigade, but soon found they could not hold the enemy in check.

He then ordered the brigade to retire to the crest of the hill, in the edge of the timber, where the charge commenced.

But a short time elapsed before *McLaw's* division came up on our left, when *General Anderson* ordered another advance, which was executed with spirit and loss to the enemy. In this charge, *General Anderson* was wounded, in consequence of which some confusion ensued, and the command fell back a short distance the second time. The third advance was made, and resulted, after a severe conflict of half an hour in the ravine, in the rout of the enemy, which was vigorously pressed to the foot of the mountain [Little Round Top]. The loss of the enemy was here very great. From the exhausted condition of the men, together with the fact that the enemy were pouring in large re-enforcements on the right, it was deemed impracticable to follow him farther. In this charge, large numbers of prisoners were taken and sent to the rear without guard. . . . The brigade retired in good order across the ravine, and went into bivouac for the night. . . . The loss of the brigade was heavy. . . . 105 killed, 512 wounded, and 146 missing." [*O.R.*, XXVII, Part 2, pp. 339, 397.]

Report of Maj. H. D. McDaniel, CSA, Eleventh Georgia Infantry, Anderson's Brigade, Hood's Division

The scene of action was reached by a march of several miles, under a burning sun, and for the distance of 1 mile under a terrific fire of the enemy's batteries. Advancing to the crest of the hill where the Emmitsburg pike enters the woods in front of the enemy's position, along a ravine near the base of the mountain, the regiment bore unflinchingly, with the remainder of the brigade, the severe enfilading fire of the enemy's batteries upon Cemetery Hill until ordered to advance.

The Eleventh Georgia is the right center regiment of the brigade, and went into action in its place. The advance was made in good order, and, upon reaching the belt of woods in front, a vigorous fire was opened upon the enemy, followed up by a vigorous charge, which dislodged them from the woods, the ravine, and from a stone fence running diagonally with the line of battle. This formidable position was occupied by the Eleventh Georgia, and a galling fire opened upon the enemy's front and flank, causing his line to recoil in confusion. At this juncture, *Brigadier-General Anderson* came in person to the regiment (a considerable distance in advance of the remainder of the brigade and in strong position, which was at the time held and might have been held against the enemy in front), and ordered *Colonel Little* to withdraw the regiment to the crest of the hill, on account of a movement of the enemy in force upon the left flank of the brigade [in the vicinity of the Stony Hill]. The regiment retired in good order, though with loss, to the point indicated.

After a short interval, a second advance was made to the stone fence, but, after a furious conflict, the failure of support on the right forced the brigade back a distance of 100 yards. The third advance was made in connection with the entire line on that part of the field, and resulted, after a conflict in the ravine of half an hour, in the rout of the enemy from the field. . . . [*O.R.*, XXVII, Part 2, p. 401.]

Report of Capt. George Hillyer, CSA, Ninth Georgia Infantry, Anderson's Brigade, Hood's Division

The regiment occupied its usual position in line on the left of the brigade and the extreme left of the division, having for nearly an hour and a half no support on its left, the advance of *McLaws'* division being for some reason thus long delayed, which left the flank while advancing nearly the distance of a mile very much exposed to an enfilading fire of the enemy's batteries, and also to the fire of a flanking party of the enemy, who were prompt to take advantage of the exposed condition of the flank. To meet this flanking party, I changed the front of three companies, and for nearly an hour, against great odds, held them in check until relieved by the advance of *McLaws'* division, which finally came up on our left.

The whole line now again pressed forward, and, though entirely without support, dispersed and scattered a fresh line of the enemy who came up against us, and pursued them 400 or 500 yards farther to the base of the mountain [Little Round Top] upon which the enemy's heavy batteries were posted, which we found to be the strongest natural position I ever saw. Our little band, now thinned and exhausted by three and a half hours' constant fighting, made a gallant attempt to storm the batteries, but the enemy being again heavily re-enforced, we were met by a storm of shot and shell, against which, in our wornout condition, we could not advance. I believe that had *McLaws'* division advanced with our line so that we could have arrived at this point before we became worn out with fatigue, we would have carried the position. In this movement the whole brigade and also several brigades of *McLaws'* division participated. [*O.R.*, XXVII, Part 2, pp. 399–400.]

Drive forward to the "T" intersection. Turn left. After you leave the Wheatfield and wind up through the woods on the stony hill, you can pull off to the right at the crest of the hill. Stop by one of the regimental monuments on your right where you can see Union artillery along **WHEATFIELD AVENUE** in your front, and the Union position in the **PEACH ORCHARD** off to your left.

Today's view of the "stony hill." (HWN)

STOP 15

You are now on "the stony hill" that remained such a vivid memory to Confederate general *Kershaw*. While there was no way that he could have anticipated its importance *before* launching his attack across the Emmitsburg road, he quickly came to appreciate the necessity of seizing and holding this vital piece of terrain. Whoever controls this ground also commands the WHEATFIELD and can enfilade the PEACH OR-CHARD, 300 yards to your left. From here riflemen from the Third South Carolina could also pick off the artillerymen working the guns supporting Union infantry in the Peach Orchard and along Wheatfield Road. In the low ground to your immediate left the three South Carolina regiments comprising *Kershaw's* left wing were caught and "cruelly punished" by the fire of batteries planted along WHEATFIELD ROAD, some 150 yards to your left front.

In an article written 20 years after the war, *Kershaw* elaborated upon the details of his after-action report. He was the only general officer in McLaws' entire division to submit a report of the battle, and his Third South Carolina regiment was the only one of 18 regiments from that division with an after-action report included in the *Official Records*. *Kershaw* describes the fighting for the "stony hill:"

The moment the line was rectified the 7th and 3rd regiments advanced into the wood and occupied the stony hill, the left of the 3d Regiment swinging around and attacking the batteries to the left of that position, which, for the reasons already stated [see above p. 66], had resumed their fire. Very soon a heavy column moved in two lines of battle across the wheat-field to attack my position in such a manner as to take the 7th Regiment in flank on the right. The right wing of this regiment was then thrown back to meet this attack, under the command of *Lieutenant-Colonel Bland*. I then hurried in person to *General Semmes*, then 150 yards in my right rear, to bring him up to meet the attack on my right, and also to bring forward my right regiment, the 15th . . . which, separated from the brigade by the artillery at the time of the attack, was cut off by *Semmes's* brigade. . . .

General Semmes promptly responded to my call, and put his brigade in motion toward the right, preparatory to moving to the front. While his troops were moving he fell, mortally wounded. Returning to the 7th Regiment, I reached it just as the advancing column of Federals [de Trobriand's brigade] had arrived at a point some two hundred yards off, whence they poured into us a volley from their whole line, and advanced to the charge. They were handsomely received . . . by this veteran regiment, which long kept them at bay in its front. One regiment of *Semmes's* brigade came at the double quick as far as the ravine in our rear, and checked the advance of the Federals in their front. There was still an interval of a hundred yards, or thereabout, between this regiment and the right of the 7th, and into this the enemy was forcing his way, causing my right to swing back more and more; still fighting, at a distance not exceeding thirty paces, until the two wings of the regiment were nearly doubled on each other.

About this time, the fire of the battery on my left having ceased, I sent for the 2d South Carolina regiment to come to the right. Before I could hear anything of them the enemy had swung around and lapped my whole line at close quarters, and the fighting was general and desperate all along the line. . . . The 7th Regiment finally gave way, and I directed *Colonel Aiken* to re-form it at the stone wall about Rose's. I passed to the 3rd Regiment, then hotly engaged on the crest of the hill, and gradually swung back its right as the enemy made progress around that flank. *Semmes's* advanced regiment had given way. One of his regiments had mingled with the 3d, and amid rocks and trees, within a few feet of each other, these brave men, Confederates and Federals, maintained a desperate conflict. The enemy could make no progress in front, but slowly extended around my right. Separated from view of my left, of which I could hear nothing, all my staff being with that wing, the position of the 15th Regiment being wholly unknown, the 7th having retreated, and nothing being heard of the other troops in the division, I feared the brave men around me would be surrounded by the large force . . . gradually enveloping us. In order to avoid such a catastrophe, I ordered a retreat to the buildings at Rose's.

On emerging from the wood . . . I saw *Wofford* riding at the head of his fine brigade, then coming in, his left being in the Peach Orchard, which was then clear of the enemy. His movement was such as to strike the stony hill on the left, and thus turn the flank of the troops that had driven us from that position. On his approach the enemy retreated across the wheatfield, where, with the regiments of my left wing *Wofford* attacked with great effect, driving the Federals upon and near to Little Round Top. I now ascertained that *Barksdale* had advanced upon the Peach Orchard after I had become engaged; that he had cleared that position with the assistance of my 8th South Carolina . . . driving all before him, and, having advanced far beyond that point . . . had fallen mortally wounded. . . . He had passed too far to my left to afford me any relief except in silencing the batteries that had so cruelly punished my left.

My losses exceeded 600 men killed and wounded—about one-half the force engaged. ["Kershaw's Brigade at Gettysburg," *Battles and Leaders*. III, p. 336–37.]

The Union forces who initially engaged *Kershaw's* troops for possession of the Stony Hill initially were the 5th Michigan and the 110th Pennsylvania, of de Trobriand's brigade. The other regiments of this brigade had already been sent to the support of Ward's brigade, to the left, and Graham's brigade in the Peach Orchard.

Report of Col. P. Regis de Trobriand, USA, commanding Third Brigade, First Division, Third Army Corps

The battle was raging on my left and right to the rear on both sides, in consequence of my advanced position . . . and soon these two attacks came converging on the angle of which I formed the summit, with the Fifth Michigan . . . and the One hundred and tenth Pennsylvania . . . the only two regiments left at that point. Fortunately my position there was a strong one, in a wood commanding a narrow ravine, which the enemy attempted in vain to cross under our fire.

The unflinching bravery of the Fifth Michigan, which sustained the loss of more than one-half of its number without yielding a foot of ground, deserves to be especially mentioned. . . . Had a sufficient force been there under my orders when the enemy gave up forcing our position, I would not have hesitated to try to break his line at that point; but two regiments from the Fifth Corps, sent there to my support, having fallen back without engaging the enemy (by what orders I could never ascertain), and some points of our line yielding under a disproportionate contest for want of timely support, I found myself in danger of being surrounded, and fell back out of the woods, where the enemy did not risk to follow us. I found the Seventeenth Maine in a wheat-field, where it had followed the receding movement of the line. As the enemy was pressing upon up on that side, I made a *retour offensif* with that regiment, re-enforced by the Fifth Michigan, keeping the enemy at bay in the woods until the arrival of sufficient re-enforcements from the Second Corps allowed us to be relieved when our ammunition was just exhausted [*O.R.*, XXVII, Part 1, p. 520.]

Longstreet's assault not only struck the Third Corps on an exposed flank; it also caught Sickles without an adequate reserve, since both of his divisions were needed to occupy his advanced and expanded line. Briga-dier General A. A. Humphreys, who had deployed his division north of the Peach Orchard, in two lines on the reserve slope "a short distance behind the crest" upon which the Emmitsburg road is located, was ordered to send his reserve brigade to Birney's support. Two of Burling's regiments were moved into the Peach Orchard; another was returned to Humphreys for picket duty, and before he could deploy his remaining three regiments in line across the Wheatfield, to fill in the gap between Ward and de Trobriand, Birney ordered him to send his largest remaining regiment to Ward's support, on his left. Meanwhile still another regiment was taken from him without his knowledge, leaving him with only a single regiment. By this time no two regiments of the brigade were together and there was no other reserve from the Third Corps.

Sykes' Fifth Corps, which Meade had initially held as his main reserve, had been moved forward soon after *Longstreet's* assault had commenced. As his column entered upon the field, the lead brigade—Vincent's—was immediately diverted to Little Round Top. The two remaining brigades of Barnes' division were ordered forward into these woods, where they were almost immediately hit by *Kershaw*.

Exactly what happened to Tilton's brigade will probably never be determined. Deployed on the right, Tilton's six regiments kept falling back in order to avoid being outflanked on their right by Confederates attacking from the direction of the Rose house. Reporting total casualties of 109—which was light in comparison to any other brigade involved in the fighting in this sector—Tilton claims that he was ordered to fall back, that he retired twice, the first time for over 300 yards, and that he had saved his brigade "from great disaster after it could no longer do any good in front." [*O.R.*, XXVII, Part 1, pp. 607–8.]

Sweitzer's brigade, which "was placed in position in a wood fronting an open field," fell back under cover of these trees once Tilton's brigade had retired to form a new line in the woods just north of WHEATFIELD AVENUE. Later they supported the attack by Caldwell's division of the Second Corps, which had been rushed over from the Union center. After "a few patriotic remarks" by the division commander Sweitzer's men moved across the Wheatfield with a cheer, the right flank resting on these woods. Halting at the stone fence defended earlier in the afternoon by the 17th Maine, they were hit by *Wofford's* brigade as it swept down from the direction of the Peach orchard. "Colonel," the color-bearer remarked, "I'll be _____ if I don't think we are faced the wrong way; the rebs are up there in the woods behind us, on the right." Finding that he was surrounded, with the Confederates sheltered by these woods while his own men were exposed in the Wheatfield, Sweitzer ordered his brigade to fall back diagonally toward the northeast corner of the Wheatfield, where it crossed another stone fence and retired to the rear of a Union battery on the elevation beyond. Of the 1010 men that Sweitzer led into action on the 2nd, 466 became casualties. [*O.R.*, XXVII, Part 1, pp. 610–12.]

Report of Brig. Gen. John C. Caldwell, USA, commanding First Division, Second Army Corps

My command arrived on the field of battle on the morning of July 2, and was placed in position by General Hancock on the left of the Second Division, in columns of regiments by brigades. . . . The battle was raging with considerable fury at the left, where, between 4 and 5 o'clock, I received orders to report with my command to General Sykes. I moved off immediately by the left flank. . . . Before reaching the position designated for me, I met a staff officer . . . who told me he had orders where to place me. I moved forward rapidly, a portion of the time at double-quick, as the Third Corps was said to be hard pressed. . . .

I ordered Colonel Cross, commanding the First Brigade, to advance in line of battle through a wheat-field, his left resting on the woods which skirted the field. He had advanced but a short distance when he encountered the enemy, and opened upon him a terrific fire, driving him steadily to the farther end of the wheat-field.

In the meantime I had put the Second Brigade in on the right of the First, and they advanced in like manner, driving the enemy before them. The Third brigade I ordered still farther to the right, to connect with the Third Corps, while I held the Fourth Brigade in reserve. The First, Second, and Third Brigades advanced with the utmost gallantry, driving the enemy before them over difficult and rocky ground, which was desperately contested by the slowly retreating foe. The First Brigade, which had been longest engaged, had expended all its ammunition, when I ordered Colonel Brooke to relieve it. He advanced . . . and drove the enemy until he gained the crest of the hill, which was afterward gained by the whole of my line. In this advantageous position I halted, and called upon General Barnes, who was some distance in the rear, to send a brigade to the support of my line. He readily complied, and ordered the brigade of Colonel Sweitzer forward into the wheat-field. I then galloped to the left to make a connection with General Ayres [commanding Second Division, Fifth Corps] and found that I had advanced some distance beyond him. He, however, gave the order to his line to move forward and connect with my left.

Thus far everything had progressed favorably. I had gained a position which, if properly supported on the flanks, I thought impregnable from the front. General Ayres was moving forward to connect with my left, but I found on going to the right that all the troops on my right had broken and were fleeing to the rear in great confusion. As soon as they broke, and before I could change front, the enemy in great numbers came in upon my right flank and even my rear, compelling me to fall back or have my command taken prisoners. My men fell back under a very heavy cross-fire, generally in good order, but necessarily with some confusion. I reformed them behind a stone wall until relieved by the Twelfth Corps. [*O.R.*, XX-VII, Part I, pp. 379–80.]

Report of Maj. St. Clair Mulholland, USA, 116 Pennsylvania Infantry, Second Brigade, First Division, Second Army Corps

Our division was ployed in mass in column of regiments. . . . Here we stacked arms, and ordered the men to rest. We remained in this position during the forenoon. . . . Heavy firing was heard at intervals on our right during the day, although everything remained quiet in the vicinity of my command until about 3 p.m.

About this time firing commenced on our left, I think about three-fourths of a mile distant. The firing had continued about an hour when orders came for us to fall in. We at once took arms, and were marched by the left flank toward the scene of action. After marching nearly 1 mile, and the division in line of battle, we advanced to support (I think) a portion of the Third Army Corps, which was then engaged. The brigade . . . advanced in line of battle. . . . As we advanced, portions of the Third Corps retired, passing through the interval of our line. Having entered a dense woods, we began to ascend a hill, where large bowlders of rocks impeded our progress, notwithstanding which we advanced in good order. We soon came within sight of the enemy, who occupied the crest of the hill, and who immediately opened fire at our approach. Our brigade returned the fire with good effect. After firing for about ten minutes, the order was given to advance, which the brigade did in excellent style, driving the enemy from their position, which we at once occupied. We took many prisoners at this point, hundreds of the enemy laying down their arms and passing to the rear. We found the position which our foe had occupied but a few moments before thickly strewn with the dead and wounded. Here we again opened fire, the enemy having rallied to oppose our farther advance. After being engaged for about twenty minutes and the enemy having re-enforced, the division began to be flanked by the enemy, who had formed a line facing the right flank of our brigade. This line was formed along the edge of a wheatfield, about a quarter of a mile in rear of our brigade. This field we had to cross to get to the rear. In doing so, we encountered the full sweep of the enemy's fire, which at this point was most destructive, Many . . . fell before this terrible fire. [*O.R.*, XXVII, Part 1, pp. 391–92.]

Now proceed to the "T" intersection and turn left on **WHEAT-FIELD ROAD**. Drive about 0.4 mile on Wheatfield Road until you come to the east edge of the **PEACH ORCHARD**. Turn left and drive around to the South side of the orchard. Stop near the 2nd New Hampshire Monument.

STOP 16

You are now on the south face of the Peach Orchard. As you look to your left, you can appreciate the field of fire for Union infantry and artillery as *Kershaw's* lines swept across the Emmitsburg road and into the woods. You can also better understand why he found it necessary to divert his left wing to attack the Peach Orchard.

Brig. Gen. Charles K. Graham's brigade occupied the Peach Orchard, supporting Ames' battery, on the higher ground a short distance to your right, and Clark's battery, farther to the east beyond Wheatfield Road. (It was Clark's battery that had initially fired on *McLaw's* division as it approached Seminary Ridge, causing him to deploy along the stone wall and forcing *Hood* in his rear to move still farther to the right.

Report of Capt. Nelson Ames, USA, Battery G, First New York Light Artillery

. . . [At] 3 p.m. . . . Captain Randolph, chief of artillery Third Army Corps, ordered me to move forward about 800 yards, take position in a thick peach orchard, and engage the enemy's batteries at a distance of 850 yards. I immediately moved forward, and, while crossing a cleared field, the enemy opened fire from one of their batteries. They got an excellent range of my battery, nearly all of their shot striking in my battery, but fortunately they did no other damage than killing 2 horses.

Trostle House with dead artillery horses littering the ground. From Miller's *Photographic History of the Civil War* (MIL).

Before gaining the position assigned me, I was obliged to halt in plain sight of the enemy, to clear away two fences which the supporting infantry had failed to throw down as they had been ordered to do. As soon as I could come into battery, I opened upon the battery in my front with spherical case and shell, and, after firing about thirty minutes, the enemy's fire greatly slackened, and in a few moments more it nearly ceased; but before I had time to congratulate myself or men upon our success . . . a four-gun battery of light 12-pounders opened upon my right from a grove [on Seminary Ridge] 500 yards distant, and at the same time a new battery opened on my front. I immediately ordered Lieutenant McClellan, commanding the right section, to turn his two pieces upon the flank battery, while Lieutenants Hazelton and Goff kept up their fire upon the battery in front, and for a short time I had as sharp an artillery fight as I ever witnessed. I was soon pleased to see one piece of the flank battery dismounted, and the cannoneers of another either killed or wounded, when the other two pieces were taken from the field. I then turned my whole attention upon the batteries in front, but was obliged to fire very slowly, as my ammunition was getting exhausted, having but a few rounds of spherical case left, with a small supply of solid shot and canister.

About this time the rebel infantry advanced in line of battle across the wheat-field to my left and front. Lieutenant Hazelton opened upon them with spherical case—he having collected all there was in the battery—with great success as long as that kind of ammunition lasted. He then ceased firing, and ordered his cannoneers to shelter themselves until the enemy advanced within canister range, when he purposed to drive them back with the unwelcome messenger—grape and canister—Lieutenants McClellan and Goff meanwhile keeping up a steady, slow fire with solid shot upon the batteries in front. After having been engaged for two and a half hours, at 5.30 p.m. I was relieved by Battery I, Fifth U.S. Artillery. My loss . . . was 7 men wounded, 1 mortally and 2 seriously; also a loss of 11 horses killed. [O.R., XXVII, Part 1, pp. 900–901.]

The best description of the fighting at this spot is found in the after-action report of the 2nd New Hampshire, one of the two regiments from Burling's brigade that Birney had ordered forward to support Graham's brigade. Reporting with 24 officers and 330 rifles, Col. Edward L. Bailey.

Report of Col. Edward L. Bailey, USA, Second New Hampshire Infantry, Third Brigade, Second Division, Third Army Corps

I was at once ordered to support Battery G, First New York Artillery, and one section of a battery unknown, all light 12-pounders, brass. In this position my left rested upon the right of the Sixty-third Pennsylvania, my right covered by a wood house [Wentz] situated upon the Emmitsburg road, line forming a right angle with that road. Two hundred yards in my front [approximately this location] the Third Maine was skirmishing with the enemy.

At 4 o'clock, while experiencing a terrific fire of spherical case and canister from batteries in my front and on my right, 650 yards distant, I directed the rolls of my companies to be called, and found but 8 of the total number absent. These had fallen out of the ranks from sunstroke and exhaustion while moving by double-quick to position.

At 4.30 p.m. the Third Maine was withdrawn from our front to our rear, and about this time a section of Rodman pieces were substituted for those we were supporting. These pieces were worked with great inefficiency, and at 5 o'clock it was observed that a brigade of the enemy was advancing on our right, in column of battalions massed, while two regiments were moving directly parallel with my front to the left, evidently with design to turn that flank.

I reported these facts to General Graham, and asked permission to charge, the enemy being close upon us—so near that the officer commanding the section of battery spiked his pieces, fearful that he should lose them. The general gave me directions to go forward, when I gave the order. My regiment started immediately, and advanced 150 yards at a run with a yell and such impetuosity as to cause the enemy to retire to a ravine 250 yards in our front, where they were covered from our fire, when I directed the fire of my battalion of the left oblique by the flank at about the same distance. My fire was so galling, assisted by that from the Third Maine, which had come up and taken part upon my left, as to cause them to break and seek shelter, when my attention was again called to my right, strengthened by the Sixty-third Pennsylvania forming at right angles with my front and parallel with the Emmitsburg road, upon which was advancing the brigade of the enemy, moving by battalion in mass, in line of battle. I immediately directed the fire of my battalion to the right oblique full upon it. Yet their line of fire, assisted by a terrible discharge of spherical case from their batteries, caused the Sixty-eighth Pennsylvania to retire, and at the same moment the Third Maine moved 200 yards to the rear, though in good order.

Finding myself thus unsupported, and the enemy steadily advancing, I ordered my regiment to fall back slowly, firing, which was fully executed. I moved to the rear 140 yards, and halted my line under the brow of the hill, halting also on the brow to give a volley to the enemy, then distant but 20 yards. The positions of the three regiments was that of *échelon* at about 20 paces, my regiment being the apex. The enemy continued advancing until they reached the brow of the hill, when their left swept toward the Sixty-third Pennsylvania in such overwhelming numbers as to cause it to give way; and fearing those regiments which had been observed marching toward my left might appear upon that flank, and knowing our efforts must prove futile against such fearful odds, I gave the order to retire, which was done quite rapidly, yet coolly, and without excitement as they went. I rejoined the brigade at about 6:30 p.m., fearfully diminished in numbers [193 casualties], yet firm and fearless still. [*O.R.*, XXVII, Part 1, pp. 573–74.]

Report of Col. Henry J. Madill, USA, One hundred and forty-first Pennsylvania Infantry, First Brigade, First Division, Third Army Corps

During the forenoon of July 2, we moved . . . to the Emmitsburg pike, and here, by command of General Graham, we then formed in line of battle, the Fifty-seventh Pennsylvania Volunteers on the right of the line, the Sixty-eighth Pennsylvania Volunteers on the left, and my regiment in the center, the One hundred and fifth and One hundred and fourteenth Pennsylvania Volunteers supporting.

The line was doubled on the center, Clark's battery in our front. They delivered a few shots, receiving but little response. The battery then moved up the hill and a little to the left, and took a position in the peach orchard, near the Emmitsburg pike. In the meanwhile our line advanced up the slope and deployed in the oat-field, some 15 rods from the pike, and were ordered to lie down. At this point we sustained a severe fire from artillery for some time, the enemy having a good range.

After remaining in this position for some twenty minutes or more, I received an order from General Graham . . . to move my regiment out, and place it in front of Clark's battery. This order was in a few minutes countermanded, and I formed my regiment in rear of that battery, and, while supporting that battery, the Second New Hampshire was ordered up to my support. They took position in my rear. Here the fire from the enemy's artillery was very severe, and we sustained a considerable loss in killed and wounded.

At this time it was observed that the enemy was advancing in strong force from across and down the Emmitsburg pike. My regiment, together with two others [3rd Michigan and 3rd Maine] were ordered to the front of the peach orchard, the battery occupying that position having withdrawn and left the field. We left, the Third Maine on my right and the Third Michigan on my left.

The enemy was advancing in two columns, one column crossing the pike beyond the stone barn and advancing in two lines in the direction of the position occupied by the Second and Third Brigades [Ward and de Trobriand], which were to our left and somewhat to our rear. When they advanced below the stone barn, they endeavored to extend their lines to the left. It was at this time that my regiment, with the two others . . . was ordered forward. We engaged the flank of the enemy, and prevented him from extending his lines this side of the small creek that runs through the field near the stone barn.

At this time the other column had advanced up to the pike and deployed, and was marching on the point we were occupying. The battery in position near the road and immediately to the left of the log house withdrew. The Third Maine, after exchanging a few shots with the enemy at this point, withdrew. Colonel Pierce's regiment [3rd Michigan] withdrew about the same time, or a few minutes before. I found myself alone, with a small regiment of about 180 men.

I continued to hold my position for a short time, when I withdrew . . . and took a position in rear of the Sixty-eighth Pennsylvania Volunteers, who were engaged with the enemy in front of the barn, near the brick house [Sherfy]. When I took this position the Sixty-eighth withdrew, the balance of the brigade having previously withdrawn. I was thus left alone on the hill occupied by the brigade in the afternoon. The enemy, after the falling back of the Sixty-eighth, advanced to the barn. I engaged them at this point, and held them in check for twenty minutes or upward, but being overpowered by the large numbers of the enemy, I was compelled to retire, which I reluctantly did.

It was at this point that my regiment suffered so severely; 25 of my men were killed here and 5 of my officers severely wounded. . . . I took 200 men into the fight, with 9 officers. Out of that number I lost 145 men and 6 commissioned officers, the largest proportionate loss in the corps in that fight . . . [*O.R.*, XXVII, Part 1, pp. 504–5.]

Drive forward to the intersection with the Emmitsburg Road. Turn right, and drive a bit more than 0.6 mile to a very sharp right turn. Turn right onto SICKLES AVENUE and stop behind the battery position (Turnbull's Battery) in the vicinity of the Carr Monument [First Brigade, 2nd Division, III Corps).

The "Brick house" where the 141st Pennsylvania took such heavy losses can be seen on your left as you drive north on the Emmitsburg road.

STOP 17

You are now on the position occupied by Humphreys' division of the Third Corps. His initial front was narrow enough to permit a defense in depth, with his forward brigade in line of battle, followed by a second brigade "in line of battalions in mass 200 yards" to the rear, and a third brigade massed 200 yards still farther to the rear. The latter, commanded by Col. Burling, was soon dispersed in a series of uncoordinated efforts to plug several gaps that had appeared along the front of Birney's division.

About 4 p.m. Sickles ordered Humphreys to move his division forward "so that the first line ran along the Emmitsburg road a short distance behind the crest upon which that road lies." Humphreys' only other brigade, commanded by Col. William R. Brewster, moved forward at the same time to a position corresponding to the continuation of this road. When *Barksdale's* Confederate brigade broke through the Union line near the Sherfy house, on *this* edge of the Peach Orchard—too far to the left to be of much help to *Kershaw*—Graham's troops still held the northern portion of the orchard, and it is apparent from reports dealing with this phase of the action that the critical blow was struck against Humphreys.

Col. Madill, whose regiment lost nearly 75% on this afternoon, expressed his opinion officially that "had the Second Division [Humphreys] maintained its position as persistently as the First did, we would not have been compelled to abandon the Peach Orchard. They gave way some time before the First Brigade was compelled to retire." [*O.R.*, XXVII, Part 1, p. 505.]

General Carr, commanding the front line in Humphreys' division, claims that the breakthrough occurred when "the regiment on my left . . . gave way" and "the enemy advanced in considerable force on my left flank, which compelled me to change my front." No sooner had this occurred when the Confederates appeared on Carr's right flank, "pouring in a most destructive cross-fire." [*O.R.*, XXVII, Part 1, p. 543.]

Report of Brig. Gen. Andrew A. Humphreys, USA, commanding Second Division, Third Army Corps

I was about to throw somewhat forward the left of my infantry and engage the enemy with it, when I received orders from General Birney (General Sickles having been dangerously wounded and carried from the field) to throw back my left, and form a line oblique to and in rear of the one I then held, and was informed that the First Division would complete the line to the Round Top ridge. This I did under a heavy fire of artillery and infantry from the enemy, who now advanced on my whole front. . . .

My infantry now engaged the enemy's, but my left was in air (although I extended it as far as possible with my Second Brigade), and, being the only troops on the field, the enemy's whole attention was directed to my division, which was forced back slowly, firing as they receded.

The two regiments sent me by General Hancock [Second Corps] were judiciously posted by Lieut. H. C. Christiancy in support of my right. At this time I received orders . . . from General Birney to withdraw to the Round Top ridge—an order previously conveyed to General Carr, commanding the First Brigade on the right, by General Birney in person. This order I complied with, retiring very slowly, continuing the contest with the enemy, whose fire of artillery and infantry was destructive in the extreme. . . . Its severity may be judged by the fact that the loss in killed, wounded and missing of my division 5,000 strong was 2,088. . . . The fortune of war rarely places troops under more trying circumstances." [*O.R.*, XXVII, Part 1, pp. 533–4.]

From this position you can view the entire area covered by the Confederate attack. *Barksdale's* bridge swept across this park road, from right to left, and charged into the woods at the bottom of the slope on the side of the TROSTLE HOUSE, some 500–600 yards to the southwest. One of *Barksdale's* regiments, the 21st Mississippi, captured a Union battery on the other side of Plum Run but lost it to the counterattack of the 39th New York, sent over from Hancock's Second Corps. *Wofford's* brigade, which initially deployed in the rear of *Barksdale*, slammed into the wedge between the Stony Hill and the Peach Orchard; his momentum carried some of his regiments all the way to the base of Little Round Top.

Anderson's division of *Hill's* Corps also took part in the attack. Notified that *Longstreet's*, line "would be in a direction nearly at right angles with mine; that he would assault the extreme left of the enemy and drive him toward Gettysburg," *Anderson* was ordered to commit his division into action "by brigades" as soon as *Longstreet's* Corps had progressed so far in the assault "as to be connected with my right flank." Wilcox's brigade, occupying the right of *Anderson's* line, attacked as ordered and crossed immediately in front of your present location.

Report of Brig. Gen. Cadmus M. Wilcox, CSA, commanding brigade, Anderson's Division, Hill's Corps

My instructions were to advance when the troops on my right should advance, and report this to the division commander, in order that the other brigades should advance in proper time. In order that I should advance with those on my right, it became necessary for me to move off by the left flank so as to uncover the ground over which they had to advance. This was done as rapidly as the nature of the ground with its opposing obstacles (stone and plank fences) would admit. Having gained 400 or 500 yards to the left by this flank movement, my command faced by the right flank, and advanced. This forward movement was made in an open field, this ground rising slightly to the Emmitsburg turnpike, 250 yards distant. Before reaching this road, a line of the enemy's skirmishers along a fence parallel to the road were encountered and dispersed. The fence being crossed, my men advanced to the road, in which infantry in line of battle were formed. A brisk musketry fight for a few minutes followed, when the enemy gave way; not however, till all save two pieces of a battery [Turnbull] that was in the road had been removed. These fell into our hands, the horses having been killed.

On the far side of the pike the ground was descending for some 600 or 700 yards. At the bottom of this descent was a narrow valley, through which ran a rocky ravine or stream, fringed with small trees and undergrowth of bushes. Beyond this, the ground rose rapidly for some 200 yards, and upon this ridge were numerous batteries of the enemy.

This ridge to my right rose into a succession of higher ridges or spurs of mountains, increasing in height to the right, but to the left gradually descending. When my command crossed the pike and began to descend the slope, they were exposed to an artillery fire from numerous pieces, both from the front and from either flank.

Before reaching the ravine at the foot of the slope, two lines of infantry were met and broken, and driven pell-mell across the ravine. A second battery of six pieces here fell into our hands. From the batteries on the ridge above referred to, grape and canister were poured into our ranks. This stronghold of the enemy, together with his batteries, were almost won, when still another line of infantry descended the slope in our front at a double quick, to the support of their fleeing comrades and for the defense of the batteries.

Seeing this contest so unequal, I dispatched my adjutant-general to the division commander, to ask that support be sent to my men, but no support came. Three . . . times did this last of the enemy's lines attempt to drive my men back, and were as often repulsed. This struggle at the foot of the hill on which were the enemy's batteries, though so unequal, was continued for some thirty minutes. With a second supporting line, the heights could have been carried. Without support on either my right or left, my men were withdrawn, to prevent their entire destruction or capture. The enemy did not pursue, but my men retired under a heavy artillery fire, and returned to their original position in line, and bivouacked for the night, pickets being left on the pike. [*O.R.*, XXVII, Part 2, p. 618.]

The troops who met *Wilcox* were the 1st Minnesota, which attacked at double-quick down the slope of the hill. "The fire we encountered here was terrible," the captain in command of the regiment reported, "and although we inflicted severe punishment upon the enemy, and stopped his advance, we there lost in killed and wounded more than two-thirds of our men and officers who were engaged." [*O.R.*, XXVII, Part 1, p. 425.]

As soon as *Wilcox* had commenced his attack, *Perry's* Florida brigade advanced on his left.

Report of Col. David Lang, CSA, Eighth Florida Infantry, commanding Perry's brigade, Anderson's Division, Hill's Corps

I was ordered to throw forward a strong line of skirmishers, and advance with *General Wilcox*, holding all the ground the enemy yielded.

At 6 p.m. *General Wilcox* having begun to advance, I moved forward, being met at the crest of the first hill with a murderous fire of grape, canister, and musketry. Moving forward at the double quick, the enemy fell back beyond their artillery, where they were attempting to rally when we reached the crest of the second hill. Seeing this, the men opened a galling fire upon them, thickly strewing the/ground with their killed and wounded. This threw them into confusion, when we charged them, with a yell, and they broke and fled in confusion into the woods and breastworks beyond, leaving four or five pieces of cannon in my front, carrying off, however, most of the horses and limbers. Following them rapidly, I arrived behind a small eminence at the foot of the heights, where, the brigade having become much scattered, I halted for the purpose of reforming, and allowing the men to catch breath before the final assault upon the heights.

While engaged in reforming here, an aide from the right informed me that a heavy force had advanced upon *General Wilcox's* brigade and was forcing it back. At the same time a heavy fire of musketry was poured upon my brigade from the woods 50 yards immediately in front, which was gallantly met and handsomely replied to by my men. A few moments later, another messenger from my right informed me that *General Wilcox* had fallen back, and the enemy was then some distance in rear of my right flank. Going to the right, I discovered that the enemy had passed me more than 100 yards, and were attempting to surround me. I immediately ordered my men back to the road, some 300 yards to the rear. Arriving here, I found there was no cover under which to rally, and continued to fall back, rallying and reforming upon the line from which we started. In this charge the brigade lost about 300 men killed, wounded, and missing. . . . [*O.R.*, XXVII, Part 2, pp. 631–32.]

Wright's brigade, still farther to the left, had been ordered to move simultaneously with *Perry's* brigade. Passing just north of the Codori farm – the first buildings that you can see on the Emmitsburg road behind you – *Wright's* object point was the clump of trees made famous by *Pickett's* charge the following day.

Report of Brig. Gen. A. R. Wright, CSA, commanding brigade, Anderson's Division, Hill's Corps

I was instructed to move simultaneously with *Perry's* brigade, which was on my right, and informed that *Posey's* brigade, on my left, would move forward upon my advance. This being the order of battle, I awaited the signal for the general advance, which was given at about 5 p.m. by the advance of *Wilcox's* and *Perry's* brigades on my right. I immediately ordered forward my brigade, and attacked the enemy in his strong position. . . . In this advance, I was compelled to pass for more than a mile across an open plain, intersected by numerous post and rail fences, and swept by the enemy's artillery, which was posted along the Emmitsburg road and upon the crest of the heights . . . a little south of Cemetery Hill. . . .

My men moved steadily forward until reaching within musket range of the Emmitsburg turnpike, when we encountered a strong body of infantry posted under cover of a fence near to and parallel with the road. Just in rear of this line of infantry were the advanced batteries of the enemy, posted along the Emmitsburg turnpike, with a field of fire raking the whole valley below. Just before reaching this position, I had observed that *Posey's* brigade, on my left, had not advanced, and fearing that, if I proceeded much farther with my left flank entirely unprotected, I might become involved in serious difficulties, I dispatched my aide-de-camp . . . with a message to *Major-General Anderson*, informing him . . . that *General Posey* had not advanced. . . . To this message I received a reply to press on; that Posey had been ordered in . . . and that he would reiterate the order.

I immediately charged upon the enemy's line, and drove him in great confusion upon his second line, which was formed behind a stone fence, some 100 or more yards in rear of the Emmitsburg turnpike. At this point we captured several pieces of artillery, which the enemy in his haste and confusion was unable to take off the field.

We again charged upon the enemy, heavily posted behind a stone fence which ran along the abrupt slope of the heights. . . . Here the enemy made considerable resistance to our farther progress, but was finally forced to retire by the impetuous charge of my command.

We were now within less than 100 yards of the crest of the heights, which were lined with artillery, supported by a strong body of infantry. . . . My men, by a well directed fire, soon drove the cannoneers from their guns, and, leaping over the fence, charged up to the top of the crest, and drove the enemy's infantry into a rocky gorge on the eastern slope . . . some 80 or 100 yards in rear of the enemy's batteries.

We were now complete masters of the field, having gained the key . . . of the enemy's whole line. Unfortunately, just as we had carried the enemy's last and strongest position, it was discovered that the brigade on our right had not only not advanced across the turnpike, but had actually given way, and was rapidly falling back to the rear, while on our left we were entirely unprotected, the brigade ordered to our support having failed to advance.

It was now evident . . . I should not be able to hold my position unless speedily and strongly re-enforced. My advanced position and the unprotected condition of my flanks invited an attack which the enemy were speedy to discover, and immediately passed a strong body of infantry under cover of a high ledge of rocks, thickly covered with stunted undergrowth, which fell away from the gorge in rear of their batteries . . . in a southeasterly direction, and, emerging on the western slope of the ridge, came upon my right and rear at a point equidistant from the Emmitsburg turnpike and the stone fence, while a large brigade advanced from the point of woods on my left, which extended nearly down to the turnpike, and, gaining the turnpike, moved rapidly to meet the party which had passed round upon our right.

We were now in a critical condition . . . A few moments more and we would be completely surrounded . . . and with painful hearts we abandoned our captured guns, faced about, and prepared to cut our way through the closing lines in our rear. This was effected in tolerable order, but with immense loss. The enemy rushed to his abandoned guns as soon as we began to retire, and poured a severe fire of grape and canister into our thinned ranks as we retired slowly down the slope into the valley below. I continued to fall back until I reached a slight depression a few hundred yards in advance of our skirmish line of the morning, when I halted, reformed my brigade, and awaited the further pursuit of the enemy. Finding that the enemy was not disposed to continue his advance, a line of skirmishers was thrown out in my front, and a little after dark my command moved to the position we had occupied before the attack was made.

In this charge, my loss was very severe, amounting to 688 in killed, wounded, and missing. . . .

I have not the slightest doubt but that I should have been able to have maintained my position on the heights, and secured the captured artillery, if there had been a protecting force on my left, or if the brigade on my right had not been forced to retire. We captured over twenty pieces of artillery, all of which we were compelled to abandon. [*O.R.*, XXVII, Part 2, pp. 623–24.]

Report of Brig. Gen. John Gibbon, USA, commanding Second Division of, and Second Army Corps

At 4 o'clock the Third Corps advanced, and, swinging round its left flank, took up a position along the Emmitsburg road. To give support to its right flank, I ordered forward two regiments . . . to occupy a position along that road and to the right of a brick house [Codori]. Here they tore down the fences and constructed breastworks, behind which they did most excellent service in checking the advance of the enemy, and preventing him from cutting off the Third Corps from our lines. For the same purpose, I sent a 12-pounder battery to the right and rear of these two regiments, to fire across the Emmitsburg road at some of the enemy's batteries established there.

No sooner was the Third Corps in position, with its right resting near the brick house and the left "in the air," than the enemy made a most furious assault with infantry and artillery on that flank, rolling it back and enfilading the whole line. Such a flank attack could not be successfully resisted, and although dispositions were made to check the advance of the enemy, he came on so rapidly as to drive everything before him. I directed solid shot to be thrown from our batteries over the heads of our own men, and, on the application of General Humphreys, sent two of my regiments to his assistance. . . . The smoke was at this time so dense that but little could be seen of the battle, and I directed some of the guns to cease firing fearing they might injure our own men or uselessly waste their ammunition.

The Eighty-second New York and Fifteenth Massachusetts, near the brick house, were overpowered, outflanked by the enemy in pursuit of the Third Corps, and forced back after heavy loss, including both commanding officers. The Nineteenth Massachusetts . . . and Forty-second New York . . . sent to the assistance of General Humphreys, finding themselves unable with that small force to stem the triumphant advance of the enemy, retired, after a short struggle, in good order.

The enemy came on with such impetuosity that the head of his column came quite through a vacancy in our line to the left of my division, opened by detaching troops to other points. By the steadiness, however, of the troops in the immediate vicinity, and the timely arrival of the Twelfth Corps, this advance was checked and driven back with considerable loss, the pursuit being continued for some distance beyond our lines, and all the guns overrun by the enemy retaken. Darkness ended the contest here, but it continued for some time on our right, in front of the Eleventh Corps. [*O.R.*, XXVII, Part 1, pp. 416–17.]

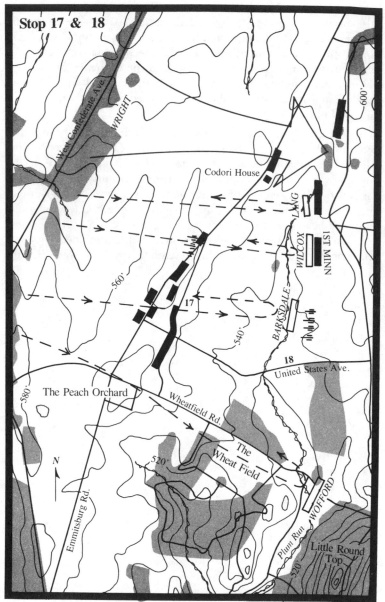

Now drive to the first intersection and turn left on UNITED STATES AVENUE. As you drive down toward the TROSTLE HOUSE, note the advantage of high ground enjoyed by defenders around the Peach Orchard, where the ground is higher than at opposite points on either Cemetery or Seminary Ridge. When you have gone about 0.1 mile beyond the Trostle house and have open fields on both sides of the road, and a clear view of a battery position in the field to your left, you may want to pause for a few minutes.

STOP 18

Sickles' original position was on the high ground several hundred yards to your front. Birney's division stretched from Little Round top to the George Weikert house, located in front of you at the intersection of this road and Sedgwick Avenue. To your left front, behind the battery you see in the field, was Humphrey's division, with each brigade formed in column of regiments. The picket line of the Third Corps was in the Emmitsburg road, with sharpshooters on Seminary Ridge until they were driven back by *Wilcox's* brigade early in the afternoon of 2 July.

By turning around and looking to the west you can appreciate why Sickles was anxious to control the high ground around the Peach Orchard, which dominates his initial position. Accordingly, about noon Sickles ordered his two divisions forward. Birney advanced through the woods on your right, placing his left about 500 yards forward at the Devil's Den and swinging around the right so it could rest in the Peach Orchard. Humphreys was ordered to form his division in line of battle near the Trostle House, in your rear: he subsequently pushed Carr's brigade forward to the Emmitsburg road, with Brewster's brigade in line of battalions in mass about half way between that road and the Trostle house. When the Union lines along the Emmitsburg road collapsed, *Barksdale's* brigade swept down the slope near the Trostle house and emerged from the woods to your left rear—which at that time was described as "small trees and undergrowth of bushes"—to encounter the concentrated fire of several Union batteries planted on the near edge of the woods in front and in the open field to your left.

Report of Lieut. Col. Freeman McGilvery, USA, First Maine Light Artillery, commanding First Volunteer Brigade, Artillery Reserve

At about a quarter to 6 o'clock the enemy's infantry gained possession of the woods immediately on the left of my line of batteries, and our infantry fell back both on our right and left, when great disorder ensued on both flanks of the line of batteries. . . . whereupon I ordered them to retire 250 yards and renew their fire. . . . The crisis of the engagement had now arrived. . . . I formed a new line of artillery about 400 yards to the rear, close under the woods, and covering the opening which led into the Gettysburg and Taneytown road, of the following batteries and parts of batteries: Battery I, Fifth Regular, and a volunteer battery which I have never been able to learn the name of; three guns of the Fifth Massachusetts and two of Captain Thompson's Pennsylvania battery, and commenced firing on the enemy's line of infantry and artillery, which had formed in the open field only about 700 or 800 yards in our front. A brook, running through low bushes parallel to our front, midway between ours and the enemy's lines, was occupied by rebel sharpshooters. As soon as the Sixth Maine Battery reported, which was just before sundown, I ordered canister to be used on the low bushes in front, which compelled them to retire. About this time Pettit's New York battery reported, and changed position on the right of the Sixth Maine.

At this time the enemy's artillery fire was very heavy and rapid. The unknown volunteer battery . . . left the field; the guns of Battery I, Fifth Regulars, were abandoned; Captain Thompson's guns, being out of ammunition, were sent to the rear; Pettit's First New York Battery [B] remained only a few minutes, and left while I was directing the fire of the Sixth Maine and one section of the Fifth Massachusetts. . . . [which] remained in position and kept up a well directed fire upon the enemy's lines, until they had ceased firing, which was about 8 o'clock. . . . During the engagement my horse was hit four times . . . by musketry . . . [O.R., XXVII, Part 1, pp. 882–83.]

Report of Lieut. Edwin B. Dow, USA, Sixth Maine Battery

I received orders . . . to report to General Sickles' (Third) corps . . . about 6 p.m. . . . I immediately marched my command to the front, meeting an ambulance with General Sickles in it, badly wounded.

I had not gone far when Major McGilvery ordered me into position in rear of the first line, remarking that he had charge of the artillery of the Third Corps. On going into position, my battery was under a heavy fire from two batteries of the enemy, situated some 1,000 yards in my front. I replied to them with solid shot and shell until the enemy's line of skirmishers and sharpshooters came out of the woods to the left front of my position, and poured a continual stream of bullets at us. I soon discovered a battle line of the enemy coming through the wood about 600 yards distant, evidently with a design to drive through and take possession of the road to Taneytown, directly in my rear. I immediately opened upon them with spherical case and canister, and, assisted by a section of Captain Phillips' (Fifth Massachusetts) battery, drove them back into the woods. Their artillery, to which we paid no attention, had gotten our exact range, and gave us a warm greeting.

We continued to shell the woods after their infantry retired, and upon visiting the spot the same night . . . found many rebels dead and wounded. It was evidently their intention, after capturing the Ninth Massachusetts Battery and Company I, Fifth Regulars, to have charged right through our lines to the Taneytown road, isolating our left wing and dividing our army; but owing to the prompt and skillful action of Maj. Freeman McGilvery, in forming this second line as soon as he found the first line lost, their plan was foiled, for they no doubt thought the woods in our rear were filled with infantry in support of the batteries, when the fact is we had no support at all. . . . It was about 7 o'clock when the enemy retired, and I was in action altogether about one hour and a half. [*O.R.*, XXVII, Part 1, p. 897.]

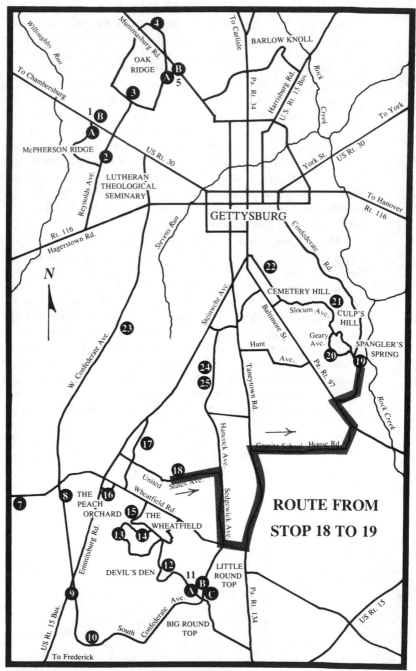

ROUTE FROM
STOP 18 TO 19

For Stop 6, see p. 5 5

Continue driving to the "T" intersection and turn right on SEDGWICK AVENUE. Follow Sedgwick Avenue south for 0.5 mile until it intersects WHEATFIELD ROAD. Turn left, and drive slightly more than 0.1 mile to the TANEYTOWN ROAD (PA 134)

Turn left, and drive about 0.7 mile until you come to the first road on your right, GRANITE SCHOOL HOUSE ROAD. Turn right.

After you have driven about 0.6 mile on this road you will notice a prominent hill on your left. This is Powers Hill, a useful Union artillery position, especially in support of Union efforts to drive Confederate infantry out of positions they would seize on Culp's Hill later in the evening of 2 July. The guns on Powers Hill, which was not heavily wooded on the northern slopes, could also have been used against *Pickett's* troops had they managed to break through the Union lines in the assault the following day.

The large open field on your right as you proceed along Granite School House Road was the location of the Union Reserve Artillery Park.

Continue another 0.15 mile. After the road winds to the left it will intersect PA Route 97, the BALTIMORE PIKE. Turn left, and drive 0.2 mile on the Baltimore Pike. Take the first road on your right, which is marked as a route to Culp's Hill and Spangler's Spring. This road winds through heavy woods for a little more than 0.3 mile before bringing you to a fork in the road marked by a ONE WAY sign pointing right. Follow the directions on the sign and continue about 0.15 mile.

You are now driving along the lines built by Brig. Gen. Thomas R. Ruger's division of the 12th Corps, and extreme right of the Union line as it existed on 2 July. Some of the breastworks remain in the dense foliage a few yards to the right of the park road. About 6 p.m. on the 2nd, Ruger's division was pulled out of these works and rushed to support Sickles corps after it had fallen back to its final position on Cemetery Ridge. The division returned late in the evening to reoccupy these lines.

As you approach the next intersection, you will see a small open field to your right. Stop in front of the 27th INDIANA MONUMENT.

Confederate skirmishers at the foot of Culp's Hill. From *Battles and Leaders of the Civil War*, 1888. (B&L)

THE THIRD DAY
FRIDAY 3 JULY 1863

STOP 19

The small field to your right was the scene of a desperate assault by two Union regiments early on the morning of 3 July. On the previous evening *Brig. Gen. G. H. Steuart's* Confederate brigade had seized a segment of breastworks on the southern slope of Culp's Hill that had just been vacated by troops of the 12th Corps sent to bolster the left of the Union line, and "before it was fairly light" on the 3rd the fighting was renewed.

The Confederate left flank was anchored behind a fence at the far side of the field to your right. While the brunt of the Union counterattack was carried by the division of Brig. Gen. John W. Geary, Ruger was ordered "to try the enemy on the right of the [Union] breastworks, to the left of the swale, with two regiments, and, if practicable, to force him out."

Report of Brig. Gen. Thomas H. Ruger, USA, commanding First Division, Twelfth Army Corps

I sent orders by a staff officer to Colonel Colgrove, commanding Third Brigade, to advance skirmishers against the enemy at that point, and, if not found in too great force, to advance two regiments, and dislodge him from the breastworks. From mistake of the staff officer, or misunderstanding on the part of Colonel Colgrove, it was attempted to carry the position without first ascertaining the force of the enemy. The regiments selected—the Second Massachusetts Volunteers and Twenty-seventh Indiana Volunteers of Third Brigade—moved forward gallantly, crossed the swale in line under a severe fire, gained the woods on the opposite side, forced the enemy back part

Breastworks of Wadsworth's Division, Culp's Hill. (NPS)

way up the slope to breastworks, but could not dislodge him, owing to the natural obstacles to the advance and heavy fire of the enemy from his well-protected position. The regiments were withdrawn. The enemy attempted to follow, but was quickly driven back by the two regiments, who turned and opened fire, assisted by their supports. About 100 prisoners were captured from the enemy at this time. . . . [O.R., XXVII, Part 1, p. 781.]

Report of Col. Silas Colgrove, USA, Twenty-seventh Indiana Infantry, commanding regiment and Third Brigade, First Division, Twelfth Army Corps

About this time the firing on our left, which had been very heavy, was fast receding, and loud cheering was heard along our lines. It was evident to me that General Geary had dislodged the enemy, and had retaken the breastworks occupied by him the day before. At this time I discovered the First Brigade, which was on my right, advance in line to the woods, forming a line at nearly right angles with my line.

At this juncture, Lieutenant Snow, of your staff, came up and said, "The general directs that you advance your line immediately." The position of the First Brigade was such that it was impossible for me to advance more than two regiments in line. Between the enemy and our line lay the open meadow, about 100 yards in width. The enemy were entirely sheltered by the breastworks and ledges of rock. It was impossible to send forward skirmishers. The enemy's advantages were such that a line of skirmishers would be cut down before they could fairly gain the open ground that intervened. The only possible chance I had to advance was to carry the position by storming it.

I selected the Second Massachusetts and Twenty-seventh Indiana for the work, and ordered the Second Massachusetts to charge the works in front of their position; the Twenty-seventh, as soon as they should gain the open ground, to oblique to the right and carry the position held in the ledges of rocks. At the command "Forward, double-quick!" our breastworks were cleared, and both regiments, with deafening cheers, sprang forward. They had scarcely gained the open ground when they were met with one of the most terrible fires I have ever witnessed.

Breastworks on Culp's Hill, Gettysburg in the distance, c. 1880's. (NPS)

Up to this time the enemy has remained entirely concealed. It had been impossible to tell anything about his strength in our immediate front, but it was now clearly ascertained that he had massed a heavy force at that point. It seemed that the two regiments were devoted to destruction. Undaunted, on they charged, officers leading and cheering their men. The Second Massachusetts succeeded in clearing the open ground to the left of the breastworks. The Twenty-seventh Indiana, having obliqued to the right, had nearly double the distance to traverse to gain the position of the enemy, but on it went; at every volley of the enemy, gaps were being cut through its ranks. It became evident to me that scarcely a man could live to gain the position of the enemy. I ordered the regiment to fall back behind the breastworks, which it did. The Second Massachusetts was also overpowered by numbers, and had to fall back.

The Twenty-seventh had scarcely gained the breastworks when the rebels in turn charged, with the intention of carrying our works. As soon as they had fairly gained the open ground, I ordered fire to be opened upon them, the Third Wisconsin, Twenty-seventh Indiana, and part of the Thirteenth New Jersey firing from the breastworks; the Second Massachusetts, from the new position on the left, had an enfilading fire upon them. At the first fire they were completely checked, and at the second they broke in confusion and fled, leaving their dead and wounded upon the field. I threw forward skirmishers from the Third Wisconsin, and ascertained that they had abandoned the breastworks. Colonel Hawley was ordered to advance his regiment (Third Wisconsin) and take position of the works, which he did, and held them during the day. During the whole day my entire line was exposed to the enemy's sharpshooters, and quite a number in all the regiments were killed and wounded by them.

In the charge, the Second Massachusetts lost about 130 killed and wounded [out of 320]. . . . The Twenty-seventh lost 112 in killed and wounded [out of 347]. [*O.R.*, XXVII, Part 1, pp. 813–14.]

Distinctive boulder at Culp's Hill. Photographer's assistant seated in foreground, Brady c. 15 July 1863, National Archives (NA).

The Confederate units involved in this action came mostly from *Smith's* Brigade, *Early's* Division, and the Second Virginia from *Walker's* (the Stonewall) Brigade, of *Johnson's* Division. *Colonel J. S. Hoffman*, commanding *Smith's* brigade, reported merely that "during most of the early part of the day the brigade was exposed to a heavy fire of artillery, and during a part to that of musketry also," which caused one of his regiments—the 49th Virginia—to lose about 40% in casualties. [*O.R.*, XXVII, Part 2, p. 490.] The most detailed account comes from the commander of the 2d Virginia.

Report of Col. J.Q.A. Nadenbousch, CSA, Second Virginia Infantry, Walker's [Stonewall] Brigade, Johnson's Division, Ewell's Corps

At 8 p.m. I rejoined the brigade with my regiment, when we marched, and, halting near Rock Creek, we remained until about 2 a.m. 3d instant, when we marched, crossing to the north bank of Rock Creek, and took position at the base of Culp's Hill on the left of the line, and in front of the enemy's breastworks some 30 yards, with our left resting on Rock Creek, with orders to support the Third Brigade . . . *[Steuart]*, then occupying said works on the extreme left.

At dawn, the enemy made a desperate attack on our lines by a heated fire of shot, shell, grape and musketry. At this time we were moved forward, and occupied the breastworks immediately in our front. It soon became apparent from the advance of the enemy that his purpose was to turn our left flank, and thus enfilade that portion of the work occupied by our troops.

Having communicated the condition of the line at this point to *Brig. Gen. G. H. Steuart*, senior brigadier-general present at the time, *Maj. Gen. E. Johnson* being engaged at another part of the line at the time, I was ordered by *Brigadier-General Walker* to support the First North Carolina Regiment . . . in the protection of our left flank. I at once detached one company (Company D, *Lieut. J. S. Harrison* commanding), and sent it to the south side of the creek (Rock Creek), for the purpose of attracting the fire of the enemy in front and turning his right flank. He continued steadily to advance, and when within some 25 yards of the left of the works, I opened a heated oblique fire from the right of the regiment upon him. For some moments he stood stubbornly. At this juncture I detached some two more of my companies, and posted some at a bend of the creek, some 60 yards to the rear and left, and in full view of the enemy. The remainder I sent on the south side of the creek to re-enforce *Lieutenant Harrison*, at that point engaging the enemy. With this concentrated fire, he was soon forced to retire in confusion.

About 7 a.m. the portion of my regiment left at the breastworks was relieved by *Brig. Gen. William Smith's* brigade.

There still being a brisk skirmish kept up on the south side of the creek with the portion of my regiment there, I at once took the remainder of my regiment to their support, reporting to *Brigadier General Walker* as to the disposition made and where to be found. I advanced some distance on the left, driving the enemy's skirmishers from and taking possession of the heights at this point, where I remained during the day, skirmishing . . . and keeping the left flank clear. [*O.R.*, XXVII, Part 2, pp. 521–22.]

The Union skirmishers came from Neill's brigade of Howe's Division, the Sixth Corps, who had been sent by Slocum to take position on the extreme right of the army to prevent the Confederates from turning the Union right flank. [*O.R.*, XXVII, Part 1, p. 680.]

Now go straight ahead toward SPANGLER'S SPRING, passing the DO NOT ENTER signs of the one-way road entering the area from your right. Follow the left fork at the junction just beyond. This is GEARY AVENUE. It swings out to the west following the contour while the other road goes straight up the hill, behind Union breastworks on the right.

Follow Geary Avenue for about 0.25 mile, until you come to another open field on your right. Stop here.

Spangler's Spring, c. 1880. (NPS)

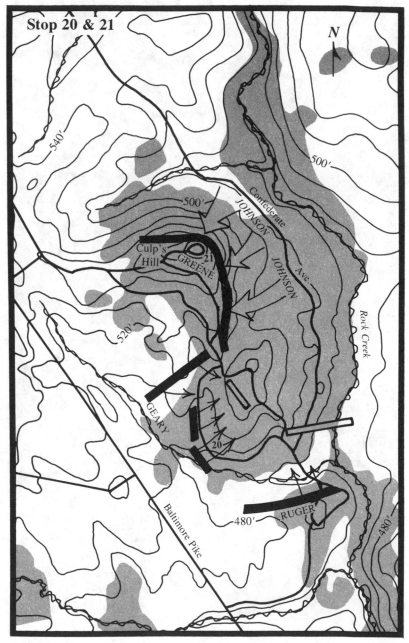

1" = 1000'

STOP 20

You are now several hundred yards behind the Geary's breastworks, "unusual facilities being afforded by the wood and rock and nature of the soil," which conform to the crest of the ridge on your right. The stone wall that you can see at the edge of the woods later became the Confederate front line after *Steuart's* brigade had captured a portion of Geary's breastworks which had been thrown up during the second day of the battle.

Report of Major General Edward Johnson, CSA, commanding division, Ewell's Corps

In obedience to an order from the lieutenant-general commanding, I . . . advanced my infantry to the assault of the enemy's strong position—a rugged and rocky mountain, heavily timbered and difficult of ascent; a natural fortification, rendered more formidable by deep intrenchments and thick abatis—*Jones'* brigade in advance, followed by *Nicholls'* and *Steuart's*. . . . The opposing force was larger and the time consumed longer than was anticipated. . . . By the time my other brigades had crossed Rock Creek and reached the base of the mountain, it was dark. . . . [Enemy] skirmishers were driven in, and the attack made with great vigor and spirit. It was as successful as could have been expected, considering the superiority of the enemy's force and position. *Steuart's* brigade, on the left, carried a line of breastworks which ran perpendicular to the enemy's main line, captured a number of prisoners and a stand of colors, and the whole line advanced to within short range, and kept up a heavy fire until late in the night. [*O.R.*, XXVII, Part 2, p. 504.]

Report of Brig. Gen. John W. Geary, USA, commanding Second Division, Twelfth Army Corps

At 5 a.m. on the 2d, having been relieved by the Third Army Corps, in obedience to orders from Major-General Slocum, the division was placed on the right of the center of the main line of battle, east of the turnpike. General Williams' division, commanded by Brigadier-General Ruger, joined ours, forming the extreme right and extending toward the Bonaughtown turnpike and at right angles to it. Here I had formed a double line of battle, fronting Rock Creek, and about 400 yards from it, along a rocky, thickly wooded ridge which

Fortifications in front of position of Greene's Brigade, Culp's Hill, c. 1865. (NPS)

sloped eastwardly to the creek. The Third Brigade (Greene's) occupied our extreme left, joining the right of the First Corps on a steep, rocky mount [Culp's Hill], which was a continuation of Cemetery Hill. Our line was nearly at a right angle with that of the First Corps. The Second Brigade (Kane's) extended from the right of Green's brigade. . . . The First Brigade (Candy) was formed in rear of the Third in line of battalions, in double column, as a support to the other two brigades.

At 4 p.m. the enemy opened with a fierce attack on the left and center of the army. . . . By a staff officer of Major-General Slocum, at 7 p.m. I received orders to move the division by the right flank, and follow the First Division, leaving one brigade to occupy the line of works of the entire corps. The First Division had gone nearly half an hour previously. Leaving Greene's brigade in the intrenchments, I rapidly moved the First and Second Brigades to the right, across Rock Creek, and, having reached the turnpike across Rock Creek Bridge, halted and reported my position, through an aide, to corps headquarters. When ordered thus to leave my intrenchments, I received no specific instructions as to the object of the move, the direction to be taken, or the point to be reached, beyond the order to move by the right flank and to follow the First Division. The First Division having gone out of sight or hearing, I directed the head of my column by the course of some of the men of that division who appeared to be following it. . . .

In the meantime General Greene had commenced to extend this brigade, as ordered along the line of entrenchments, and had barely occupied General Kane's original position when a vigorous attack was made upon his front and right by the enemy, who quickly occupied the intrenchments left by the First Division. . . . As soon as the attack commenced, Generals Wadsworth and Howard were petitioned by General Greene for support, to which they promptly responded—the Sixth Wisconsin . . . Fourteenth Brooklyn . . . and One hundred and forty-seventh New York Volunteers . . . (in all 355 men) being sent from Wadsworth's division, and . . . about 400 men from the Eleventh Corps. These regiments rendered good service, relieving temporarily regiments of Greene's brigade whose ammunition was exhausted, and by whom they were again in turn relieved.

The enemy, meeting with so determined a resistance, discontinued their attack at about 10 p.m., and remained in occupancy of the ridge. . . General Greene still holding all his original position, with the One hundred and thirty-seventh New York Volunteers placed in line perpendicularly to the rest of the brigade, its left resting on the intrenchments and its right near a stone wall, which extended parallel to General Ruger's and Kane's intrenchments and about 200 yards in rear of them. This stone wall was occupied by a force of the enemy as a protection against attack from the direction of the turnpike. [O.R., XXVII, Part 1, pp. 826–27.]

Report of Brig. Gen. George H. Steuart, CSA, commanding brigade, Johnson's Division

The left of the brigade now rested very near one line of the enemy's breastworks, which extended up the hill at right angles to the creek and then parallel with it on the summit. The enemy's attention being called more especially to our right, this fortification was not occupied in force. The Twenty-third Virginia . . . immediately charged the work, and scattered the enemy which was behind it. This regiment then filed to the right, until it reached the portion of the breastworks which was at right angles to the part first captured [near the point where GEARY AVENUE rejoins SLOCUM AVENUE a short distance ahead]. Forming in line on the flank and almost in rear of the enemy . . . it opened fire upon them, killing, wounding, and capturing quite a number. The Thirty-seventh and Tenth Virginia and First Maryland Battalion then came to the assistance of the Twenty-third Virginia, and fully occupied the works . . .

The brigade, with the exception of the two North Carolina regiments, was then formed in line of battle between the captured breastwork and a stone wall on the left of and parallel to it, from which position it was enabled to open a cross-fire upon the enemy, doing considerable execution. More, however, might have been done had not the impression at this time prevailed that we were firing upon our friends, and the fire been discontinued at intervals. . . . The whole command rested from about 11 p.m. till about daylight, when the enemy opened a terrific fire of artillery and a very heavy fire of musketry upon us . . . occasioning no loss to the brigade.

At about 10 a.m. [3 July] the . . . enemy was discovered in the woods, drawn up in line of battle, at not over 300 yards from the west of the stone wall. The brigade then formed in line of battle . . . and charged toward the enemy's second breastworks [on the high ground to your left], partly through an open field and partly through a wood, exposed to a very heavy fire of artillery and musketry, the latter in part a cross-fire. The left of the brigade was the most exposed at first, and did not maintain its position in line of battle. The right, thus in advance, suffered very severely, and, being unsupported, wavered, and the whole line fell back, but in good order. The enemy's position was impregnable, attacked by our small force, and any further effort to storm it would have been futile, and attended with great disaster, if not total annihilation.

The brigade rallied quickly behind rocks, and reformed behind the stone wall . . . where it remained about an hour, exposed to a fire of artillery and infantry more terrific than any experienced during the day, although less disastrous. Ultimately, in accordance with orders from the major-general commanding, the brigade fell back to the creek. . . . [*O.R.*, XXVII, Part 2, pp. 510–11.]

Report of Brig. Gen. John W. Geary, USA, *continued*

At 9 p.m. I ordered Kane's brigade to return to its original position and Candy's to follow it. On entering the woods, and when within 200 yards of the breastworks, Kane's brigade was met by a sharp fire, which, in the midst of the surrounding darkness, was at first supposed to be from General Greene's troops. Without replying, the brigade was withdrawn to the turnpike, taken in past the rear of Greene's brigade and past Greene's right, when it was again met with a volley, thus proving that the enemy still occupied the ground to Greene's right; a fact of which in the dark night there remained some doubt.

It being injudicious to attack the enemy in the night in their new position, I formed the Second Brigade in double line perpendicular to the Third Brigade, and joining its right, thus relieving the One hundred and thirty-seventh New York Volunteers, which had so long and so well held that position. Between this new line of the Second Brigade and that of the enemy in their front was a shallow ravine. The whole ground was very rough and rocky, affording some shelter on both sides for infantry. I devoted the rest of the night, after consultation with Major-General Slocum and Brigadier-General Williams [commanding the Right Wing and the 12th Corps respectively, to such an arrangement of my troops as, by a vigorous attack at daylight, to drive the enemy from the ground they had gained.

The "shallow ravine" mentioned in Geary's report is where GEARY AVENUE is now located. *Steuart's* front line is behind that stone wall at the far end of the field on your right. The brigades of Kane and Candy were deployed along a much smaller ridge line a hundred feet or so to your left, parallel to the road. The line that Greene threw up at right angles to his front line, which the 137th New York defended so stoutly and which had blocked any farther penetration by the Confederates along the rear of Greene's position on Culp's Hill, was located a short distance to your left when this road joins SLOCUM AVENUE a short distance ahead.

At 1 a.m. . . . . the First Brigade, which had been held in readiness on the [Baltimore] turnpike, was placed in position on the right of Kane's brigade, in extension of Kane's line, its right resting on an orchard near the turnpike. Immediately in front of the First Brigade was a narrow lane running from the turnpike to the stone wall. . . . Along this lane Candy's brigade was placed in double line of battle, and screened from the enemy's observation by the woods. All these dispositions were made with the utmost silence and secrecy and within a few rods of the enemy's lines.

By your order, Lieut. E. D. Muhlenberg, chief of artillery of the [12th] corps, reported with fourteen pieces of artillery. These were posted on a hill west of the turnpike and about 500 yards in rear of the intrenchments gained by the enemy, and I trained them so as to command the enemy's position without injury to our own troops. To Knap's . . . battery, which was in position on the hill near corps headquarters, I gave similar directions regarding their line of fire. At my request, General Williams, commanding corps, readily sent to my support Lockwood's brigade. . . . [which] I placed in position to support the artillery.

Everything being thus in readiness, at 3.30 a.m. (early dawn) a simultaneous attack was made by artillery and the infantry of the Second and Third Brigades. This attack was most furious, but was stubbornly met. Our artillery fire continued, by previous arrangement, for ten minutes. This tremendous assault at first staggered the enemy, by whom it was seemingly unexpected; but, rallying as my troops charged at the close of the artillery fire, *Johnson's* division . . . massed in three lines, advanced, charging heavily upon our front and right, and yelling in their peculiar style. They were met at every point by the unswerving lines and deadly fire of my Second and Third

Brigades, our men cheering loudly and yielding not an inch of ground. Line after line of the enemy broke under this steady fire, but the pressing masses from behind rushed forward to take their places.

During this contest, Greene's brigade was protected by his breastworks, while Kane's fought without shelter, excepting such as might be afforded by inequalities of the ground. After a lapse of twenty minutes, I directed the artillery fire again to open, having myself sighted the pieces so as to bear directly upon the masses of the enemy in the woods. This artillery fire lasted about fifteen minutes. A part of it being directed to the valley of Rock Creek, where the enemy's left rested, prevented them from flanking the troops of the First Division [Ruger] which were engaging the enemy in front. This flank movement the enemy made repeated attempts to effect, but they were driven back by well-directed shells from our artillery. Meanwhile the musketry fire continued with unabated fierceness.

At 5 a.m. the One hundred and forty-seventh Volunteers, of Candy's brigade, was ordered to charge and carry the stone wall occupied by the enemy. This they did in handsome style, their firing causing heavy loss to the enemy, who then abandoned the entire line of the stone wall. At this time the Fifth Ohio, on Candy's left, was exposed to a severe enfilading fire from the enemy, but they held their position, punishing the enemy severely.

At 5.45 a.m. the Sixty-sixth Ohio was ordered to advance outside of Greene's entrenchments and perpendicular to them, in order to harass the enemy by a raking fire. This they accomplished with great gallantry, driving the enemy and holding the ground until recalled by an order at 11 a.m.

At 6 a.m. the Twenty-eighth Pennsylvania, and Fifth, Seventh, and Twenty-ninth Ohio, of Candy's brigade, were ordered into the intrenchments to relieve some of Greene's regiments which were out of ammunition, and went in with loud cheering, keeping up the continuous fire while the relieved regiments passed to the rear between the files.

At 7.30 o'clock Lockwood's brigade, of the First Division, 1,700 strong, reported to me as a support, and was rested in line in the woods about 25 yards in rear of Greene's breastworks. This brigade, composed almost entirely of untried troops . . . rendered efficient service.

About 8 a.m. the enemy redoubled their efforts, and, massing all the force against us that the ground would admit, pressed forward with an evident determination to carry the position at all hazards. Our entire line was hotly engaged, and, fearing that the overwhelming force might prove too much for us, General Slocum was solicited for re-enforcements, and General Alexander Shaler's (First) brigade, Third Division, Sixth Corps, reported at 8.45 o'clock and was posted as a reserve. Ten minutes before the arrival of this brigade, the Fourteenth Brooklyn and One hundred and forty-seventh New York Volunteers (both together about 150 strong) reported again from General Wadsworth's division, and were sent in to re-enforce Kane's brigade on the right. They were shortly afterward relieved by Candy's and Lockwood's troops. . . . Our troops, cheered by the arrival of supports, soon repulsed the fierce attack. . . .

At 10.15 o'clock two brigades of *Johnson's* division, having formed in column by regiments, charged upon our line on the right. They met the determined men of Kane's little brigade, which, though only 650 strong, poured into them so continuous a fire that when within 70 paces their columns wavered and soon broke to the rear. The First Maryland Battalion (rebel) was in the advance, and their dead lay mingled with our own.

This was the last charge. As they fell back, our troops rushed forward with wild cheers of victory, driving the rebels in confusion over the intrenchments, the ground being covered with their dead and wounded. . . .

With great gallantry our troops sustained for seven hours and a half a battle fraught with persistent and obstinate effort and unremitting fire of an intensity seldom prolonged beyond a limited period. . . . I estimate upon personal observation . . . their killed in front of our lines at nearly . . . 1,200, of which we succeeded in burying 900, and wounded in the ratio of at least four to one killed, the greater portion of whom were carried off during the night by the enemy. We took over 500 prisoners, independent of those who were wounded. . . . About 5,000 small-arms were left upon the field by the enemy. . . . The efficiency of our intrenchments was clearly demonstrated . . . in the action. . . . The command in the fight on July 3, and in subsequent skirmishing, 277,000 rounds of ammunition. [*O.R.*, XXVII, Part 1, pp. 826–33.]

Now continue to the "T" intersection beyond the field. Turn left on SLOCUM AVENUE. Bear right at the next fork in the road and follow the line of monuments toward the summit of Culp's Hill. Turn right at the next "T" intersection so that you can drive up to the parking lot at the base of the tower on the summit. Park here and dismount.

STOP 21

Report of Brig. Gen. George S. Greene, USA, commanding Third Brigade, Second Division, Twelfth Army Corps

On the 2d, we took position at about 6 a.m. on the right of the First Corps, on the crest of the steep and rocky hill, being thrown back nearly at right angles with the line of the First Corps, Rock Creek running past our front at the distance of 200 to 400 yards. Our position and the front were covered with a heavy growth of timber, free from undergrowth, with large ledges of rock projecting above the surface. These rocks and trees offered good cover for marksmen. The surface was very steep on our left, diminishing to a gentle slope on our right. . . .

By 12 o'clock we had good cover for the men. The value of this defense was shown in our subsequent operations by our small loss compared with that of the enemy during the continuous attacks by a vastly superior force. Our skirmishers were thrown out immediately on taking position, and moved toward the creek in our front, when they came to the enemy's pickets.

We remained in this position, with occasional firing of the pickets, until 6.30 p.m., when the First [Ruger's] Division and the First and Second Brigades of the Second Division were ordered from my right, leaving the intrenchments of Kane's brigade and [Ruger's] division unoccupied on the withdrawal of the troops.

I received orders to occupy the whole of the intrenchments previously occupied by the Twelfth Army Corps with my brigade. This movement was commenced, and the One hundred and thirty-seventh Regiment, on my right, was moved into the position occupied by Kane's brigade. Before any further movements could be made, we were attacked on the whole of our front by a large force a

Breastworks on Culp's Hill, Brady, c. 15 July 1863. (USAMHI)

few minutes before 7 p.m. The enemy made four distinct charges between 7 and 9.30 p.m., which were effectually resisted. . . .

Not more than 1,300 were in the lines at any one time. The loss of the enemy greatly exceeds ours. [*O.R.*, XXVII, Part 1, pp. 858–59.]

If you were to walk 100 feet or so into the woods along the unimproved path by the 76th NEW YORK INFANTRY marker, directly across the park road from the monument to Battery K, Fifth US Artillery, you would quickly encounter "the large ledges of rock" that offered shelter to *Johnson's* Confederates as they neared the top of the hill. Here *Nicholls'* brigade "reached a line about 100 yards" from the Union works and engaged Greene's brigade in "an almost incessant" fire fight for about four hours, during which several attempts to carry the works by assault: "being entirely unsupported on the right," *Nicholls'* attacks were "attended with more loss than success." [*O.R.*, XXVII, Part 2, p. 513.]

Jones' brigade, on the right, advanced "in good order" up the "steep, heavily timbered, rocky, and difficult" terrain. His men "gained ground steadily . . . under a heavy fire of musketry from the enemy, protected by intrenchments." For his part, *Jones* reported "some confusion toward the left," which was "perhaps unavoidable from the lateness of the hour . . . the darkness in the woods, and the nature of the hill." [*O.R.*, XXVII, Part 2, p. 533.] One of *Jones'* regiments, the 48th Virginia, "bravely maintained its ground till within about 10 paces of the enemy's works, when, from its reduced numbers in ranks, together with the strength of the enemy and his strong position" it was ordered to fall back about 200 yards. This regiment "went into action with about 210 men and officers, and came out with a loss of 76." [*O.R.*, XXVII, Part 2, p. 533.] The 42nd Virginia "got within 30 paces" of Greene's works but after an hour's firing "the line was ordered to fall back slowly." [*O.R.*, XXVII, Part 2, p. 537.] The commander of the 50th Virginia reported that "the fighting was kept up with great fury" well into the night: "we tried again and again to drive the enemy from their position, but at length we were compelled to fall back, worn down and exhausted, but not till every round of cartridge had been discharged. At one time we were within a few feet of their works, but the fire was so heavy we could not stand it. . . . When we fell back we carried every one of our killed and wounded with us to the base of the hill." [*O.R.*, XXVII, Part 2, p. 539.]

The fighting on Culp's Hill on the morning of 3 July has already been described by General Geary, the division commander. Before leaving the area you may wish to climb the tower for a good overview of the northern portion of the battlefield. This tower was erected by the US Army about the turn of the century to enable officers visiting the battlefield to study the terrain.

Now drive down the western slope of Culp's Hill toward Cemetery Hill. About 0.4 mile from the tower the road forks. The park tour turns left; you should turn *right* and proceed another 300 yards. Stop at the far side of the patch of woods on your right, in the turnout directly opposite the monument to the 25th and 75th Ohio infantry regiments. In 1863 there were only a few trees that lined this lane connecting the town with the spring you will shortly pass on your right. The terrain over which the Confederates attacked Cemetery Hill on the evening of 2 July was largely open fields.

STOP 22

As soon as *General Early* learned that *Johnson's* division had commenced the attack against Culp's Hill on the evening of 2 July, he ordered two of his own brigades forward against Cemetery Hill. *General Rodes*, whose division was drawn up in two lines in the town of Gettysburg—one along one of the main streets and the other along the railroad—was ordered to cooperate with the attacking force. The plan was to attack "just at dark." *Rodes* could not move his men through the town and make the necessary changes in direction "and then to traverse a distance of 1,200 or 1,400 yards" before *Early's* brigades, which "had to move only half that distance without change of front" had launched their attack." [*O.R.*, XXVII, Part 2, p. 556.]

The two brigades had spent the entire day in the open fields some 500 yards to your right, at the base of the hill that offered some shelter from the guns on Cemetery Hill although the Confederates were "prominently exposed to the fire of the enemy's skirmishers and sharpshooters."

Report of Brig. Gen. Harry T. Hays, CSA, commanding brigade, Early's Division, Ewell's Corps

During the afternoon . . . I was directed by *Major-General Early* to hold my brigade in readiness at a given signal to charge the enemy in the works on the summit of the hill before me, with the information that a general advance of our entire line would be made at the same time.

A little before 8 p.m. I was ordered to advance with my own and *Hoke's* brigade on my left, which had been placed for the time under my command. I immediately moved forward, and had gone but a short distance when my whole line became exposed to a most terrific fire from the enemy's batteries from the entire range of hills in front, and to the right and left; still, both brigades advanced steadily up and over the first hill, and into a bottom at the foot of Cemetery Hill.

Here we came upon a considerable body of the enemy, and a brisk musketry fire ensued; at the same time his artillery, of which we were now within canister range, opened upon us, but owing to the darkness of the evening, now verging into night, and the deep obscurity afforded by the smoke of the firing, our exact locality could not be discovered by the enemy's gunners, and we thus escaped what in the full light of day could have been nothing else than horrible slaughter.

Taking advantage of this, we continued to move forward until we reached the second line, behind a stone wall at the foot of a fortified hill. We passed such of the enemy who had not fled, and who were still clinging for shelter to the wall, to the rear, as prisoners. Still advancing, we came upon an abatis of fallen timber and the third line, disposed in rifle-pits. This line we broke, and, as before, found many of the enemy who had not fled hiding in the pits for protection. These I ordered to the rear as prisoners, and continued my progress to the crest of the hill.

Arriving at the summit, by a simultaneous rush from my whole line, I captured several pieces of artillery, four stand of colors, and a number of prisoners. At that time every piece of artillery which had been firing upon us was silenced.

A quiet of several minutes now ensued. Their heavy masses of infantry were heard and perfectly discerned through the increasing darkness, advancing in the direction of my position. Approaching within 100 yards, a line was discovered before us, from the whole length of which a simultaneous fire was delivered. I reserved my fire, from the uncertainty of this being a force of the enemy or of our men, as I had been cautioned to expect friends both in front, to the right, and to the left. *Lieutenant-General Longstreet*, *Major-General Rodes*, and *Major-General Johnson*, respectively, having been assigned to these relative positions; but after the delivery of a second and third volley, the flashing of the musketry disclosed the still-advancing line to be one of the enemy.

I then gave the order to fire; the enemy was checked for a time, but discovering another line moving up in rear of this one, and still another force in rear of that, and being beyond the reach of support, I gave the order to retire to the stone wall at the foot of the hill, which was quietly and orderly effected. From this position I subsequently fell back to a fence some 75 yards distant from the wall, and awaited the further movement of the enemy.

Only contemplating, however, to effect an orderly and controlled retreat before a force which I was convinced I could not hope to withstand—at all events, where I then was—I was on the point of retiring to a better position when . . . the brigade quartermaster, informed me that *Brigadier-General Gordon* was coming to my support.

I immediately dispatched an officer to hasten *General Gordon* with all possible speed, but this officer returning without seeing *General Gordon*, I went back myself, and finding *General Gordon* occupying the precise position in the field occupied by me when I received the order to charge, . . . and not advancing, I concluded that any assistance from him would be too late . . . I therefore moved my brigade by the right flank, leading it around the hill, so as to escape the observation of the enemy, and conducted it to the right of my original position. . . . This was about 10 o'clock. I remained in this position for the night. [*O.R.*, XXVIII, Part 2, pp. 480–81.]

The Union infantry defending Cemetery Hill were commanded by Brig. Gen. Adelbert Ames, who reported only that "on the evening of the 2d, an attempt was made to carry the position we held, but the enemy was repulsed with loss. Colonel Carroll, with a brigade from the Second Corps, rendered timely assistance. The batteries behaved admirably. [*O.R.*, XXVII, Part 1, p. 713.] Colonel Andrew Harris, commanding Ames' Second Brigade, explained in his after-action report that the 75th Ohio had been placed "at the stone wall south of the hill, with the Seventeenth Connecticut immediately on our left. Just before the attack was made, the Seventeenth was thrown to the extreme right of the line [probably upon hearing sounds of the fighting on Culp's Hill] and the space at the wall where they had been was left unoccupied, excepting by a few of the Twenty-fifth Ohio Volunteers. About dusk the enemy attacked the regiment in front and on the flank and rear at nearly the same time, having come through the space which had been vacated by the removal of the Seventeenth Connecticut Volunteers. From this attack but few escaped, and those only in the darkness and smoke. . . ." [*O.R.*, XXVII, Part 1, p. 715.]

Report of Maj. Allen G. Brady, USA, Seventeenth Connecticut Infantry, Second Brigade, First Division

We remained in . . . position [behind the rail fence], exposed to the enemy's batteries and sharpshooters, until 7 p.m. when we were ordered to the extreme right, behind a stone wall on each side of the lane, below the battery opposite the cemetery entrance. Two companies were advanced to the grain field near the woods, through which the enemy were rapidly advancing. We covered the wall on each side of the line by compelling about 300 stragglers, who had no commander, to fall into our line. We had not more than time to form behind the wall before the enemy were discovered advancing rapidly upon us on our right and a full brigade obliquely toward our left. When within 150 paces of us, we poured a destructive fire upon them, which thinned their ranks and checked their advance. We fired several volleys by battalion, after which they charged upon us. We had a hand-to-hand conflict with them, firmly held our ground, and drove them back. The firing ceased excepting occasional shots from their sharpshooters. [*O.R.*, XXVII, Part 1, p. 718.]

Report of Col. Charles S. Wainwright, USA, commanding Artillery Brigade, First Army Corps

At dusk . . . their column filed out of town. . . . Wheeling into line, they swung around, their right resting on the town, and pushed up the hill, which is quite steep at this corner. As their line became fully unmasked, all the guns which could be brought to bear were opened on them, at first with shrapnel and afterward with canister, making a total of fifteen guns in their front and six on their left flank. Their center and left never mounted the hill at all, but their right worked its way up under cover of the houses, and pushed completely through Wiedrich's battery into Ricketts' The cannoneers of both these batteries stood well to their guns, driving the enemy off with fence-rails and stones and capturing a few prisoners. I believe it may be claimed that this attack was almost entirely repelled by the artillery." [*O.R.*, XXVII, Part 1, p. 358.]

Colonel Wainwright was less restrained in his journal:

About an hour after sundown, the moon shining brightly, the enemy made a push for our position. Dr. Mosser [Wainright's surgeon], who was in the town, tells me that the attack was made by the "Louisiana Tigers" and another brigade, the lines being formed in the streets running north and south, and marching out by the left flank. . . . They marched straight out of the town, and then facing to their right rushed for the hill. So soon as the rebels began to fire, the two lines of Deutschmen in front of the batteries began to run, and nearly the whole of them cleared out. As the enemy advanced we commenced firing canister, depressing the guns more and more, until it was one continual shower straight down the hill. The night was heavy, and the smoke lay so thick that you could not see ten yards ahead; seventeen guns vomiting it as fast as they can will make a good deal of smoke. Feeling sure that no enemy could get up that front, I now passed down the road beyond Stewart's four pieces, so as to get a view townward, for I could not get over my fear of an attack from that quarter. All was quiet, and Stewart keeping a sharp lookout. . . .

I pitied General Ames most heartily. His men would not stand at all, save one. I believe not a single regiment of the Eleventh Corps exposed to the attack stood fire, but ran away almost to a man. Stewart stretched his men along the road, with fence rails! to try to stop the runaways but could do nothing. Officers and men were both alike. . . . But on the other hand, the men of "I" Battery, also Germans, fought splendidly, sticking to their guns, and finally driving the rebs out with their handspikes and fence rails. . . . This would show that the Germans have got fight in them; the fault must be in the officers, most of whom are adventurers, political refugees, and the like. . . . After the charge of Carroll's brigade [General Howard] . . . himself tried to get two strong regiments to push down the hill near to the town so as to cut off some three hundred rebs who had sought shelter from our fire behind a little knoll. Some had escaped from them there, and knew just where they were. Not an officer of rank in either regiment could be found when the order was given to advance. I said to General Howard, why don't you have them shot? The General answered, "I should have to shoot all the way down; they are all alike." [Allan Nevins, ed., *A Diary of Battle: The Personal Journals of Colonel Charles S. Wainwright, 1861–1865*, New York, Harcourt, Brace and World, Inc., 1962, pp. 245–48.]

Now follow the park road to the first city street and turn left. Turn left again at the stop sign, and stay to the left on BALTIMORE STREET until you reach the entrance to the NATIONAL CEMETERY on your right.

Turn right and drive through the Cemetery, exiting onto the TANEYTOWN ROAD in front of the National Park Service VISITOR CENTER. Turn left on the TANEYTOWN ROAD, and then take the next right, into the Visitor Center Parking Lot. You can stop here if you need a break, but you will be returning to this area at the end of the tour. We are now ready to move on to the central events of the third day at Gettysburg.

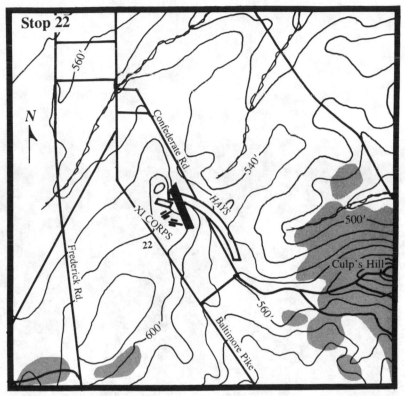

Drive through the Visitor Center parking lot toward the highway on the far side (the Emmitsburg Road). Turn left onto the **EMMITSBURG ROAD** and follow it 1.25 mile. Turn right as you approach the **PEACH ORCHARD** and follow **WHEATFIELD ROAD** 0.3 mile to **WEST CONFEDERATE AVENUE**. Turn right and drive nearly 1.0 mile to the large equestrian statue of General Lee (the Virginia Monument). Turn right into the circular drive around this monument and park in the small parking lot.

727 Gettysburg, Pa., Sept., 1885. From Little Round Top. Confederate Position, and scene of Pickett's charge, July 3, 1863.

View from Little Round Top of Confederate position and scene of Pickett's charge, 1885. (USAMHI)

STOP 23

Historians have debated *Lee's* motives in ordering *Pickett's* Charge; soldiers visiting the ground have wondered what could have prompted him to send ten brigades across these fields against an intrenched position well supported by artillery; authorities can not even agree upon the actual number of men involved in the attack—estimates vary from 10,500 to 15,000, with the truth probably somewhere in between. *Lee* never offered an explanation beyond that contained in his official papers, and his anxiety to avoid dissension among subordinates caused him to request *Pickett* and perhaps others to destroy the initial after-action report. [*O.R.*, XXVII, Part 3, p. 1075.] His own two reports on the campaign raise as many questions as they answer, beginning with his rationale for ordering *Longstreet's* attack on the 2nd.

Report of General R. E. Lee of the operations of the Army of Northern Virginia. July 31, 1863

The enemy held a high and commanding ridge, along which he had massed a large amount of artillery. . . . In front of *General Longstreet* the enemy held a position [the Peach Orchard?] from which, if he could be driven, it was thought our artillery could be used to advantage in assailing the more elevated ground beyond, and thus enable us to reach the crest of the ridge. . . . After a severe struggle, *Longstreet* succeeded in getting possession of and holding the desired ground. *Ewell* also carried some of the strong positions which he assailed, and the result was such as to lead to the belief that he would ultimately be able to dislodge the enemy. . . .

These partial successes determined me to continue the assault next day. *Pickett*, with three of his brigades, joined *Longstreet* the following morning, and our batteries were moved forward to the positions gained by him the day before. The general plan of attack was unchanged, excepting that one division and two brigades of *Hill's* corps were ordered to support *Longstreet*. The enemy, in the meantime, had strengthened his lines with earthworks. [*O.R.*, XXVII, Part 2, p. 308.]

*Report of General R. E. Lee of the Operations of the Army of
Northern Virginia, January 1864*

The result of this day's operations [2 July] induced the belief
that, with proper concert of action, and with the increased support that the positions gained on the right would enable the
artillery to render the assaulting columns, we should ultimately
succeed, and it was accordingly determined to continue the attack. *Longstreet*, re-enforced by *Pickett's* three brigades, which
arrived near the battle-field during the afternoon of the 2d, was
ordered to attack the next morning, and *General Ewell* was
directed to assail the enemy's right *at the same time.* The latter,
during the night, re-enforced *General Johnson* with two brigades
from *Rodes'* and one from *Early's* division.

General Longstreet's dispositions were not completed as early
as was expected, but before notice could be sent to *General Ewell,*
General Johnson had already become engaged [at Culp's Hill] and
it was too late to recall him. . . .

General Longstreet was delayed by a force occupying the high,
rocky hills on the enemy's extreme left; from which his troops
could be attacked in reverse as they advanced. His operations had
been embarrassed the day previous by the same cause, and he
now deemed it necessary to defend his flank and rear with the
divisions of *Hood* and *McLaws.* He was, therefore, reinforced by
Heth's division and two brigades of *Pender's,* to the command of
which *Major-General Trimble* was assigned. *General Hill* was
directed to hold his line with the rest of his command, afford
General Longstreet further assistance, if required, and avail himself
of any success that might be gained.

A careful examination was made of the ground secured by
Longstreet, and his batteries placed in positions, which, it was
believed, would enable them to silence those of the enemy. *Hill's*
artillery and part of *Ewell's* was ordered to open simultaneously,
and the assaulting column to advance under cover of the combined fire of the three. The batteries were directed to be pushed
forward as the infantry progressed, protect their flanks, and support their attacks closely.

About 1 p.m., at a given signal, a heavy cannonade was opened, and continued for about two hours with marked effect upon the enemy. His batteries replied vigorously at first, but toward the close their fire slackened perceptibly, and *General Longstreet* ordered forward the column of attack, consisting of *Pickett's* and *Heth's* divisions, in two lines, *Pickett* on the right. *Wilcox's* brigade marched in rear of *Pickett's* right, to guard that flank, and *Heth's* was supported by *Lane's* and *Scales'* brigades, under *General Trimble.*

The troops moved steadily on, under a heavy fire of musketry and artillery, the main attack being directed against the enemy's left center. [*O.R.*, XXVII, Part 2, pp. 320–21.]

Report of Brigadier General William N. Pendleton, CSA, Chief of Artillery

By direction of the commanding general, the artillery along our entire line was to be prepared for opening, as early as possible on the morning of the 3d, a concentrated and destructive fire, consequent upon which a general advance was to be made. The right, especially, was, if practicable, to sweep the enemy from his stronghold on that flank. Visiting the lines at a very early hour toward securing readiness for this great attempt, I found much (by *Colonel Alexander's* energy) already accomplished on the right. *Henry's* battalion held about its original position on the flank. *Alexander's* was next, in front of the peach orchard. Then came the Washington Artillery Battalion, under *Major Eshleman,* and *Dearing's* battalion on his left, these two having arrived since dusk of the day before; and beyond *Dearing, Cabell's* battalion had been arranged, making nearly sixty guns for that wing, all well advanced in a sweeping curve of about a mile. In the posting of these there appeared little room for improvement, so judiciously had they been adjusted. To *Colonel Alexander,* placed here in charge by *General Longstreet,* the wishes of the commanding general were repeated. The battalion and battery commanders were also cautioned how to fire so as to waste as little ammunition as possible.

To the Third Corps artillery attention was also given. *Major Poague's* battalion had been advanced to the line of the right wing, and was not far from its left. His guns also were well posted. . . . The other battalions of his corps . . . held their positions of the day before, as did those of the Second Corps, each group having specific instructions from its chief. Care was also given to the convenient posting of ordnance trains, especially for the right, as most distant from the main depot, and due notice given of their position. . . .

At length, about 1 p.m., on the concerted signal, our guns in position, nearly one hundred and fifty, opened fire along the entire line from right to left, salvos by battery being much practiced, as directed, to secure greater deliberation and power. The enemy replied with their full force. . . . The average distance between contestants was about 1,400 yards, and the effect was necessarily serious on both sides. With the enemy, there was advantage of elevation and protection from earthworks; but his fire was unavoidably more or less divergent, while ours was convergent. His troops were massed, ours diffused. We, therefore, suffered apparently much less. . . .

Proceeding again to the right, to see about the anticipated advance of the artillery, delayed beyond expectation, I found, among other difficulties, many batteries getting out of or low in ammunition, and the all-important question of supply received my earnest attention. Frequent shell endangering the First Corps ordnance train in the convenient locality I had assigned it, it had been removed farther back. This necessitated longer time for refilling caissons. What was worse, the train itself was very limited, so that its stock was soon exhausted, rendering requisite demand upon the reserve train, farther off. The whole amount was thus being rapidly reduced. Without our means, to keep up supply at the rate required . . . proved practically impossible. There had to be, therefore, some relaxation of the protracted fire, and some lack of support for the deferred and attempted advance. Night closed upon our guns in their advanced position. [*O.R.*, XXVII, Part 2, pp. 351–53.]

Part of the ground occupied by Hancock at the time of Longstreet's charge, 1880's. (NPS)

Now retrace your path back toward the Visitor Center, leaving the Emmitsburg Road where you entered it. But now, as you approach the parking lot from the west, turn right on Hancock Avenue so that you can drive down the Union main line of resistance to THE ANGLE. Turn right into the angle and park wherever you can get a good view.

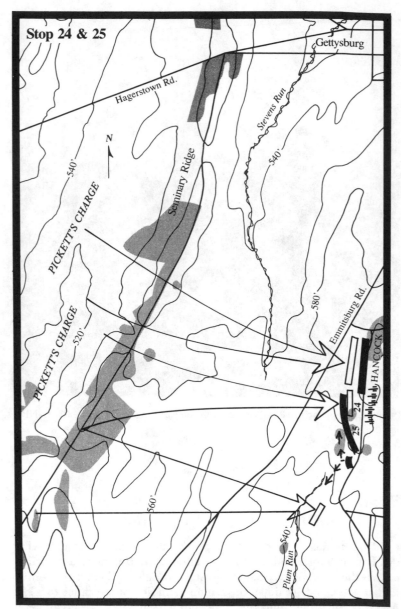

Stop 24 & 25

Gettysburg

Hagerstown Rd.

Stevens Run

Seminary Ridge

PICKETT'S CHARGE

PICKETT'S CHARGE

Emmitsburg Rd.

HANCOCK

Plum Run

1" = 1500'

STOP 24

You are now at what is popularly called "the high water mark of the Confederacy." All of the Confederate guns and the attacking lines of Pickett, Pettigrew *and* Trimble *were directed upon this point.*

Report of Brig. Gen. Henry J. Hunt, USA, Chief of Artillery, Army of the Potomac

There was but little firing during the morning. At 10 a.m. I made an inspection of the whole line, ascertaining that all the batteries — only those of our right serving with the Twelfth Corps being engaged at the time — were in good condition and well supplied with ammunition. As the enemy was evidently increasing his artillery force in front of our left, I gave instructions to the batteries and to the chiefs of artillery not to fire at small bodies, nor to allow their fire to be drawn without promise of adequate results; to watch the enemy closely, and when he opened to concentrate the fire of their guns on one battery at a time until it was silenced; under all circumstances to fire deliberately, and to husband their ammunition as much as possible.

I had just finished my inspection, and was with Lieutenant Rittenhouse on the top of [Little] Round Top, when the enemy opened, at about 1 p.m., along his whole right, a furious cannonade on the left of our line. I estimated the number of his guns bearing on our west front at from one hundred to one hundred and twenty. . . . To oppose these we could not, from our restricted position, bring more than eighty to reply effectively. Our fire was well withheld, until the first burst was over, excepting from the extreme right and left of our positions. It was then opened deliberately and with excellent effect. As soon as the nature of the enemy's attack was made clear, and I could form an opinion as to the number of his guns, for which my position afforded great facility, I went to the park of the Artillery Reserve, and ordered all the batteries to be ready to move at a moment's notice. . . . I then proceeded along the line, to observe the effects of the cannonade and to replace such batteries as should become disabled.

About 2.30 p.m., finding our ammunition running low and that it was very unsafe to bring up loads of it, a number of caissons and limbers having been exploded, I directed that the fire should be gradually stopped, which was done, and the enemy soon slackened his fire also. I then sent orders for such batteries as were necessary to replace exhausted ones, and all that were disposable were sent me.

About 3 p.m., and soon after the enemy's fire had ceased, he formed a column of attack in the edge of the woods in front of the Second Corps. At this time Fitzhugh's (K, First New York, six 3-inch), Parsons' (A, First New Jersey, six 10-pounder), Weir's (C, Fifth United States, six 12-pounders), and Cowan's (First New York Independent, six 3-inch) batteries reached this point, and were put in position in front of the advancing enemy. I rode down to McGilvery's batteries [still in the open ground north of the Weikert house], and directed them to take the enemy in flank as they approached.

The enemy advanced magnificently, unshaken by the shot and shell which tore through his ranks from his front and from our left. The batteries of the Second Corps on our right, having nearly exhausted their supply of ammunition, except canister, were compelled to withhold their fire until the enemy, who approached in three lines, came within its range. When our canister fire and musketry were opened upon them, it occasioned disorder, but still they advanced gallantly until they reached the stone wall behind which our troops lay. Here ensued a desperate conflict, the enemy succeeding in passing the wall and entering our lines, causing great destruction of life, especially among the batteries. Infantry troops were, however, advanced from our right; the rear line of the enemy broke, and the others, who had fought with a gallantry that excited the admiration of our troops, found themselves cut off and compelled to surrender. As soon as their fate was evident, the enemy opened his batteries upon the masses of our troops at this point without regard to the presence of his own. Toward the close of this struggle . . . [3] batteries which had lost heavily in men and horses were withdrawn, and as soon as the affair was over their places were filled with fresh ones.

Soon the necessary measures had been taken to restore this portion of the line to an efficient condition. It required but a few minutes, as the batteries, as fast as withdrawn from any point, were sent to the Artillery Reserve, replenished with ammunition, reorganized, returned to the rear of the lines, and there awaited assignment.

I then went to the left, to see that proper measures had been taken there for the same object. On my way, I saw that the enemy was forming a second column of attack to his right of the point where the first was formed, and in front of the position of the First Corps. I gave instructions to . . . Major McGilvery to be ready to meet the first movements of the enemy in front, and, returning to the position of the Second Corps, directed the batteries there, mostly belonging to the Artillery Reserve, to take the enemy in flank as he advanced. When the enemy moved . . . and before he reached our line he was brought to a stand. The appearance of a body of our infantry moving down in front of our lines from the direction of the Second Corps caused the enemy to move off by his right flank, under cover of the woods and undergrowth, and, a few minutes after, the column had broken up, and in the utmost confusion the men . . . fled . . . and took refuge behind their batteries.

The attacks on the part of the enemy were not well managed. Their artillery fire was too much dispersed, and failed to produce the intended effect. . . . The two assaults, had they been simultaneous, would have divided our artillery fire. As it was, each attack was met by a heavy front and flank fire of our artillery. . . .

The losses of the artillery . . . were very large. The destruction of *materiel* was large. The enemy's cannonade, in which he must have almost exhausted his ammunition, was well sustained, and cost us a great many horses and the explosion of an unusually large number of caissons and limbers. The whole slope behind our crest, although concealed from the enemy, was swept by his shot, and offered no protection to horses or carriages. . . . The marks of the shot in the trees on both crests bear conclusive evidence of the superiority of our practice. . . .

The expenditure of ammunition in the three days amounted to 32,781 rounds, averaging over 100 rounds per gun. [*O.R.*, XXVII, Part 2, pp. 238–41.]

Report of Maj. Gen. Winfield S. Hancock, USA, commanding
Second Army Corps

After an hour and forty-five minutes, the [artillery] fire of the enemy became less furious, and immediately their infantry was seen in the woods beyond the Emmitsburg road, preparing for the assault. A strong line of skirmishers soon advanced (followed by two deployed lines of battle), supported at different points by small columns of infantry. Their lines were formed with precision and steadiness that exhorted the admiration of the witnesses of that memorable scene. The left of the enemy extended slightly beyond the right of General Alexander Hays' division, the right being about opposite the left of General Gibbon's. Their line of battle thus covered a front of not more than two of the small and incomplete divisions of the corps. The whole attacking force is estimated to have exceeded 15,000 men.

No attempt was made to check the advance of the enemy until the first line had arrived within about 700 yards of our position, when a feeble fire of artillery was opened upon it, but with no material effect, and without delaying for a moment its determined advance. The column pressed on, coming within musketry range without receiving immediately our fire, our men evincing a striking disposition to withhold it until it could be delivered with deadly effect.

Two regiments of Stannard's Vermont Brigade (of the First Corps), which had been posted in a little grove in front of and at a considerable angle with the main line, first opened with an oblique fire upon the right of the enemy's column, which had the effect to make the troops on that flank double in a little toward their left. They still pressed on, however, without halting to return the fire. The rifled guns of our artillery, having fired away all their canister, were now withdrawn, or left on the ground inactive, to await the issue of the struggle between the opposing infantry.

Arrived at between 200 and 300 yards, the troops of the enemy were met by a destructive fire from the divisions of Gibbon and Hays, which they promptly returned, and the fight at once became fierce and general. In front of Hays' division it was not of very long duration. Mowed down by canister from Woodruff's battery, and by the fire from two regiments judiciously posted by General Hays in his extreme front and right, and by the fire of different lines in the rear, the enemy broke in great disorder, leaving fifteen colors and nearly 2,000 in the hands of this division. Those . . . who did not fall into disorder in front of the Third Division [Hays] were moved to the right, and re-enforced the line attacking Gibbon's division. The right of the attacking line having been repulsed by Hall's and Harrow's brigades of the latter division, assisted by the fire of the Vermont regiments. . . . doubled to its left and also re-enforced the center, and thus the attack was its fullest strength opposite the brigade of General Webb.

This brigade was disposed in two lines. Two regiments . . . the Sixty-ninth and Seventy-first Pennsylvania Volunteers, were behind a low stone wall and a slight breastwork hastily constructed by them, the remainder of the brigade being behind the crest some 60 paces to the rear, and so disposed as to fire over the heads of those in front.

When the enemy's line had nearly reached the stone wall, led by *General Armistead*, the most of that part of Webb's brigade posted here abandoned their position, but fortunately did not retreat entirely. They were, by the personal bravery of General Webb and his officers, immediately formed behind the crest . . . which was occupied by the remainder of the brigade.

Emboldened by seeing this indication of weakness, the enemy pushed forward more pertinaciously, numbers of them crossing over the breastwork abandoned by the troops. The fight here became very close and deadly. The enemy's battle-flags were soon seen waving on the stone wall. Passing at this time, Colonel Devereux, commanding the Nineteenth Massachusetts Volunteers [Hall's brigade], anxious to be in the right place, applied to me for permission to move his regiment to the right and to the front, where the line had been broken. I granted it, and his regiment and Colonel Mallon's (Forty-second New York Volunteers, on his right) proceeded there at once; but the enemy having left Colonel Hall's front, as described before, this officer promptly moved his command by the right flank to still further re-enforce the position of General Webb, and was immediately followed by Harrow's brigade. The movement was executed, but not without confusion, owing to many men leaving their ranks to fire at the enemy from the breastwork.

Today's view of the "copse of trees" from the southwest. (HWN)

The situation was now very peculiar. The men of all the brigades had in some measure lost their regimental organization, but individually they were firm. The ambition of individual commanders to promptly cover the point penetrated by the enemy, the smoke of battle, and the intensity of the close engagement, caused this confusion. The point, however, was now covered. In regular formation our line would have stood four ranks deep.

The colors of the different regiments were now advanced, waving in defiance of the long line of battle-flags presented by the enemy. The men pressed firmly after them, under the energetic commands and example of their officers, and after a few moments of desperate fighting the enemy's troops were repulsed, threw down their arms, and sought safety in flight or by throwing themselves on the ground to escape our fire. The battle-flags were ours and the victory was won.

While the enemy was still in front of Gibbon's division, I directed Colonel [General] Stannard to send two regiments of his Vermont Brigade, First Corps, to a point which would strike the enemy on the right flank. [*O.R.*, XXVII, Part i, pp. 373–74.]

To get a better view of Stannard's maneuver, either walk several hundred yards along the path *in front* of the Copse marking the "High Water Mark" of Confederate penetration that day—and perhaps the high water mark of southern hopes as well—or else return to your car and drive 0.1 mile beyond the Copse. Stop where the park road bends to the right, dismount, and walk to the fence overlooking the Codori farm.

Cemetery Ridge looking toward Codori's house, Gibbon's position. (USAMHI)

Seated is Maj. Gen. Winfield Scott Hancock, commanding officer of the II Corps. Behind Hancock is Maj. Gen. David Birney, division commander in the III Corps; at the left is Brig. Gen. Francis Barlow, division commander in the XI Corps; at the right is Brig. Gen. John Gibbon, division commander in the II Corps. All were wounded at Gettysburg. (MIL)

STOP 25

The troops entrusted with holding this portion of the line came from the First Corps. Biddle's brigade, which two days earlier had been out-flanked and pushed back from the field south of the HERBST WOODS at a cost of 440 killed or wounded and 457 missing out of 1,287, [O.R., XXVII, Part 1, p. 315] had the remnants of two regiments in line at this spot.

Report of Colonel Theodore B. Gates, USA, commanding Twentieth New York State Militia, First Brigade, Third Division, First Army Corps.

About 5 p.m. on *July 2*, the brigade was ordered to the left center, to support the Second Corps, which had been advanced to the relief of the Third. Two regiments only of the brigade . . . reached the front line, where they were halted on the last and lowest of the ridges running nearly north and south between the Taneytown and Emmitsburg roads. Some 300 yards on our right was a bluff, on which were standing a few trees and a battery. The trees on the westerly face of the bluff had been felled to clear a range for the guns. A rail fence stood at the foot of the bluff and extended along the ridge southerly. A little in advance and to our left was a small grove. The ground in front descended gradually to a little valley, wet and marshy, and then by a corresponding ascent reached the Emmitsburg Road and the position occupied by the enemy. . . . On my right was one regiment of Stannard's brigade [First Corps]; on my left two others, and one in rear and partly to my left. Receiving no orders, and finding myself the senior officer of the brigade present, I assumed command of the two regiments, and in . . . the evening constructed a breastwork of the fence . . . and of such other material as could be procured.

About 5 a.m. on the 3d the enemy opened with artillery, and for some time kept up a brisk fire upon our position. This finally ceased, and until about 1 p.m. no further firing took place on this part of the line.

During this interval, the Vermont troops threw up a breastwork to my left and about 100 feet in advance of my line, masked by the small grove. . . . The regiment of that brigade on my right took position in rear of this new work, leaving open the space between my right and the bluff, on which was the nearest battery.

At 1 o'clock the enemy opened from his right-center battery, which was soon followed by all his guns on the right and center, and the position occupied by my command was swept by a tempest of shot and shell from upward of one hundred guns for nearly three hours. When the cannonading subsided, the enemy's infantry debouched from the orchard and woods on his right center, and moved in two lines of battle across the fields toward the position. . . . Our skirmishers (from the Vermont brigade) fell back before them, and sought cover behind the breastworks on my left.

The enemy came forward rapidly, and began firing as soon as they were within range of our men. When they had approached within about 200 feet of the bottom of the valley . . . the troops of my command opened a warm fire upon them. Almost immediately the first line faced by the left flank, and moved at a double-quick up the valley and toward Gettysburg. The second line followed the movement. Reaching a position opposite the bluff, they faced to the right, and moved forward rapidly in line of battle.

Perceiving that their purpose was to gain the bluff, I moved my command by the right flank up to the foot of the bluff, delivering our fire as we marched, and keeping between the enemy and the object of his enterprise. He succeeded in reaching the fence at the foot of the bluff, but with ranks broken and his men evidently disheartened. Some succeeded in getting over the fence into the slashing, from which and behind the fence they kept up a murderous fire. The men were now within a quarter pistol-range, and, as the fence and fallen trees gave the enemy considerable cover, I ordered the Twentieth New York State Militia and the One hundred and fifty-first Pennsylvania Volunteers to advance to the fence, which they did, cheering, and in gallant style, and poured a volley into the enemy at very short range, who now completely broke, and those who did not seek to escape by flight threw down their arms. Very few of those who fled reached their own lines. Many turned after having run several rods and surrendered themselves. . . . During the latter part of this struggle, and after it ceased, the enemy's batteries played upon friend and foe alike. . . .

The two regiments I had the honor to command were either actually engaged with the enemy or occupying a position in the front line from the beginning of the battle . . . until its close . . . excepting only about six hours on the 2d . . . My loss in killed in wounded [in the 20th New York Militia] was two-thirds of my officers and half of my men. [*O.R.*, XXVII, Part 1, pp. 321-22.]

As Hunt mentioned in his report, the Confederates attacked in two successive columns. The action just described refers to the main assault by the brigades of *Brockenbrough (Mayo), Davis, Pettigrew (Marshall), Archer (Fry), Scales (Lowrance), Lane, Garnett, Kemper,* and *Armistead.* The last three crossed the Emmitsburg pike *south* of the Codori farm, which is plainly visible from here, and then obliqued to the left to add weight to the assault at the clump of trees. To their right and rear, with brigades of *Wilcox* and *Perry* moved some time after the others (*Wilcox* thought it was about 20 minutes later) and attacked straight forward. This in fact — and effect — amounted to a separate attack, for as *Wilcox* subsequently reported, when the two brigades reached the Emmitsburg road "not a man of the division that I was ordered to support could I see; but as my orders were to go to their support, one of my men went down the slope until they came near the hill upon which were the enemy's batteries and intrenchments. Here they were exposed to a close and terrible fire of artillery. Two lines of the enemy's infantry were seen moving by the flank toward the rear of my left. I ordered my men to hold their ground until I could get artillery to fire upon them. I then rode back rapidly to our artillery, but could find none near that had ammunition. After some little delay . . . knowing that my small force could do nothing save to make a useless sacrifice of themselves, I ordered them back. [*O.R.*, XXVII, Part 2, p. 620.]

The troops attacking *Wilcox's left* flank were the same Vermonters that had just hit the first column on its *right*. The brigade had reached the battle-ground too late on 1 July to participate in the fighting with the rest of the First Corps, and just before dark on 2 July Hancock had thrown one of the Vermont regiments against *Perry's* brigade near the clump of trees perhaps 500 yards to the south of your present location. Early on the morning of 3 July, General Stannard moved the other regiment to the front of the main line about 75 yards" and "selected a position to occupy, if attacked with infantry, some distance in front of the main line."

Report of Brig. Gen. George J. Stannard, USA, commanding Third Brigade, Third Division, First Army Corps

At about 2 p.m. the enemy . . . commenced a vigorous attack upon my position. After subjecting us for one and one-half hours to the severest cannonade of the whole battle . . . the enemy charged with a heavy column of infantry, at least one division, in close column by regiments. The charge was aimed directly upon my command, but owing apparently to the firm shown them, the enemy diverged midway, and came upon the line on my right [the near clump of trees]. But they did not thus escape the warm reception prepared for them by the Vermonters. During this charge the enemy suffered from the fire of the Thirteenth and Fourteenth, the range being short. At the commencement of the attack, I called the Sixteenth from the skirmish line, and placed them in close column by division in my immediate rear. As soon as the change of the point of attack became evident, I ordered a flank attack upon the enemy's column. Forming in the open meadow in front of our lines [opposite the Codori house], the Thirteenth changed front forward on first company; the Sixteenth, after deploying, performed the same, and formed on the left of the Thirteenth, at right angles to the main line of our army, bringing them in line of battle upon the [right] flank of the charging division of the enemy, and opened a destructive fire at short range, which the enemy sustained but a very few moments before the large portion of them surrendered and marched in—not as conquerors, but as captives. I then ordered the two regiments into their former position. The order was not filled when I saw another rebel column [*Wilcox* and *Perry*] charging immediately upon our left. Colonel Veazey, of the Sixteenth, was at once ordered to attack it in its turn upon the flank. This was done as successfully as before. The rebel forces, already decimated by the fire of the Fourteenth Regiment . . . were scooped almost *en masse* into our lines. . . .

The movements . . . were executed in the open field, under a very heavy fire of shell, grape, and musketry, and they were performed with the promptness and precision of battalion drill. They ended the contest in the center and substantially closed the battle. Officers and men behaved like veterans, although it was for most of them their first battle. . . . There were 350 killed, wounded and missing from my three regiments engaged; of the missing, only 1 is known to have been taken prisoner. [*O.R.*, XXVII, Part 1, pp. 349–50.]

Given the heavy casualties, it is understandable why so few after-action reports were written by Confederate infantry commanders involved in *Pickett's* Charge and most of those were scanty in their specific detail. *Pickett's* initial report was returned by *Lee* with the request that "you destroy both copy and original, substituting one confined to casualties merely." [*O.R.*, Part 3, p. 1075.]; he is not known to have submitted another. Of the few reports that are preserved, the following best communicate what happened to *Pickett's* men.

Report of Maj. Charles S. Peyton, CSA, Nineteenth Virginia Infantry, commanding Garnett's Brigade, Pickett's Division, Longstreet's Corps

At about 12 p.m. we were ordered to take position behind the crest of the hill on which the artillery, under *Colonel [E. Porter] Alexander*, was planted, where we lay during a most terrific cannonading, which . . . was kept up without intermission for one hour. During the shelling we lost about 20 killed and wounded. . . .

At 2.30 p.m. the artillery fire having to some extent abated, the order to advance was given, first by *Major-General Pickett* in person, and repeated by *General Garnett* with promptness, apparent cheerfulness, and alacrity. The brigade moved foward at quick time. The ground was open, but little broken, and from 800 to 1,000 yards from the crest whence we started to the enemy's line. The brigade moved in good order, keeping up its line almost perfectly, notwithstanding it had to climb three high post and rail fences, behind the last of which the enemy's skirmishers were first met and immediately driven in. Moving on, we soon met the advance line of the enemy, lying concealed in the grass on the slope, about 100 yards in front of his second line, which consisted of a stone wall about breast-high, running nearly parallel to and about 30 paces from the crest of the hill, which was lined with their artillery.

The first line . . . after offering some resistance, was completely routed, and driven in confusion back to the stone wall. Here we captured some prisoners, which were ordered to the rear without a guard. Having routed the enemy here, *General Garnett* ordered the brigade forward, which it promptly obeyed, loading and firing as it advanced.

Up to this time we had suffered but little from the enemy's batteries, which apparently had been much crippled previous to our advance, with the exception of one posted on the mountain [Little Round Top], about 1 mile to our right, which enfiladed nearly our entire line with fearful effect, sometimes as many as 10 men being killed and wounded by the bursting of a single shell. From the point it had first routed the enemy, the brigade moved rapidly forward toward the stone wall, under a galling fire from both artillery and infantry, the artillery using grape and canister. We were now within about 75 paces of the wall, unsupported on the right and left, *General Kemper* being some 50 or 60 yards behind and to the right, and *General Armistead* coming up in our rear. *General Kemper's* line was discovered to be lapping on ours, when, deeming it advisable to have the line extended on the right to prevent being flanked, a staff officer rode back to the general to request him to incline to the right. *General Kemper* not being present (perhaps wounded at the time), *Captain [W. T.] Fry*, of his staff, immediately began his exertions to carry out the request, but, in consequence of the eagerness of the men in pressing forward, it was impossible to have the order carried out.

Our line, much shattered, still kept up the advance until within about 20 paces of the wall, when, for a moment, it recoiled under the terrific fire that poured into our ranks both from their batteries and from their sheltered infantry. At this moment, *General Kemper* came up on the right and *General Armistead* in rear, when the three lines, joining in concert, rushed forward with unyielding determination and an apparent spirit of laudable rivalry to plant the Southern banner on the walls of the enemy. His strongest and last line was instantly gained; the Confederate battle-flag waved over his defenses, and the fighting over the wall became hand to hand, and of the most desperate character; but more than half having already fallen, our line was found too weak to rout the enemy. We hoped for a support on the left (which had started simultaneously with ourselves), but hoped in vain. Yet a small remnant remained in desperate struggle, receiving a fire in front, on the right, and on the left, many even climbing over the wall, and fighting the enemy in his own trenches until entirely surrounded; and those who were not killed or wounded were captured, with the exception of about 300 who came off slowly, but greatly scattered, the identity of every regiment being entirely lost, and every regimental commander killed or wounded.

The brigade went into action with 1,287 men and about 140 officers . . . and sustained a loss . . . of 941 killed, wounded, and missing. . . . Never had the brigade been better handled, and never has it done better service in the field of battle. There was scarcely an officer or man in the command whose attention was not attracted by the cool and handsome bearing of *General Garnett*, who, totally devoid of excitement or rashness, rode immediately in rear of his advancing line, endeavoring by his personal efforts, and by the aid of his staff, to keep his line well closed and dressed. He was shot from his horse while near the center of the brigade, within about 25 paces of the stone wall. [*O.R.*, XXVII, Part 2, pp. 385–87.]

This is the appropriate place and time to end the tour. To get back to the Visitor's Center, take the next left turn (just before you reach the PENNSYLVANIA STATE MEMORIAL, and drive to the STOP sign. This is the TANEYTOWN ROAD. Turn left. At 0.7 you will reach the entrance to the CYCLORAMA CENTER on your left. Another 0.1 mile and you will be at the VISITOR'S CENTER.

The cavalry battle on 3 July between Brig. Gen. D. M. Gregg and *Maj. Gen. J.E.B. Stuart* is not included in this tour, but will be a part of a future study of cavalry operations during the Gettysburg campaign. The cavalry battlefield site, however, is well marked and can be visited 3 miles east of Gettysburg on Pa. 116.

General Robert E. Lee (MIL)

EPILOGUE

Report of R. E. Lee, (continued)

The trains, with such of the wounded as could bear removal, were ordered to Williamsport on 4 July, part of moving through Cashtown and Greencastle, escorted by *General Imboden*, and the remainder by the Fairfield road.

The army retained its position until dark [on 4 July], when it was put in motion for the Potomac by the last-named route.

A heavy rain continued throughout the night, and so much impeded its progress that *Ewell's* corps, which brought up the rear, did not leave Gettysburg until late in the afternoon of the following day. The enemy offered no serious interruption, and, after an arduous march, we arrived at Hagerstown in the afternoon of the 6th and morning of 7 July. The great length of our trains made it difficult to guard them effectually in passing through the mountains, and a number of wagons and ambulances were captured. They succeeded in reaching Williamsport. . . . but were unable to cross the Potomac on account of the high stage of water. . . . The rains that had prevailed almost without intermission since our entrance into Maryland . . . had made the Potomac unfordable, and the pontoon bridge left at Falling Waters had been partially destroyed by the enemy. . . .

Nothing but occasional skirmishing occurred until 12 July, when the main body of the enemy arrived. The army then took a position previously selected, covering the Potomac from Williamsport to Falling Waters, where it remained for two days, with the enemy immediately in front, manifesting no disposition to attack, but throwing up intrenchments along his whole line.

By 13 July, the river . . . though still deep, was fordable, and a good bridge was completed at Falling Waters. . . . Orders were accordingly given to cross the Potomac that night. . . . [*O.R.*, XXVII, Part 2, pp. 322-23.]

Maj. Gen. Henry W. Halleck (MIL)

Report of Major General Henry W. Halleck, General-in-Chief, U.S. Army

The opposing forces in this sanguinary contest were nearly equal in numbers, and both fought with the most desperate courage. The commanders were also brave, skillful, and experienced, and they handled their troops on the field with distinguished ability; but to General Meade belongs the honor of a well-earned victory in one of the greatest and best-fought battles of the war.

On the morning of 4 July, the enemy apparently occupied a new line in front of our left, but in reality his army had commenced its retreat, carrying off a part of his wounded. His lines, however, were not entirely evacuated until the morning of 5 July, when the cavalry and the Sixth Corps were sent in pursuit.

The days of 5 and 6 July were employed by General Meade in succoring the wounded and burying the dead left on the battlefield. He then started in pursuit of *Lee* by a flank movement upon Middletown. In the meantime General French [commanding a division in the Third Corps] had reoccupied Harper's Ferry, destroyed the enemy's pontoon train at Williamsport and Falling Waters, and captured its guards.

Halting a day at Middletown, General Meade crossed South Mountain, and on 12 July found the enemy occupying a strong position on the heights of Marsh Run, in front of Williamsport. Not being attacked in this position, with the swollen waters of the Potomac in his rear, without any means of crossing his artillery, and where a defeat must have cased the surrender of his entire army, Lee had time to construct a pontoon bridge with lumber collected from canal-boats and the ruins of wooden houses, and on the morning of 14 July his army had crossed to the south side of the river. His rear guard, however, was attacked by our cavalry and suffered considerable loss. Thus ended the rebel campaign north of the Potomac, from which important political and military results had been expected. [*O.R.*, XXVII, Part 1, pp. 16-17.]

Maj. Gen. George G. Meade (LC)

Meade to his wife, 5 July 1863

It was a grand battle, and is in my judgment a most decided victory, though I did not annihilate or bag the Confederate Army. This morning they retired in great haste into the mountains, leaving their dead unburied and their wounded on the field. They awaited one day, expecting that, flushed with success, I would attack them when they would play their old game of shooting us from behind breastworks—a game we played this time to their entire satisfaction. The men behaved splendidly; I really think they are becoming soldiers. They endured long marches, short rations, and stood one of the most terrific cannonadings I ever witnessed. . . . The army are in the highest spirits, and of course I am a great man. The most difficult part of my work is acting without correct information on which to predicate action.

Headquarters, Army of the Potomac, 5 July, 1863, General Orders, No. 68.

The Commanding General, in behalf of the country, thanks the Army of the Potomac for the glorious result of the recent operations.

An enemy superior in numbers and flushed with the pride of a successful invasion, attempted to overcome and destroy this Army. Utterly baffled and defeated, he has now withdrawn from the contest. The privations and fatigue the Army had endured, and the heroic courage and gallantry it has displayed will be matters of history to be remembered.

Our task is not yet accomplished, and the Commanding General looks to the Army for greater efforts to drive from our soil every vestige of the presence of the invader. [*The Life and Letters of George Gordon Meade* by (Captain) George Meade (2 vols., New York, Charles Scribner's Sons, 1913) II, 122-23, 125, 307]

Lincoln to Major General Halleck, 6 July, 1863

I left the telegraph office a good deal dissatisfied. You know I did not like the phrase, in Orders, No. 68, I believe, "Drive the invaders from our soil." Since that, I see a dispatch from General French, saying the enemy is crossing his wounded over the river in flats, without saying why he does not stop it, or even intimating a thought that it ought to be stopped. Still later, another dispatch from General Pleasonton, by direction of General Meade, to General French, stating that the main army is halted because it is believed the rebels are concentrating "on the road toward Hagerstown, beyond Fairfield," and is not to move until it is ascertained that the rebels intend to evacuate Cumberland Valley.

These things all appear to me to be connected with a purpose to cover Baltimore and Washington, and to get the enemy across the river again without a further collision, and they do not appear connected with a purpose to prevent his crossing and to destroy him. I do fear the former purpose is acted upon, and the latter is rejected.

If you are satisfied the latter purpose is entertained and is judiciously pursued, I am content. If you are not so satisfied, please look to it. [O.R., XXVII, Part 3, p. 567.]

Halleck to Meade, 7 July, 1863

You have given the enemy a stunning blow at Gettysburg, follow it up and give him another before he can cross the Potomac.

Meade to his wife, 8 July, 1863

I claim no extraordinary merit for this last battle, and would prefer waiting a little while to see what my career is to be before making any pretensions. I did and shall continue to do my duty to the best of my abilities, but knowing as I do that battles are often decided by accidents, and that no man of sense will say in advance what their result will be, I wish to be careful in not bragging before the right time. . . . From the time I took command till today, now over ten days, I have not changed my clothes, have not had a regular night's rest, and many nights not a wink of sleep, and for several days did not even wash my face and hands, no regular food, and all the time in a great state of mental anxiety. Indeed, I think I have lived as much in this time as in the last thirty years. . . . I never claimed a victory, though I stated that *Lee* was defeated in his efforts to destroy my army. I am going to move as soon as I can get the army supplied with subsistence and ammunition.

Meade to his wife, 14 July, 1863

I found *Lee* in a very strong position, intrenched. I hesitated to attack him, without some examination of the mode of approaching him. I called my corps commanders together, and they voted against attacking him. This morning, when I advanced to feel his position and seek for a weak point, I found he had retired in the night and was nearly across the river. I immediately started in pursuit, and my cavalry captured two thousand prisoners, two guns, several flags, and killed *General Pettigrew*. On reporting these facts to General Halleck, he informed me the President was very much dissatisfied at the escape of Lee. I immediately telegraphed I had done my duty to the best of my ability, and that the expressed dissatisfaction of the President I considered undeserved censure, and asked to be immediately relieved. In reply he said this was not intended to censure me, but only to spur me on to an active pursuit. . . .

I start tomorrow to run another race with *Lee*. [Meade, *Life and Letters*, II, 122-23, 132-34.]

Headquarters Army of Northern Virginia, Bunker Hill, Va., July 16, 1863

Mr. President:

The army is encamped around this place. . . . The men are in good health and spirits, but want shoes and clothing badly. I have sent back to endeavor to procure a supply of both, and also horseshoes, for want of which nearly half our cavalry is unserviceble. As soon as these necessary articles are obtained, we shall be prepared to resume operations. [*O.R.*, XXVII, Part 2, p. 302.]

APPENDIX I
CAPABILITIES AND
DOCTRINE IN THE
CIVIL WAR

When today's soldiers first encounter Civil War battlefield accounts, they are usually appalled by the slaughter. This first impression is valid, but it should not obscure the fact that the military leaders of the 1860's who fought those battles were trying to use modern, professional methods to make use of lethal instruments. The measure of effectiveness was the same as now: protect key elements of your own force while destroying those portions of the enemy's force that render him unable or unwilling to continue the fight.

The means used to achieve those ends centered on tactics and technology, both of which were similar in the armies of the North and the South. Of course the use of technology and the execution of tactical designs depended largely on the quality of troops and their leaders—factors that varied widely within both armies. But no matter how perfect the leader's decision might be, it had to be communicated on the battlefield by the age-old means of messenger, drum or bugle, supplemented only at the strategic level by semaphore flags or telegraph. Industrial production allowed societies to clothe, feed, equip, and move much larger armies into battle, but generals still directed the efforts of those armies in ways that had already been barely adequate when much smaller forces were engaged.

Decentralized execution and specialization had been important parts of the solution to this problem of battle management long before the Civil War. To understand these battles we need general knowledge of the way armies were organized, and then we need a bit more detailed information on the armament and tactics of the subordinate organizations that were the specialized building blocks from which armies were formed.

ORGANIZATION

The armies that we see on battlefields (Army of the Potomac, Army of Northern Virginia, etc.) were only parts of the total forces available to the warring powers. As separate entities, these armies contained all the elements necessary for independent, sustained operations throughout a campaign. Because they were so large, they could be concentrated only for battles and were habitually divided into separate corps for routine operations and for decentralized execution in large battles. By 1863, both armies generally formed a corps of three divisions, but Union corps usually were significantly smaller than those in the Confederate armies because the Union brigades, and therefore divisions, were smaller. As the table below indicates, strengths of units varied widely within each army.

UNIT	USA	CSA
COMPANY	35–40 men	35–40 men
REGIMENT	350–400 (10 companies)	350–400 (10 companies)
BRIGADE	800–1700	1400–2000
DIVISION	3,000–7,000	6,000–14,000
CORPS	12,000–14,000	24,000–28,000

Corps and divisions were combined arms teams having their own field artillery batteries, and divisions as well as corps often had limited cavalry assets. Cooperation among the three combat arms was far from perfect, and battles are generally best understood by studying the role played by each arm. But the "ideal battle" that Civil War generals would have been trying to fight has few similarities to the battles we see on our visits to actual battlefields. The image of a battle that follows was actually translated from a French source, even though it appeared in an American handbook during the Civil War. In terms of weapon ranges, battlefield lethality, and numerical strength of the armies, it depicts Napoleonic battle rather than the conditions on a Civil War battlefield.

When approaching the enemy, the army is drawn up in four or five lines, viz., an advanced guard, a battle corps in two lines, a reserve, and a rear-guard. The infantry of the battle corps marches in front with its pieces of artillery. . . . The mounted artillery does not immediately precede the columns of infantry, but it should have a single battalion in front of it, for at the first signal, it should take up its position. After the infantry comes the mass of the cavalry and the reserve, followed by the materiel of the battalions and the parks; the rear-guard keeps distant about half a march. . . . The advanced guard takes a defensive position, deploying its columns, in order to arrest the enemy and hold him in check by a destructive fire until the main body has taken a position for battle; the duty of the advanced guard being to act strictly on the defensive while the main body is making its dispositions for battle.

The general commanding examines the ground and the enemy when he arrives in his presence; he immediately sends his aids to the main body to direct the heads of columns, and give the generals the first instructions for entering the line of battle. The divisions quicken their pace, separating as they reach the field of battle, and move to their designated positions.

The cavalry hastens to the wings, to take its proper duties in the battle. The infantry first deploys by battalions en masse, upon two lines, 300 yard apart, a proper distance of the second line to be beyond musket range of the enemy's lines, and not to be cut up if the first line is routed, but still sufficiently near to be well in hand. It should take advantage as far as possible of all natural covers. Each division is usually in a single line.

The [battalion] masses are next deployed, either to move toward the enemy in this order, preceded by the skirmishers, or to form double columns at deployment distance, a disposition always taken by the second line, the centre of its battalions being opposite the intervals of the first.

If the columns are not very deep, they may, in debouching, deploy at once, without the preliminary formation into battalions en masse, The reserve, or third line, usually forms by battalions en masse, and takes up a position to the rear, while the first two lines are engaged.

The action is begun by skirmishers, who halt as soon as they are within good range of the enemy's skirmishers, and hold them in check. The main body halts at the same time, and being soon unmasked by the skirmishers, the first line opens fire. If this is not simply a demonstration, the second line does not halt, but passes into the intervals of the first, and attacks in column with the bayonet, protected by skirmishers, which are spread among the intervals. The first line being thus passed by, ceases its fire, forms in double columns, in order to be ready in turn to succor the second line, now become first. If the latter overthrows the enemy, it reforms after the charge, and the skirmishers follow the enemy, supported by detachments; if not the columns of the second line again advance, and are replaced by those of the reserve, which prepares to move while the first line is retiring. There is in this way a constant passage of lines, in which consists the mechanical part of battles.

. . . Artillery, upon reaching the field of battle, separates from the columns of infantry, and marches upon their flanks to take up its positions, the reserve being left in temporary positions, that of each battery following the movements of the troops to which it belongs, keeping safe from the fire and attacks of the enemy, that of each corps being placed in some central position, from two to five miles from the troops, and under a good escort.

. . . The object of artillery is to harass the enemy and cause disorder in his ranks at distances where musketry is useless or nearly so. It takes position on the wings in front of the line of battle, or opposite the intervals, especially while the troops of the first line are not yet deployed, but it should not go to a greater distance to the front than 150 yards, nor approach the enemy within 300 yards. If the enemy makes a decided forward movement, it retires to the neighborhood of the second line.

It may happen that the second line cannot give the artillery immediate protection. In this case supports are provided for, and these place themselves a little to the rear, and upon the flanks of the battery, but never behind it . . . in order not to furnish a double mark for the enemy's artillery.

[William P. Craighill, *Army Officer's Pocket Companion*, (1862), pp. 174–188.]

INFANTRY IN BATTLE

Civil War infantry could use its bayonets for shock action but generally depended on the firepower of its rifled muskets. Commanders recognized that infantry was capable of fighting over all kinds of ground in all weather conditions. They also shared the time-worn belief that infantry was the arm most easily recruited, instructed, and maintained. Since infantry could, if necessary, survive without the support of other arms, and could take and hold ground, it was the central element in any operational plan.

Weapons. The principal weapon of the infantry in both armies throughout the war was the muzzle-loading rifled musket firing a non-spherical projectile. This weapon incorporated several significant improvements over the musket of the Napoleonic era: the flintlock had been replaced by a percussion cap, simplifying the loading drill, reducing the frequency of misfires, and making the weapon more reliable in damp weather; the rifled bore gave the common infantryman a weapon with much greater range and accuracy; and the non-spherical projectile (the Minie ball is best-known, but there were many competing designs) gave the rifled musket the same speed in loading familiar in the old smooth-bores. It still produced great clouds of smoke from its black powder propellant, and the ammunition was still so heavy that a soldier carried a basic load of only 60 rounds.

Weapon effectiveness for 19th century infantry was gauged in terms of "musketry"—the effect of volley fire from a unit's weapons against an area target. By this measure, effectiveness was a function of accuracy, range, penetration, and rate of fire. The rifled musket matched the old smoothbore in rate of fire and exceeded its capability in all other categories. The superiority of the rifled musket became obvious at ranges greater than 150 yards, and musketry could be used to good effect against lines of infantry at ranges greater than 400 yards. Ammunition consumption was a problem if units opened fire at such great range, but contemporary calculations indicated that the new rifled muskets gave defenders the range necessary to deliver at least five more aimed volleys against infantry attacking at the quick time than would have been possible with the smoothbore. This increased lethal range of the standard infantry weapon was a major factor transforming the tactical problems confronting an attacker.

Tactics. Since rate of fire had not improved, well-trained infantrymen could sustain a rate of fire of little more than two shots per minute. Adequate volume of fire could be generated by deploying infantry in the close-order linear formations that had been familiar features of battlefields for more than a century. These formations could only deliver that high volume of fire to their front—the flank was shallow, weak, and therefore a vulnerable point against which the enemy army could naturally be expected to maneuver.

Whether attacking or defending, tactics and drill were virtually identical for Civil War soldiers, and the key evolution was from column to line and back again. Troops were formed in columns whenever speed and convenience were more important than firepower. Infantry columns were easily controlled by the officers, could move rapidly on roads, and could clear obstacles quickly. But only a few soldiers in a column could fire their weapons, so trained soldiers knew numerous drills to maintain unit integrity while changing from column to line. If time and terrain allowed, commanders might march the entire column at right angles to the direction the line was to face, allowing the subordinate elements to go through relatively simple evolutions to form the line. In other situations tactical constraints might force far more complex movements to achieve the same end. In any case, the unit was vulnerable while going through these inevitably time-consuming evolutions. A tactically-proficient commander could choose the correct evolution for the situation confronting him. A tactically-proficient unit could execute the required move without error, in spite of terrain obstacles or enemy fire. And once the line was formed, proficient units maintained contact with flank units so that their own flank did not become the vulnerable point at which an enemy could seize the advantage, penetrate, and roll up their entire army.

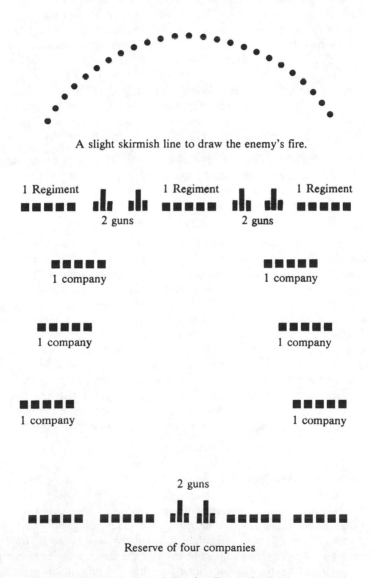

A slight skirmish line to draw the enemy's fire.

"Colonel Wilder's Preferred Cavalry Formation" (see page 214).

FIELD ARTILLERY IN BATTLE

The Napoleonic Wars were characterized by significant improvements in the military discipline of artillery and its integration into a proficient general's plan for attack and defense. In the U.S. Army, the field artillery had shown its ability to meet the high modern standards in the war with Mexico, and the necessity for competent artillery organizations was recognized by both sides at the outset of the Civil War. In general, Northern armies were able to bring more artillery pieces to bear in battle, and these pieces had better ammunition supplies and better draught horses. Both armies had high standards for their gunners and fielded fine batteries able to establish local fire superiority on a battlefield.

In the 1860's, "The principal object of artillery [was] to sustain the troops in attack and defense; to facilitate their movement and oppose the enemy's; to destroy his forces as well as the obstacles which protect them; and to keep up the combat until an opportunity is offered for a decisive blow." [John Gibbon, *The Artillerist's Manual*, 1860, p. 389.]

In early campaigns much of the artillery was distributed to support individual infantry brigades. As the war progressed, both armies eventually realized that artillery missions could be best performed if control of batteries was centralized at division and higher levels, with special artillery staff officers of sufficient rank advising their generals on the placement and use of artillery assets. The battery of six guns remained the basic unit, although smaller batteries were not uncommon, especially in the Confederate force. Before the war, U.S. artillery organization had called for standard batteries having 4 guns and 2 howitzers, but new technology was pushing the army toward batteries having 6 pieces of one type. The Northern organization followed this trend, but Confederate batteries often were organized around pieces of more than one type or caliber. On a full war-time footing, a standard battery would have about 150 men and 110 horses.

Weapons. In the 1850's, design improvements in the standard bronze (commonly called "brass") 12 pound gun had reduced its weight while improving its reliability. The resulting Model 1857 12-pounder gun-howitzer (Napoleon) was a smooth-bore muzzle-loader that could fire a 12 pound round cast-iron shot nearly a mile. This solid shot was useful against artillery, cavalry, and infantry in column and could be fired for direct hits or ricocheting impact in front of the target. The latter method was preferred against attacking infantry when the ground allowed, for it unnerved survivors while inflicting heavy casualties (contemporary handbooks estimated that a round shot would carry through six ranks of infantry). The new 12 pound gun also fired shells—special projectiles that in the past had required the use of howitzers, pieces having powder chambers with a diameter smaller than that of the bore. The resulting reduction in powder charge made howitzers useless with the solid shot projectile but allowed construction of a lighter piece perfectly suited for firing the more fragile shell. A shell was a hollow cast iron sphere filled with black powder and armed with a black powder fuze that was ignited by the flame of the burning propellant. Accurate and reliable fuzes were not quite "state of the art" during the Civil War, and several patents competed for the gunner's acceptance. If a shell was properly aimed and its fuze functioned, it burst over the target, showering the area with cast iron fragments and unsettling men and horses. Preferred range for shell was 300–1300 yards, and it was useful against cavalry, artillery, and infantry in the open or in trenches. The "high tech" projectile fired by the Civil War gunner was case shot. This round was a hollow cast iron sphere like the shell, but it was filled with lead balls and a small black powder bursting charge. The fuze problems in its employment were the same as those encountered in firing shell, but the effects over the target area were potentially more lethal. Like the shell, the spherical case projectile was seldom fired much beyond 1300 yards. Inside 400 yards, but especially at ranges of 100 to 200 yards, the preferred round was canister. This was a cylindrical tin can filled with cast iron balls. When fired, the can fell away, and the balls spread in a sheaf like giant shotgun pellets. While Civil War accounts are filled with references to "grape and canister," the larger grape shot—which had been far more prevalent in naval warfare—was no longer in use by the 1860's.

Rifled guns coexisted with smoothbores in both armies throughout the Civil War. These were of various calibers and patents, the most common for field use being the 3 inch Ordnance Rifle and the 10 pound Parrott. These rifled guns fired all of the projectile types associated with the 12 pound Napoleon, but the comparable projectiles for the rifles were elongated, using various systems to engage the rifling. The main advantage of the rifled gun was range: their firing tables normally ran beyond 3500 yards, although effective firing at 3000 yards was extremely difficult. In addition, impact (percussion) fuzes could be used with the rifled gun, and these were improved as the war continued.

All Civil War field artillery was used for direct fire—the gunner aimed the gun, sensed the strike of the shot, and then repositioned the piece to move the next shot to the target. This procedure was more art than science since the entire gun rolled backward with the force of recoil, depriving the gunner of fixed reference points. The clouds of smoke from the black powder propellant charges further complicated his task by obscuring his vision of the projectile in flight. A well-trained crew could be expected to fire two rounds per minute, or three rounds of canister, since pointing was simpler for the latter.

For movement, each gun in a battery was attached to a two-wheeled limber pulled by six horses. It was accompanied by another six-horse team pulling a limber and a caisson. The limbers and caisson carried ammunition chests with capacity for 128 rounds per piece, with additional rounds in the battery wagons and reserve artillery ammunition trains. This arrangement made the guns mobile while giving them adequate ammunition for brief independent action.

Tactics. Field artillery tactics were based upon selecting ground suitable for the use of guns, moving batteries into firing position rapidly, and delivering fire accurately and efficiently against targets imposed by the overall situation. Artillery positions generally were interspersed with infantry or were placed on the flank. Often the artillery was pushed forward 50 to 100 yards beyond the infantry line, in an arrangement that one contemporary authority compared to fortress design, with the artillery as the bastion and the infantry as the curtain. Whatever the arrangement, it had to allow the batteries to range their selected targets without interfering with the fire and movement of the infantry. If the tactical disposition placed no cavalry or infantry close to a battery, supports were detailed from one of these arms to protect the guns from direct attack.

Cannoneers drilled to become proficient in occupying a position rapidly, removing the horses and limbers to a safe distance, and bringing effective fire to bear on the designated target. Fire could be delivered against enemy artillery, infantry and cavalry, but the highest priority target normally was that which posed the greatest risk to the supported force. In the attack, artillery would be used against both infantry and artillery. In the defense, initial artillery efforts would be aimed at artillery, with priority shifting to the infantry attackers as they moved into easier range. These passages from a contemporary handbook give the flavor of the classic tactical problem facing the gunner:

Suppose cavalry to be advancing to attack infantry, and first observed at the distance of a mile, passing over the first half mile at a trot; the next quarter of a mile at the maneuvering gallop, and the remaining distance at an increasing gallop, terminating with the charge; occupying altogether about six minutes: during the last 1500 yards of their advance how many rounds per piece might a battery fire in that time?

Eleven rounds with effect, thus:

From 1500 to 650 yards
3 min, 32 sec—spherical case 7

From 650 to 350
0 min, 48 sec—solid shot 2

From 350 to close quarters
0 min, 34 sec—canister 2

What number of rounds could a piece fire against infantry, supposing them to pass over 1500 yards in about 16¼ minutes?

Thirty-six rounds with effect, viz.:

From 1500 to 650 . . . Quick step
9 min, 45 sec—spherical case 19

From 650 to 350
3 min, 50 sec—solid shot 7

From 350 to 100
2 min, 30 sec—canister 8

From 100 to close quarters

Double Quick and the Charge
0 min, 40 sec—canister 2

[Joseph Roberts, *Handbook of Artillery*, 1863, pp. 50–51.]

Batteries sometimes fought until overrun, but more often casualties among cannoners and horses forced the battery to displace before the enemy closed. When that occurred, the gun sections rejoined the battery wagons in a sheltered section of the battlefield, cross-leveled manpower and equipment, refilled their ammunition chests, and reported to higher authority to be assigned a new place in the line.

CAVALRY IN BATTLE.

Early in the Civil War, General Scott stated that, "Owing to the broken and wooded Character of the terrain in the field of operations, and the improvement of rifled weapons, the role of cavalry will be secondary and unimportant." [George H. Morgan, "General Study of Cavalry in the Eastern Armies in 1862," U.S. Army War College, 1914.]

This attitude, together with the shortage of skilled riders in the Northeast, tended to give the Confederacy the advantage early in the war. Southern cavalry in the early campaigns was more numerous, better organized, and better led. But Northern cavalry leaders recognized the deficiencies in their combatant arm and sought improvements, as the following memorandum from General Pleasonton, dated December 1, 1862, indicates:

To obviate some of the defects existing at present in our cavalry organization, the following sugestions are respectfully submitted:

1st. That portion of the army whose duties are to cover the front and flanks of the army, form advanced guards, rear guards, gain information of the enemy's movements, and, in fact, perform all the functions of cavalry as a corps, should be organized as such into brigades and divisions, with a common commander, under the direct orders of the commander of the army. The cavalry is a distinct arm of the service, having specific duties to perform, that can only be properly discharged under an organization conformable to those duties. It is, therefore, recommended that such legislation be obtained as will give the cavalry a corps organization.

2d. For the orderly, escort and detachment service of infantry corps, divisions, grand divisions &c., a certain amount of cavalry is needed, depending on the service required. This service can be very well discharged by cavalry regiments just entering the service, and as these men learn their duties, it is much better to keep them as such than transfer them to the new and trying duties of the cavalry to the front of the army. In each army corps an officer should be especially assigned to take charge of the cavalry on duties as orderlies, escorts, &c., and in no case should it ever be permitted to take men from the army corps and transfer them to the cavalry corps, or the reverse, unless with the approval of the several commanders concerned, and by the order of the commanding general of the army.

3d. To insure uniformity and accuracy in the reports to the commanding general of the army, the cavalry used in obtaining the information must be under the orders of the same person. The same report made through two different sources rarely reaches a third party as it started. Besides, under different independent commanders, each gets mistrustful in the field, is soon confounded, frequently fires on the other through mistake, and eventually becomes timid. Such has been the experience of this war up to this time. Our cavalry can be made superior to any now in the field by organization. The rebel cavalry owe their success to their organization, which permits great freedom and responsibility to its commanders, subject to the commanding general.

4th. The horse artillery should invariably belong and serve with the cavalry. Eight batteries would be a proper allowance to a corps of two divisions of cavalry. This would allow for four in constant field service, and on the day of battle one horse battery is equal to two foot batteries, by reason of its mobility. The remaining four would render the most important service. These eight batteries should be formed into a corps, having a brigadier-general at its head, and no horse battery should be commanded by an officer of less rank than a lieutenant-colonel.

A. PLEASONTON
Brigadier-General
[O.R. Series I—Vol. XXI, p. 815]

Pleasonton understood the organization that was needed to perform the missions that inevitably fell to cavalry, and he was willing to copy Southern approaches when they produced results. All of his proposed reforms were not implemented, but by 1863 the North had made enough improvements in its cavalry forces to neutralize the South's early advantage. In the last two years of the war, Union cavalry outnumbered its Southern foe, and it was better mounted and far better supplied.

Cavalry was raised and maintained in regiments, having ten companies (or troops) each authorized 60 privates in the South, 72 in the North. Two troops formed a squadron, and the squadrons were in turn formed into battalions of varying size. Originally, both sides sought cavalry volunteers bringing their own mounts. This practice was quickly dropped in the North in favor of a centralized remount system. It persisted much longer in the South, where a veteran trooper's loss of a mount often deprived his unit of an able-bodied soldier for extended periods while the young man returned home to find another horse.

As General Pleasonton's memo indicates, the cavalry had numerous missions: reconnaissance, intelligence gathering, protection of flanks, head and rear of the army on the march, local security of headquarters and other key points, and movement control. Any of these might lead to clashes with the enemy that would, in theory, result in quick victory for the cavalry detachment, rapid reinforcement by nearby infantry, or rapid retreat by outnumbered cavalry if no infantry support was near. In every case, the strength of the cavalry lay in its mobility. Independent cavalry operations by large organizations (generally divisions) placed the same emphasis on mobility, but they also called for significant firepower if the force was to avoid becoming decisively engaged by an overwhelming foe.

Weapons. Experiments with lances for cavalry failed in the Civil War because these traditional weapons were hard to handle in the woods and underbrush that covered so much of the country the armies traversed. The other traditional weapon, the saber, was much in evidence. Combined with the weight of horse and rider at the charging gallop, it gave the cavalry the shock effect needed to break the enemy line. Bringing that shock to bear had always been difficult, and rifled weapons in the hands of infantry did not simplify the task. In fact, the cavalry charge was virtually reserved for use against enemy cavalry.

But new technology favored cavalrymen as well. The revolver was a vast improvement over the old horse pistols of earlier wars, giving cavalry patrols far greater firepower for the short-range, sharp exchanges that were so important in their routine small-unit actions. As the war progressed, the traditional dragoon concept—cavalry trained to fight in the traditional fashion but also trained and equipped to fight as infantry—gained greater prominence. Many cavalrymen were then issued rifled muskets, carbines, or repeating rifles. As the repeating rifles became more widespread among Union cavalrymen they became a far more formidable force, no matter what mission they might be performing.

Horse artillery batteries provided a mount for every cannoneer to achieve greater mobility. They were still far less mobile than the fighting edge of a cavalry regiment because the gun carriages could not handle rough fords and steep inclines with the same ease enjoyed by a mounted man. But the additional saddle horses gave the batteries the same mobility as a cavalry regiment's trains, and this was the deciding difference. Horse artillery could be found in various calibers, but the 12 pound Napoleon was ideally suited to most requirements. Six pound guns and 12 pound howitzers were lighter, but they were too easily outgunned in any serious engagement with properly-supported infantry.

Tactics. Cavalry drill was rooted in the same basic needs as infantry drill: Column formations were mandatory for mobility, the line was the key to delivering fire or shock. Given ample maneuver room, cavalry could conduct rapid evolutions from one formation to another, but such conditions were difficult to find. Since firepower was often the key ingredient in the cavalry contribution to battle, dragoon tactics sought opportunity for the cavalry force to approach the ground to be used in column at right angles to the line to be formed, dismount leaving the horses with a few designated men, and then rapidly form a single rank of riflemen. The account that follows gives a straightforward account of cavalry tactics in a typical engagement:

My brigade, composed of the 17th and 72d Indiana Infantry and the 92d, 98th and 123d Illinois Infantry and the 18th Indiana Battery, were mounted in February, 1863. They were all pretty well drilled under Hardie's tactics, and as we nearly always fought dismounted, we simply kept that manner of movement, except that we made a single line with the men at intervals of six feet, as we had Spencer rifles, a magazine gun with seven rounds in the magazine, and could use a single round without drawing on the magazine, which was kept full for fighting at short range. The calibre was 52 and carried an ounce bullet, and had a range of one mile. We always tried to get close to our opponents, as we then got the benefit of rapid fire, which was very effective then. I trained my command to hold their rapid fire until our opponents were within 300 yards, when our rapid fire with aim never failed to break their charge, and if it was desirable to advance, we did so at once, and in that way lost less men than we otherwise would have done.

Magazine guns are most effective at close range. I do not believe in long range fighting, as my most effective work was done at short ranges.

My command had little time for drill, as we were kept close to the enemy and our movements were mostly in firing range of our opponents, and that I found to be the most useful drill we could have. My lines *were never broken*, as we had so many shots at close quarter no troops, however capable, could withstand the fire we could give, and I always tried to compel our opponents to charge us and then our plan of action was most effective.

I tried to keep our men down under cover or lying down until attacked, and then orders were to fire and load at will, always taking aim.

Volley fire was mostly a waste of ammunition, and I hardly ever practiced it. I enclose a diagram of my favorite formation when in action.

This formation was used when I had time to make it, and the topography suitable, and if I had another regiment, it was used for flanking purposes or for prolonging the battle line.

My usual artillery ammunition was 80% canister and 20% percussion shells and we always exhausted the canister first.

The three companies on the flanks were in echelon, and this formation was very effective and very mobile. I had six Rodman guns, 10 pounders of 3-inch calibre, and always kept 20 ammunition wagons with eight horses to each, so as never to be short of ammunition, or power to move them over any ground.

(signed)
J.T. Wilder
Colonel, 17th Indiana, and
Brevet Brig. Gen. of Volunteers

[George H. Morgan, "Cavalry in the Eastern Theater, 1862," U.S. Army War College, 1913–14]

APPENDIX II
ORDER OF BATTLE

The listing of units that follows has been drawn from the *Official Records*, but several significant categories of data found in that source have been omitted. Since this listing is designed to help users of this guide in following the development of the battle, it includes only unit entries. Staffs were not extensive in the Civil War, but listing staff officers would make this aid far more cumbersome. Names of commanders down through brigade level have been retained, because these names appear frequently in the extracts from the *Official Records* that form the bulk of this guide. Note that changes in command are indicated by placing the successor's name beneath that of the commander who was incapacitated or relieved. The entry for the Union First Army Corps at the beginning of the listing is illustrative: Doubleday replaced Reynolds when Reynolds was killed early on the first day. Doubleday was then relieved and replaced by Newton. The consequences of these changes are reflected in the changes in the units from which successors were drawn, in this case, First Corps' Third Division and its First Brigade. This listing of commanders and their successors has not been carried down into regiments because that detail is seldom needed and is voluminous.

Few other details have been omitted, but not all indications of partial regiments have been included, and units detailed to provost guard or headquarters security have been omitted. In the former instance, the number of companies available is only included when it is significantly below a standard regimental complement of ten companies. Regimental strength was usually a function of company strength and freedom from straggling and details, not a result of the number of companies assigned. Units providing rear area security were important, but they have no direct influence on the aspects of the battle addressed in this tour.

If additional information on units present at the battle of Gettysburg is required, the full order of battle listing is found in the *Official Records* XXVII, Part I, pp. 155–168 and Part II, pp. 283–291.

H.W.N.

ORDER OF BATTLE
UNITED STATES ARMY

ARMY OF THE POTOMAC
Maj. Gen. George G. Meade, Commanding

FIRST ARMY CORPS (Maj. Gen. John R. Reynolds)
(Maj. Gen. Abner Doubleday)
(Maj. Gen. John Newton)

First Division (Brig. Gen. James S. Wadsworth)

First Brigade (Brig. Gen. Solomon Meredith)
19th Indiana
24th Michigan
2d Wisconsin
6th Wisconsin
7th Wisconsin

Second Brigade (Brig. Gen. Lysander Cutler)
7th Indiana
76th New York
84th New York (14th Militia)
95th New York
147th New York
56th Pennsylvania

Second Division (Brig. Gen. John C. Robinson)

First Brigade (Brig. Gen. Gabriel R. Paul)
(Col. Samuel H. Leonard)
(Col. Adrian R. Root)
(Col. Richard Coulter)
(Col. Peter Lyle)
(Col. Richard Coulter)
16th Maine
13th Massachusetts
94th New York
104th New York
107th Pennsylvania

Second Brigade (Brig. Gen. Henry Baxter)
12th Massachusetts
83rd New York (9th Militia)
97th New York
11th Pennsylvania
88th Pennsylvania
90th Pennsylvania

Third Division (Brig. Gen. Thomas A. Rowley)
(Maj. Gen. Abner Doubleday)

First Brigade (Col. Chapman Biddle)
(Brig. Gen. Thomas Rowley)
(Col. Chapman Biddle)
80th New York (20th Militia)
121st Pennsylvania
142nd Pennsylvania
151st Pennsylvania

Second Brigade (Col. Roy Stone)
(Col. Langhorne Wister)
(Col. Edmund L. Dana)
143d Pennsylvania
149th Pennsylvania
150th Pennsylvania

Third Brigade (Brig. Gen. George J. Stannard)
(Col. Francis Randall)
13th Vermont
14th Vermont
16th Vermont

Artillery Brigade (Col. Charles S. Wainwright)
4th United States, Battery B
Maine Light, 2d Battery (B)
Maine Light, 5th Battery (E)
1st New York Light, Batteries E and L
1st Pennsylvania Light, Battery B

SECOND ARMY CORPS (Maj. Gen. Winfield S. Hancock)
(Brig. Gen. John Gibbon)
(Maj. Gen. Winfield S. Hancock)

First Division (Brig. Gen. John C. Caldwell)

First Brigade (Col. Edward E. Cross)
(Col. H. Boyd McKeen)
5th New Hampshire
61st New York
81st Pennsylvania
148th Pennsylvania

Second Brigade (Col. Patrick Kelly)
28th Massachusetts
63rd New York (two companies)
69th New York (two companies)
88th New York (two companies)
116th Pennsylvania (four companies)

Third Brigade (Brig. Gen. Samuel K. Zook)
(Lieut. Col. John Fraser)
52nd New York
57th New York
66th New York
140th Pennsylvania

Fourth Brigade (Col. John R. Brooke)
27th Connecticut (two companies)
2d Delaware
64th New York
53rd Pennsylvania
145th Pennsylvania (seven companies)

Second Division (Brig. Gen. John Gibbon)
(Brig. Gen. William Harrow)
(Brig. Gen. John Gibbon)

First Brigade (Brig. Gen. William Harrow)
(Col. Francis E. Heath)
19th Maine
15th Massachusetts
1st Minnesota
2nd Company Minnesota Sharpshooters
82nd New York (2d Militia)

Second Brigade (Brig. Gen. Alexander S. Webb)
69th Pennsylvania
71st Pennsylvania
72d Pennsylvania
106th Pennsylvania

Third Brigade (Col. Norman J. Hall)
19th Massachusetts
20th Massachusetts
7th Michigan
42nd New York
59th New York (four companies)

Third Division (Brig. Gen. Alexander Hays)

First Brigade (Col. Samuel S. Carroll)
14th Indiana
4th Ohio
8th Ohio
7th West Virginia

Second Brigade (Col. Thomas A. Smyth)
(Lieut. Col. Francis E. Pierce)
14th Connecticut
1st Delaware
12th New Jersey
10th New York (battalion)
108th New York

Third Brigade (Col. George L. Willard)
(Col. Eliakim Sherrill)
(Lieut. Col. James M. Bull)
39th New York (four companies)
111th New York
125th New York
126th New York

Artillery Brigade (Capt. John G. Hazard)
1st United States, Battery I
4th United States, Battery A
1st New York, Battery B and 14th New
York Battery
1st Rhode Island Light, Battery A
1st Rhode Island Light, Battery B

THIRD ARMY CORPS (Maj. Gen. Daniel E. Sickles)
(Maj. Gen. David B. Birney)

First Division (Maj. Gen. David B. Birney)
(Brig. Gen. J.H. Hobart Ward)

First Brigade (Brig. Gen. Charles K. Graham)
(Col. Andrew H. Tippin)
57th Pennsylvania
63rd Pennsylvania
68th Pennsylvania
105th Pennsylvania
114th Pennsylvania
141st Pennsylvania

Second Brigade (Brig. Gen. J. H. Hobart
Ward)
(Col. Hiram Berdan)
1st United States Sharpshooters
2d United States Sharpshooters
20th Indiana
3rd Maine
4th Maine
86th New York
124th New York
99th Pennsylvania

Third Brigade (Col. P. Regis de Trobriand)
17th Maine
3d Michigan
5th Michigan
40th New York
110th Pennsylvania (six companies)

Second Division (Brig. Gen. Andrew A. Humphreys)

First Brigade (Brig. Gen. Joseph B. Carr)
1st Massachusetts
11th Massachusetts
16th Massachusetts
12th New Hampshire
11th New Jersey
26th Pennsylvania

Second Brigade (Col. William R.
Brewster)
70th New York
71st New York
72nd New York
73rd New York
74th New York
120th New York

Third Brigade (Col. George C. Burling)
2d New Hampshire
5th New Jersey
6th New Jersey
7th New Jersey
8th New Jersey
115th Pennsylvania

Artillery Brigade (Capt. George E.
Randolph)
(Capt. A. Judson Clark)
4th United States, Battery K
New Jersey Light, 2d Battery
1st New York Light, Battery D
New York Light, 4th Battery
1st Rhode Island Light, Battery E

FIFTH ARMY CORPS (Maj. Gen. George Sykes)

First Division (Brig. Gen. James Barnes)

First Brigade (Col. William S. Tilton)
18th Massachusetts
22d Massachusetts
1st Michigan
118th Pennsylvania

Second Brigade (Col. Jacob B. Sweitzer)
9th Massachusetts
32d Massachusetts
4th Michigan
62nd Pennsylvania

Third Brigade (Col. Strong Vincent)
(Col. James C. Rice)
20th Maine
16th Michigan
44th New York
83d Pennsylvania

Second Division (Brig. Gen. Romeyn B. Ayres)

First Brigade (Col. Hannibal Day)
3d United States (six companies)
4th United States (four companies)
6th United States (five companies)
12th United States (eight companies)
14th United States (eight companies)

Second Brigade (Col. Sidney Burbank)
2d United States (six companies)
7th United States (four companies)
10th United States (three companies)
11th United States (six companies)
17th United States (seven companies)

Third Brigade (Brig. Gen. Stephen H. Weed)
(Col. Kenner Garrard)
140th New York
146th New York
91st Pennsylvania
155th Pennsylvania

Third Division (Brig. Gen. Samuel W. Crawford)

First Brigade (Col. William McCandless)
1st Pennsylvania Reserves
2nd Pennsylvania Reserves
6th Pennsylvania Reserves
13th Pennsylvania Reserves

Third Brigade (Col. Joesph W. Fisher)
5th Pennsylvania Reserves
9th Pennsylvania Reserves
10th Pennsylvania Reserves
11th Pennsylvania Reserves
12th Pennsylvania Reserves

Artillery Brigade (Capt. Augustus P. Martin)
5th United States, Battery D
5th United States, Battery I
Massachusetts Light, 3d Battery (C)
1st New York Light, Battery C
1st Ohio Light, Battery L

SIXTH ARMY CORPS (Maj. Gen. John Sedgwick)

First Division (Brig. Gen. Horatio G. Wright)

First Brigade (Brig. Gen. A. T. A. Torbert)
1st New Jersey
2d New Jersey
3d New Jersey
15th New Jersey

Second Brigade (Brig. Gen. Joseph J. Bartlett)
5th Maine
121st New York
95th Pennsylvania
96th Pennsylvania

Third Brigade (Brig. Gen. David A. Russell)
6th Maine
49th Pennsylvania (four companies)
119th Pennsylvania
5th Wisconsin

Second Division (Brig. Gen. Albion P. Howe)

Second Brigade (Col. Lewis A. Grant)
2d Vermont
3d Vermont
4th Vermont
5th Vermont
6th Vermont

Third Brigade (Brig. Gen. Thomas H. Neill)
7th Maine (six companies)
33rd New York (detachment)
43rd New York
49th New York
77th New York
61st Pennsylvania

Third Division (Maj. Gen. John Newton)
(Brig. Gen. Frank Wheaton)

First Brigade (Brig. Gen. Alexander Shaler)
65th New York
67th New York
122d New York
23d Pennsylvania
82d Pennsylvania

Second Brigade (Col. Henry L. Eustis)
7th Massachusetts
10th Massachusetts
37th Massachusetts
2d Rhode Island

Third Brigade (Brig. Gen. Frank Wheaton)
(Col. David J. Nevin)
62d New York
93d Pennsylvania
98th Pennsylvania
139th Pennsylvania

Artillery Brigade (Col. Charles H. Tompkins)
2d United States, Battery D
2d United States, Battery G
5th United States, Battery F
Massachusetts Light, 1st Battery (A)
New York Light, 1st Battery
New York Light, 3rd Battery
1st Rhode Island Light, Battery C
1st Rhode Island Light, Battery G

ELEVENTH ARMY CORPS (Maj. Gen. Oliver O. Howard)
(Maj. Gen. Carl Schurz)
(Maj. Gen. Oliver O. Howard)

First Division (Brig. Gen. Francis C. Barlow)
(Brig. Gen. Adelbert Ames)

First Brigade (Col. Leopold von Gilsa)
41st New York
54th New York
68th New York
153d Pennsylvania

Second Brigade (Brig. Gen. Adelbert Ames)
17th Connecticut
25th Ohio
75th Ohio
107th Ohio

Second Division (Brig. Gen. Adolph von Steinwehr)

First Brigade (Col. Charles R. Coster)
134th New York
154th New York
27th Pennsylvania
73rd Pennsylvania

Second Brigade (Col. Orlando Smith)
33d Massachusetts
136th New York
55th Ohio
73d Ohio

Third Division (Maj. Gen. Carl Schurz)
(Brig. Gen. Alexander Schimmelfennig)
(Maj. Gen. Carl Schurz)

First Brigade (Brig. Gen. Alexander Schimmelfennig)
(Col. George von Amsberg)
82d Illinois
45th New York
157th New York
61st Ohio
74th Pennsylvania

Second Brigade (Col. W. Krzyzanowski)
58th New York
119th New York
82d Ohio
75th Pennsylvania
26th Wisconsin

Artillery Brigade (Maj. Thomas W. Osborn)
4th United States, Battery G
1st New York Light, Battery I
New York Light, 13th Battery
1st Ohio Light, Battery I
1st Ohio Light, Battery K

TWELFTH ARMY CORPS (Maj. Gen. Henry W. Slocum)
(Brig. Gen. Alpheus S. Williams)

First Division (Brig. Gen. Alpheus S. Williams)
(Brig. Gen. Thomas H. Ruger)

First Brigade (Col. Archibald L. McDougall)
5th Connecticut
20th Connecticut
3d Maryland
123d New York
145th New York
46th Pennsylvania

Second Brigade (Brig. Gen. Henry H. Lockwood)
1st Maryland, Potomac Home Brigade
1st Maryland, Eastern Shore
150th New York

Third Brigade (Brig. Gen. Thomas H. Ruger)
(Col. Silas Colgrove)
27th Indiana
2d Massachusetts
13th New Jersey
107th New York
3d Wisconsin

Second Division (Brig. Gen. John W. Geary)

First Brigade (Col. Charles Candy)
5th Ohio
7th Ohio
29th Ohio
66th Ohio
28th Pennsylvania
147th Pennsylvania

Second Brigade (Col. George A. Cobham, Jr.)
(Brig. Gen. Thomas L. Kane)
(Col. George A. Cobham, Jr.)
29th Pennsylvania
109th Pennsylvania
111th Pennsylvania

Third Brigade (Brig. Gen. George S. Greene)
60th New York
78th New York
102nd New York
137th New York
149th New York

Artillery Brigade (Lieut. Edward D. Muhlenberg)
4th United States, Battery F
5th United States, Battery K
1st New York Light, Battery M
Pennsylvania Light, Battery E

CAVALRY CORPS (Maj. Gen. Alfred Pleasonton)

First Division (Brig. Gen. John Buford)

First Brigade (Col. William Gamble)
8th Illinois
12th Illinois (four companies)
3d Indiana (six companies)
8th New York

Second Brigade (Col. Thomas C. Devin)
6th New York
9th New York
17th Pennsylvania
3d West Virginia (two companies)

Reserve Brigade (Brig. Gen. Wesley Merritt)
1st United States
2d United States
5th United States
6th United States
6th Pennsylvania

Second Division (Brig. Gen. David McM. Gregg)

First Brigade (Col. John B. McIntosh)
1st Maryland
Purnell (Maryland) Legion, Company A
1st Massachusetts
1st New Jersey
1st Pennsylvania
3d Pennsylvania
3d Pennsylvania Artillery, Section Battery H

Third Brigade (Col. Irvin Gregg)
1st Maine
10th New York
4th Pennsylvania
16th Pennsylvania

Third Division (Brig. Gen. Judson Kilpatrick)

First Brigade (Brig. Gen. Elon J. Farnsworth)
(Col. Nathaniel P. Richmond)
5th New York
18th Pennsylvania
1st Vermont
1st West Virginia

Second Brigade (Brig. Gen. George A. Custer)
1st Michigan
5th Michigan
6th Michigan
7th Michigan

Horse Artillery

First Brigade (Capt. James M. Robertson)
2d United States, Batteries B, L and M
4th United States, Battery E
9th Michigan Battery
6th New York Battery

Second Brigade (Capt. John C. Tidball)
1st United States, Batteries E, K and G
2d United States, Battery A

ARTILLERY RESERVE (Brig. Gen. Robert O. Tyler)
(Capt. James M. Robertson)

First Regular Brigade (Capt. Dunbar R. Ransom)
1st United States, Battery H
3rd United States, Batteries F and K
4th United States, Battery C
5th United States, Battery C

First Volunteer Brigade (Lieut. Col. Freeman McGilvery)
Massachusetts Light, 5th Battery (E) and 10th New York Battery
Massachusetts Light, 9th Battery
New York Light, 15th Battery
Pennsylvania Light, Batteries C and F

Second Volunteer Brigade (Capt. Elijah D. Taft)
Connecticut Light, 2d Battery
New York Light, 5th Battery

Third Volunteer Brigade (Capt. James F. Huntington)
New Hampshire Light, 1st Battery
1st Ohio Light, Battery H
1st Pennsylvania Light, Batteries F and G
West Virginia Light, Battery C

Fourth Volunteer Brigade (Capt. Robert H. Fitzhugh)
Maine Light, 6th Battery (F)
Maryland Light, Battery A
New Jersey Light, 1st Battery
1st New York Light, Battery G
1st New York Light, Battery K and 11th New York Battery

CONFEDERATE STATES ARMY

THE ARMY OF NORTHERN VIRGINIA
(General Robert E. Lee)

FIRST ARMY CORPS (Lieut. Gen. James Longstreet)
McLaws' Division (Maj. Gen. Lafayette McLaws)

Kershaw's Brigade (Brig. Gen. J. B. Kershaw)
2d South Carolina
3d South Carolina
7th South Carolina
8th South Carolina
15th South Carolina
3d South Carolina Battalion

Barksdale's Brigade (Brig. Gen. William Barksdale)
(Col. B. G. Humphreys)
13th Mississippi
17th Mississippi
18th Mississippi
21st Mississippi

Semmes' Brigade (Brig. Gen. P. J. Semmes)
(Col. Goode Bryan)
10th Georgia
50th Georgia
51st Georgia
53rd Georgia

Wofford's Brigade (Brig. Gen. W. T. Wofford)
16th Georgia
18th Georgia
24th Georgia
Cobb's (Georgia) Legion
Philips (Georgia) Legion

Artillery (Col. H. C. Cabell)
1st North Carolina Artillery, Battery A
Pulaski (Georgia) Artillery
1st Richmond Howitzers
Troup (Georgia) Artillery

Pickett's Division (Maj. Gen. George E. Pickett)

Garnett's Brigade (Brig. Gen. R. B. Garnett)
(Maj. C. S. Peyton)
8th Virginia
18th Virginia
19th Virginia
28th Virginia
56th Virginia

Kemper's Brigade (Brig. Gen. J. L. Kemper)
(Col. Joseph Mayo, Jr.)
1st Virginia
3d Virginia
7th Virginia
11th Virginia
24th Virginia

Armistead's Brigade (Brig. Gen. L. A. Armistead)
(Col. W. R. Aylett)
9th Virginia
14th Virginia
38th Virginia
53d Virginia
57th Virginia

Artillery (Maj. James Dearing)
Fauquier (Virginia) Battery
Hampden (Virginia) Battery
Richmond Fayette Artillery
Virginia Battery

Hood's Division (Maj. Gen. John B. Hood)
(Brig. Gen. E. M. Law)

Law's Brigade (Brig. Gen. E. M. Law)
  (Col. James L. Sheffield)
  4th Alabama
  15th Alabama
  44th Alabama
  47th Alabama
  48th Alabama

Robertson's Brigade (Brig. Gen. J. B. Robertson)
  3d Arkansas
  1st Texas
  4th Texas
  5th Texas

Anderson's Brigade (Brig. Gen. George T. Anderson)
  (Lieut. Col. William Luffman)
  7th Georgia
  8th Georgia
  9th Georgia
  11th Georgia
  59th Georgia

Benning's Brigade (Brig. Gen. Henry L. Benning)
  2d Georgia
  15th Georgia
  17th Georgia
  20th Georgia

Artillery (Maj. M. W. Henry)
  Branch (North Carolina) Artillery
  German (South Carolina) Artillery
  Palmetto (South Carolina) Light Artillery
  Rowan (North Carolina) Artillery

Artillery Reserve (Col. J. B. Walton)

Alexander's Battalion (Col. E. P. Alexander)
  Ashland (Virginia) Artillery
  Bedford (Virginia) Artillery
  Brooks (South Carolina) Artillery
  Madison (Louisiana) Light Artillery
  Virginia Battery
  Virginia Battery

Washington (Louisiana) Artillery (Major B. F. Eshleman)
  First Company
  Second Company
  Third Company
  Fourth Company

SECOND ARMY CORPS (Lieut. Gen. Richard S. Ewell)

Early's Division (Maj. Gen. Jubal A. Early)

Hays' Brigade (Brig. Gen. Harry T. Hays)
  5th Louisiana
  6th Louisiana
  7th Louisiana
  8th Louisiana
  9th Louisiana

Smith's Brigade (Brig. Gen. William Smith)
  31st Virginia
  49th Virginia
  52d Virginia

Hoke's Brigade (Col. Isaac E. Avery)
  (Col. A. C. Goodwin)
  6th North Carolina
  21st North Carolina
  57th North Carolina

Gordon's Brigade (Brig. Gen. J. B. Gordon)
  13th Georgia
  26th Georgia
  31st Georgia
  38th Georgia
  60th Georgia
  61st Georgia

Artillery (Lieut. Col. H. P. Jones)
Charlottesville (Virginia) Artillery
Courtney (Virginia) Artillery
Louisiana Guard Artillery
Staunton (Virginia) Artillery

Johnson's Division (Maj. Gen. Edward Johnson)

Steuart's Brigade (Brig. Gen. George H. Steuart)
1st Maryland Battalion Infantry
1st North Carolina
3d North Carolina
10th Virginia
23d Virginia
37th Virginia

Nicholl's Brigade (Col. J. M. Williams)
1st Louisiana
2d Louisiana
10th Louisiana
14th Louisiana
15th Louisiana

Stonewall's Brigade (Brig. Gen. James A. Walker)
2d Virginia
4th Virginia
5th Virginia
27th Virginia
33d Virginia

Jones's Brigade (Brig. Gen. John M. Jones)
(Lieut. Col. R. H. Duncan)
21st Virginia
25th Virginia
42d Virginia
44th Virginia
48th Virginia
50th Virginia

Artillery (Maj. J. W. Latimer)
(Capt. C. I. Raine)
1st Maryland Battery
Alleghany (Virginia) Battery
Chesapeake (Maryland) Artillery
Lee (Virginia) Battery

Rodes's Division (Maj. Gen. R. E. Rodes)

Daniel's Brigade (Brig. Gen. Junius Daniel)
32d North Carolina
43d North Carolina
45th North Carolina
53d North Carolina
2d North Carolina Battalion

Iverson's Brigade (Brig. Gen. Alfred Iverson)
5th North Carolina
12th North Carolina
20th North Carolina
23d North Carolina

Doles's Brigade (Brig. Gen. George Doles)
4th Georgia
12th Georgia
21st Georgia
44th Georgia

Ramseur's Brigade (Brig. Gen. S. D. Ramseur)
2d North Carolina
4th North Carolina
14th North Carolina
30th North Carolina

O'Neal's Brigade (Brig. Gen. E. A. O'Neal)
3d Alabama
5th Alabama
6th Alabama
12th Alabama
26th Alabama

Artillery (Lieut. Col. Thomas H. Carter)
Jeff. Davis (Alabama) Artillery
King William (Virginia) Artillery
Morris (Virginia) Artillery
Orange (Virginia) Artillery

Artillery Reserve (Col. J. Thompson Brown)

First Virginia Artillery (Captain Willis J. Dance)
2d Richmond (Virginia) Howitzers
3d Richmond (Virginia) Howitzers
Powhatan (Virginia) Artillery
Rockbridge (Virginia) Artillery
Salem (Virginia) Artillery

Nelson's Battalion (Lieut. Col. William Nelson)
Amherst (Virginia) Artillery
Fluvanna (Virginia) Artillery
Georgia Battery

THIRD ARMY CORPS (Lieut. Gen. Ambrose P. Hill)

Anderson's Division (Maj. Gen. R. H. Anderson)

Wilcox's Brigade (Brig. Gen. Cadmus M. Wilcox)
8th Alabama
9th Alabama
10th Alabama
11th Alabama
14th Alabama

Wright's Brigade (Brig. Gen. A. R. Wright)
(Col. William Gibson)
(Brig. Gen. A. R. Wright)
3d Georgia
22d Georgia
48th Georgia
2d Georgia Battalion

Mahone's Brigade (Brig. Gen. William Mahone)
6th Virginia
12th Virginia
16th Virginia
41st Virginia
61st Virginia

Perry's Brigade (Col. David Lang)
2d Florida
5th Florida
8th Florida

Posey's Brigade (Brig. Gen. Carnot Posey)
12th Mississippi
16th Mississippi
19th Mississippi
48th Mississippi

Artillery (Sumter Battalion) (Maj. John Lane)
Company A
Company B
Company C

Heth's Division (Maj. Gen. Henry Heth)
(Brig. Gen. J. J. Pettigrew)

First Brigade (Brig. Gen. J. J. Pettigrew)
(Col. J. K. Marshall)
11th North Carolina
26th North Carolina
47th North Carolina
52d North Carolina

Second Brigade (Col. J. M. Brockenbrough)
40th Virginia
47th Virginia
55th Virginia
22d Virginia Battalion

Third Brigade (Brig. Gen. James J. Archer)
   (Col. B. D. Fry)
   (Lieut. Col. S. G. Shepard)
   13th Alabama
   5th Alabama Battalion
   1st Tennessee (Provisional Army)
   7th Tennessee
   14th Tennessee

Fourth Brigade (Brig. Gen. Joseph R. Davis)
   2d Mississippi
   11th Mississippi
   42d Mississippi
   55th North Carolina

Artillery (Lieut. Col. John J. Garnett)
   Donaldsonville (Louisiana) Artillery
   Huger (Virginia) Artillery
   Lewis (Virginia) Artillery
   Norfolk Light Artillery Blues

Pender's Division (Maj. Gen. William D. Pender)
   (Brig. Gen. James H. Lane)
   (Maj. Gen. William D. Pender)
   (Brig. Gen. James H. Lane)

First Brigade (Col. Abner Perrin)
   1st South Carolina (Provisional Army)
   1st South Carolina Rifles
   12th South Carolina
   13th South Carolina
   14th South Carolina

Second Brigade (Brig. General James H. Lane)
   (Col. C. M. Avery)
   (Brig. Gen. James H. Lane)
   (Col. C. M. Avery)
   7th North Carolina
   18th North Carolina
   28th North Carolina
   33d North Carolina
   37th North Carolina

Third Brigade (Brig. Gen. Edward L. Thomas)
   14th Georgia
   35th Georgia
   45th Georgia
   49th Georgia

Fourth Brigade (Brig. Gen. A. M. Scales)
   (Lieut. Col. G. T. Gordon)
   (Col. W. Lee J. Lowrance)
   13th North Carolina
   16th North Carolina
   22d North Carolina
   34th North Carolina
   38th North Carolina

Artillery (Maj. William T. Poague)
   Albemarle (Virginia) Artillery
   Charlotte (North Carolina) Artillery
   Madison (Mississippi) Light Artillery
   Virginia Battery

Artillery Reserve (Col. R. Lindsay Walker)

MacIntosh's Battalion (Maj. D. G. McIntosh)
   Danville (Virginia) Artillery
   Hardaway (Alabama) Artillery
   2d Rockbridge (Virginia) Artillery
   Virginia Battery

Pegram's Battalion (Maj. W. J. Pegram)
   (Capt. E. B. Brunson)
   Crenshaw (Virginia) Battery
   Fredericksburg (Virginia) Artillery
   Letcher (Virginia) Artillery
   Pee Dee (South Carolina) Artillery
   Purcell (Virginia) Artillery

CAVALRY

Stuart's Division (Maj. Gen. J. E. B. Stuart)

Hampton's Brigade (Brig. Gen. Wade Hampton)
   (Col. L. S. Baker)
   1st North Carolina
   1st South Carolina
   2d South Carolina
   Cobb's (Georgia) Legion
   Jeff. Davis Legion
   Phillips (Georgia) Legion

Robertson's Brigade (Brig. Gen. Beverly H. Robertson)
   4th North Carolina
   5th North Carolina

Jones's Brigade (Brig. Gen. William E. Jones)
   6th Virginia
   7th Virginia
   11th Virginia

Fitz. Lee's Brigade (Brig. Gen. Fitzhugh Lee)
   1st Maryland Battalion
   1st Virginia
   2d Virginia
   3d Virginia
   4th Virginia
   5th Virginia

Jenkins' Brigade (Brig. Gen. A. G. Jenkins)
   (Col. M. J. Ferguson)
   14th Virginia
   16th Virginia
   17th Virginia
   34th Virginia Battalion
   36th Virginia Battalion
   Jackson's (Virginia) Battery

W. H. F. Lee's Brigade (Col. J. R. Chambliss, Jr.)
   2d North Carolina
   9th Virginia
   10th Virginia
   13th Virginia

Stuart Horse Artillery (Maj. R. F. Beckham)
   Breathed's (Virginia) Battery
   Chew's (Virginia) Battery
   Griffin's (Maryland) Battery
   Hart's (South Carolina) Battery
   McGregor's (Virginia) Battery
   Moorman's (Virginia) Battery

Imboden's Command (Brig. Gen. J. D. Imboden)
   18th Virginia Cavalry
   62d Virginia Infantry, Mounted
   Virginia Partisan Rangers
   Virginia Battery

APPENDIX III
RECAPITULATION OF CASUALTIES

The Army of the Potomac

Command	Killed	Wounded	Captured or Missing	Aggregate
General Headquarters	–	4	–	4
First Army Corps	666	3,231	2,162	6,059
Second Army Corps	797	3,194	378	4,369
Third Army Corps	593	3,029	589	4,211
Fifth Army Corps	365	1,611	211	2,187
Sixth Army Corps	27	185	30	242
Eleventh Army Corps	369	1,922	1,510	3,801
Twelfth Army Corps	204	812	66	1,082
Cavalry Corps	91	354	407	852
Artillery Reserve	43	187	12	242
Total Army of the Potomac	3,155	14,529	5,365	23,049

The Army of Northern Virginia

Command	Killed	Wounded	Captured or Missing	Aggregate
First Army Corps	910	4,339	2,290	7,539
Second Army Corps	809	4,823	1,305	5,937
Third Army Corps	837	4,407	1,491	6,735
Stuart's Cavalry Division	36	140	64	240
Total Army of Northern Virginia	2,592	12,709	5,150	20,451

INDEX TO REPORTS

INDEX